THE

GRAND JURY

An Essay

Awarded the Peter Stephen Duponceau Prize by the
Law Academy of Philadelphia

BY

GEORGE J. EDWARDS, JR.

OF THE PHILADELPHIA BAR.

THE LAWBOOK EXCHANGE, LTD.
Clark, New Jersey

ISBN 978-1-58477-432-7

Lawbook Exchange edition 2004, 2025

The quality of this reprint is equivalent to the quality of the original work.

THE LAWBOOK EXCHANGE, LTD.
33 Terminal Avenue
Clark, New Jersey 07066-1321

*Please see our website for a selection of our other publications
and fine facsimile reprints of classic works of legal history:*
www.lawbookexchange.com

Library of Congress Cataloging-in-Publication Data

Edwards, George J. (George John), b. 1875
    The grand jury : an essay awarded the Peter Stephen Duponseau
    Prize by the Law Academy of Philadelphia / by George J. Edwards.
        p. cm.
    Originally published: Philadelphia: G.T. Bisel Co., 1906.
    ISBN 1-58477-432-0 (cloth: alk. paper)
        1. Grand jury--United States. 2.Grand Jury--Great Britian. I. Title.

KF9642.E3 2004
345.73'072--dc22   2004041801

Printed in the United States of America on acid-free paper

THE

GRAND JURY

An Essay

Awarded the Peter Stephen Duponceau Prize by the
Law Academy of Philadelphia

BY

GEORGE J. EDWARDS, JR.

OF THE PHILADELPHIA BAR.

Philadelphia:
GEORGE T. BISEL COMPANY
Law Booksellers, Publishers and Importers
1906

To the Law Academy of Philadelphia:

As the Committee of your Faculty requested to examine and report upon the essays submitted for the Annual Prize offered by the Law Academy, we desire to inform you that we have carefully read and compared the two essays which have been placed in our hands, one submitted under the *nom de plume* "Lawyer," and the other under that of "American," and that the result of our examination is as follows:—

1. We find that both essays are in form and substance excellent and very creditable to the Academy.

2. We find that, of the two, the essay signed "Lawyer" is the better, and evinces the greater labor and research and is worthy of the prize offered.

· 3. We, therefore, recommend that the prize offered by the Academy be awarded to the writer of the essay signed "Lawyer," whoever he may be.

Although in strictness, it does not fall within our province, we feel that we ought not to omit this opportunity of expressing our approval of the subject chosen for this year's prize essay. Not only is it extremely interesting, from an historical standpoint, but it is one of great practical importance. Since Mr. Furman Sheppard prepared his "Manual for Grand Juries" in 1875, of which but a few copies are now in existence, no work of any importance, which deals in a practical way with the Grand Jury System as it is in force in this Commonwealth, has been published. The essay to which we have recommended the award of this prize contains a vast amount of valuable information on the subject and with a few slight alterations and additions (incorporating the points decided by the Superior Court in the case of Commonwealth *vs.* Brown, which was decided after these essays were handed in) might be made a useful handbook for those concerned with practice in the Criminal Courts, and we suggest that the Academy, if it sees its way clear to do so, take steps to have it printed for the use of the Bar.

(Signed)   CHAS. Y. AUDENRIED,
                  ROBERT N. WILLSON,
                  ABRAHAM M. BEITLER.

Philadelphia, May 11, 1904.

PREFACE.

THIS essay was originally written with particular reference to the law relating to the grand jury in England, Pennsylvania and the United States Courts. After the committee by whom it was read had reported favorably upon it, the suggestion was made that its scope be enlarged so as to make the work applicable to all of the states. This suggestion was communicated to Judge Audenried, the Chairman of the Committee, and received his approval.

In effecting this change it has been found necessary to make few alterations in the text. So far as the common law principles relating to the grand jury are in force in the various states, the law and the decisions thereon are generally uniform. In such states as have adopted a code of criminal procedure, the common law principles relating to the grand jury constitute an important part of the code, and the decisions thereunder, in such instances, will be found to be in harmony with the decisions at the common law. Only where the common law has been superseded by statute do we find any material conflict in the decisions, and this is due, in large measure, to differences in the constitutions or statutes of the various states. By adding the citations of the state court decisions in the foot notes, with occasional additions to the text where the rulings of the courts may be regarded as of local application only, the author trusts the work has been made of more general utility than when originally submitted to the committee.

While the subject of juries has received careful attention from legal writers, and within the scope of their work the law as to grand juries has been considered fully, sufficient attention has not been given to the historical growth of the grand jury. In this essay the origin, history and development of the grand jury have been, therefore, considered at length. The history of the grand jury is closely interwoven with that of the petit jury, while the judicial records during its infancy are very meagre and confusing.

In tracing its historical development, much must be left to surmise, and this necessarily has resulted in conflicting opinions. Where doubt has arisen, the author has endeavored to present the reasons upon which his conclusions are based, and in all cases has sought to treat his subject in the light of the conditions which he conceives existed at the period of which he treats. To present the matter as clearly as possible, the method has been adopted of showing the character of trial awarded with relation to the manner of instituting the prosecution. By so doing, it becomes possible to trace the development of the grand jury separate and apart from the petit jury and thus the likelihood of confusing the action of these bodies in the early stages of their existence is in large measure avoided.

The author desires to express his thanks to Carlyle H. Ross, Esq., of the Philadelphia Bar, for his valuable assistance in the preparation of the index to this book.

He also acknowledges his appreciation of the criticism and suggestions of John M. Gest, Esq., and his obligation to Luther E. Hewitt, Esq., Librarian of the Law Association, for his interest in the preparation of this work.   G. J. E., Jr.

March 20, 1906.

Table of Contents

PART I.

vii

PART II.

ORGANIZATION AND QUALIFICATIONS.

PART III.

THE OATH, POWERS AND DUTIES OF GRAND JURORS.

PART IV.

How the Grand Jury Transacts Business and Its Relation to the Court.

Table of Text Books and Miscellaneous Articles

xvi

Table of Statutes and Constitutions

xviii

Table of Cases

3

4

THE GRAND JURY

PART I

ITS ORIGIN, HISTORY AND DEVELOPMENT.

The grand jury is an institution of English-speaking countries, of historic interest by reason of the obscurity surrounding its origin, its gradual development, and the part it has played in some of the most stirring events in the history of the Anglo-Saxon race; of political interest by its effectual protection of the liberty of the subject from the arbitrary power of the government; of legal interest in that its power and action is utterly repugnant to "the experience and theory of English law."[1]   It has been extravagantly praised as the "security of Englishmen's lives,"[2] the conserver of his liberties,[3] and the noblest check upon the malice and oppression of individuals and states;[4] it has been bitterly assailed as "purely mischievous"[5] and a "relic of barbarism."[6]

The origin of the grand jury has given rise to protracted discussion on the part of learned writers and has been productive of widely differing conclusions.   Some have claimed to find traces of the institution among the Athenians,[7] but if such an institution ever existed in Athens it had become extinct before

1 An Essay on the Law of Grand Juries, (E. Ingersoll, Philadelphia, 1849).

2 The Security of Englishmen's Lives, etc., (Lord Somers, London, 1694).

3 4 Bl. Com. 349; Judge King, in Case of Lloyd and Carpenter, 3 Clark (Pa.) 188.

4 Addison, App. 18.

5 Bentham—Rationale of Judicial Evidence, Vol. II, p. 312.

6 Grand Juries, 29 L. T. 21.

7 Jas. Wilson's Works, Vol. II. p. 361.

I

the existence of Britain became known to the Mediterranean Countries.   And although Athenian history makes mention of customs similar to the Norman appeal with the wager of battle and also of a trial by a large number of jurors, it is silent concerning a body whose duty was to accuse.

Other writers claim for the institution an Anglo-Saxon origin,[8] and in confirmation of their opinion point to the law of Ethelred II[9] (A. D. 978-1016), while still others urge that juries were unknown to the Anglo-Saxons and were introduced into England by the Normans after the conquest.[10]

Strictly speaking there is no obscurity surrounding the origin of the "grand jury," for it was not until the 42nd year of the reign of Edward III (A. D. 1368) that the modern practice of returning a panel of twenty-four men to inquire for the county was established and this body then received the name *"le graunde inquest."*[11]   Prior to this time the accusing body was known only as an inquest or jury, and was summoned in each hundred by the bailiffs to present offences occurring in that hundred. When, therefore, this method of proceeding was enlarged by the sheriff returning a panel of twenty-four knights to inquire of and present offences for the county at large, we see the inception of the grand jury of the present day.   But while it is true that our grand jury was first known to England in the time of Edward the Third, it is nevertheless not true that it was an institution of Norman origin or transplanted into England by the Normans.

That the petit jury was a Norman institution and by them brought into England cannot well be doubted.   Mr. Reeves[12]

---

8 Crabb's Hist. Eng. Law, 35; Spence—Equitable Jurisdiction of the Court of Chancery, Vol. I, p. 63; Grand Juries and the Pleas of Criminals, (John Lascelles) Law Mag. & Rev. Vol. 4 (N. S.) 767; Grand Jury in Ireland, etc. (Wm. G. Huband) 5.

9 Wilkins Leges Anglo Saxonicae 117; Note to Grand Juries and the Pleas of Criminals (John Lascelles) Law Mag. & Rev. Vol. 4 (N. S.) 767.

10 1 Reeves Hist. Eng. Law 23.

11 3 Reeves Hist. Eng. Law 133; Growth of the Grand Jury System (J. Kinghorn) 6 Law Mag. & Rev. (4th S.) 367.

12 Hist. Eng. Law, Vol. I, p. 84.

shows that the trial by twelve jurors was anciently in use among the Scandinavians, and became disused, but "was revived, and more firmly established by a law of Reignerus, surnamed Lodbrog, about the year A. D. 820. It was about seventy years after this law, that Rollo led his people into Normandy, and, among other customs, carried with him this method of trial; it was used there in all causes that were of small importance." At the time the Normans were using the Scandinavian *nambda,* the Anglo-Saxons were proceeding with *sectatores,* that is suitors of the court, to whom were referred all questions of law and of fact. The number of *sectatores* was indeterminate[13] and we have no record that unanimity was required in their verdict. While, therefore, we see that in Normandy, the *nambda,* and in England, the *sectatores,* were performing similar functions in determining questions of fact, we further find their jurisdiction extending only to civil causes.

The ancient modes of bringing offenders to justice in Normandy and in England were as radically different as they are to-day.

The Norman method was by appeal, (from the French *appeler,* to call)[14] the direct individual accusation, the truth of which was determined by the wager of battle. The *nambda* took no cognisance of criminal pleas, and crimes, where no appellor appeared, went unpunished. The English method was designed to prevent the escape of any who had violated the law. This was sought to be accomplished first, by prevention through the system of frank pledge, by which in every tithing the inhabitants were sureties to the king for the good behavior of each other;[15] and, second, by prosecution instituted by the presentment of the twelve senior thanes in every hundred or wapentake, whose duty was, according to the law of Ethelred, to accuse such persons as they found had committed any

13 1 Reeves Hist. Eng. Law 22.

14 Bouvier's Law Dictionary (Rawle's Revision).

15 1 Bl. Com. 114; Bouvier's Law Dictionary (Rawle's Revision); Growth of the Grand Jury System (J. Kinghorn) 6 Law Mag. & Rev. (4th S.) 367.

crime.[16]   There was also the hue and cry, which was raised
when any offence was discovered and the offender was pursued
until taken; if he escaped, then the hundred in which he was in
frank-pledge was liable to be amerced.[17]   Inasmuch as in this
period all offences were regarded as of purely private concern,
the offender could escape trial and punishment upon payment to
the person wronged, or, if he was dead, to his next of kin, of
a sum of money, varying in accordance with the enormity of
the offence, and the rank of the person injured.   This was
known as the custom of *weregild*.[18]   If, however, the defendant either could not or would not pay *weregild,* then the truth
of the charges prosecuted by these methods was determined by
compurgation, by the *corsned* or morsel of execration, or by the
ordeal of fire or water.[19]   Where the accused failed to clear
himself by compurgation, which occurred when he failed to obtain the necessary number of persons who were willing to swear
their belief in his innocence, he was obliged to purge himself
by the ordeal.[20]

It will therefore be seen that the grand jury was not a Norman institution brought into England by the conquest, for an
accusing body was wholly unknown among the Normans; and
while the Normans did introduce the *nambda* into England,
where its similarity to the *sectatores* caused it to firmly impress
itself into the English customs,[21] in the land which sent it forth
to England it gradually sank into disuse.[22]

The English system of frank-pledge, with the holding of the
sheriff's tourn semi-annually in the county, and the court-leet

16 Wilkins Leges Anglo Saxonicae 117; The Grand Jury, etc., in Ireland (Wm. G. Huband) 11; Spence—Equitable Jurisdiction of the Court of
Chancery, Vol. I, p. 63; Crabb Hist. Eng. Law 35.

17 4 Bl. Com. 294.

18 For the amount to be paid as weregild, see Stubbs Select Charters, 65;
Reeves Hist. Eng. Law 14 et. seq.

19 4 Bl. Com. 414; 1 Reeves Hist. Eng. Law 15, 20, 21.

20 Forsyth Trial by Jury 159.

21 An Essay on the Law of Grand Juries (E. Ingersoll, Philadelphia,
1849); Origin of Grand Juries (Hon. E. Anthony), 1 Chic. L. News, 20.

22 The Jury and Its Development, (Prof. J. B. Thayer), 5 Harv. L. Rev.
251.

or view of frank-pledge, annually in the hundred, when offenders appear to have been punished,[23] were supplemented in their purpose of preventing crime and bringing offenders to justice by the accusing body of twelve thanes of each hundred as ordained by the law of Ethelred.[24] Whether this law created the accusing body or was merely declaratory of a custom then in use in parts of the kingdom with the intent to make it of universal application, is a matter of much doubt. It is more probable, however, that the statute of Ethelred was declaratory of the law then subsisting and this view is strengthened by the statement of Blackstone,[25] that "the other general business of the leet and tourn was to present by jury all crimes whatsoever that happened within their jurisdiction," although he cites no authority in support of his opinion.

That the accusing body was the result of a slow growth, eventually being confirmed by statute, would seem to receive support from the nature of the institution of frank-pledge. Twice each year the sheriff would visit each hundred in the county and keep a court leet where he would view the frank-pledges,[26] and as wrongdoers were at such times awarded punishment, it is manifest that some method must have been employed to make the offenders known. The principal thanes and freeholders of the hundred being responsible for their subordinates, would most naturally be the ones upon whom would devolve the duty of presenting the offenders. We see these customs substantially appearing in the law of Ethelred, which provides that a *gemot*,[27] that is, a meeting be held in every wapentake (hundred) and the twelve senior thanes go out and the reeve (sheriff) with them, to accuse those who have committed any offence.[28]

The statute would merely seem to have made secure that which the very nature of frank-pledge had of necessity pre-

23 4 Bl. Com. 273.
24 Wilkins Leges Anglo Saxonicae 117.
25 4 Bl. Com. 274.
26 4 Bl. Com. 273.
27 Bouvier's Law Dictionary (Rawle's Revision).
28 Wilkins Leges Anglo Saxonicae 117.

viously brought forth. That it was but declaratory of the existing law would seem to be further verified by the fact that the statute was ordained as "frith-bot for the whole nation at Woodstock in the land of the Mercians, according to the law of the English,"[29] thereby indicating such to have been the existing law in some parts of the kingdom at least. Whether the number composing this accusing body had by usage been fixed at twelve or whether it was first definitely fixed by the statute cannot be determined, but the statute is the only evidence we have of the number necessary to present offenders, until the time of Glanville, nearly two hundred years later. It is probable, however, that, like the *sectatores,* the number was indeterminate until the statute of Ethelred reduced it to a certainty, although there is one instance even as late as the reign of Henry III (A. D. 1221) where a presentment was made to the itinerant justices by seven jurors.[30] That the number should be fixed at twelve is perhaps due to the superstition of the period which tolerated the trial by the corsned and the ordeal, believing God would miraculously intervene to protect the innocent. Lord Coke[31] thinks "that the law in this case delighteth herself in the number of twelve . . . . and that number of twelve is much respected in holy writ, as twelve apostles, twelve stones, twelve tribes, &c."

The Norman conquest, while it brought into England the customs and laws of the conquerors, did not materially alter the Saxon laws and customs relating to the detection and punishment of crime. With them came the barbarous trial by battle,[32] but they also brought what afterward became a blessing in the trial by jury.[33]

Under the Norman occupation the system of frank-pledge still continued, although not perhaps of its former importance

---

29 Note to Grand Juries and the Pleas of Criminals, (John Lascelles), 4 Law Mag. & Rev. (N. S.) 767. Stubbs Select Charters 72.

30 Select Pleas of the Crown, (Selden Society) Case No. 162.

31 Coke on Littleton 155a.

32 The Older Modes of Trial, (Prof. J. B. Thayer) 5 Harv. Law Rev. 65.

33 Id. p. 45.

now that the accusing body in each hundred regularly made its presentments, and its importance was still further lessened by the Norman appeal with its wager of battle. The appeal materially promoted the importance of the accusing body, for unless the appellor himself suffered the injury, there was no incentive to him to risk his life or liberty in the trial by battle, when the crime could equally well be presented by the inquest.[34]

In the period of one hundred years following the conquest, the Normans were actively engaged in introducing their laws and customs in the stead of the Saxon laws and customs. It is therefore of interest that at the close of this period, the accusing body should receive its second statutory confirmation and at the hands of a descendant of William the Conqueror. By the Assize of Clarendon A. D. 1166, it was enacted "that inquiry be made in each county and in each hundred, by twelve lawful men of the hundred and four lawful men of every township—who are sworn to say truly whether in their hundred or township there is any man accused of being or notorious as a robber, or a murderer or a thief, or anybody who is a harborer of robbers, or murderers or thieves, since the king began to reign. And this let the justices and the sheriffs inquire, each (officer) before himself."[35] All persons thus presented were to be tried by ordeal.

This statute marks an important change in the administration of the criminal law. Prior to this all offences were tried in the county or hundred courts, but now those offences named in the statute became offences against the peace of the king and were cognizable only in the itinerant courts which this same statute created. It is thought by some writers that these courts were not created by this statute,[36] but were first provided for by the statute of Northampton A. D. 1176, but it would rather seem that they were created by the Assize of Clar-

34 An Essay on the Law of Grand Juries, (E. Ingersoll, Philadelphia, 1849) ; Lesser, Hist. Jury System 136.

35 Lesser's Hist. Jury System 138.

36 Forsyth Trial by Jury 81.

endon,[37] that of Northampton merely dividing the kingdom
into six circuits as the Assize of 1179 subsequently divided the
kingdom into four circuits.[38]   The Assize of Clarendon marks
still another important event in the history of the administration of the criminal law in England, for by reason of what was
called "the implied prohibition" in this statute, (the statute
provided for trial by the ordeal) compurgation in criminal
cases disappears in the king's courts although it continued until a later period in the hundred courts where the sheriff pre-
sided.[39]   The system of frank-pledge while itself falling into
disuse, really formed the root of a broader scheme for administering justice.

The idea of itinerant justices was not in use among the Normans at the time of the conquest, nor does it seem to have ever
been adopted in Normandy.   Under the Saxon law the sheriff
was the king's officer in the county, and was appointed each
year.   During his term, his authority in the county was supreme except when directed otherwise by the king.[40]   It, therefore, was an easy matter in order to increase the influence of
the crown, and to insure the administration of Norman laws
and customs, to appoint sheriffs chosen by the king from the
justices of the *curia regis*.[41]   We consequently have the king's
judicial officer acting in the capacity of sheriff and, in accordance with the Saxon custom, viewing the frank-pledges in each
hundred of his county and blazing the way for the system of
itinerant justices, who came into the county to hold the eyre
and, like the sheriff, administered the pleas of the crown in
each hundred.   The inhabitants gathered before the itinerant
justices as the frank-pledges gathered before the sheriff; and
the twelve knights made their presentments to the justices in
the same manner in which the twelve thanes had, under the
Saxon law, presented offenders before the sheriff.

By the Assize of Northampton, A. D. 1176, the institution of

37 4 Bl. Com. 422.
38 Forsyth Trial by Jury 82.
39 The Older Modes of Trial, (Prof. J. B. Thayer) 5 Harv. L. Rev. 59.
40 Bl. Com. Book 1, p. 343; Bispham Equity (5th Ed.) Sec. 5.
41 Bispham Equity (5th Ed.) Sec. 5.

the accusing body was again confirmed[42] by the following provision: that "anyone charged before the king's justices with the crime of murder, theft, robbery or receipt of such offenders, of forgery, or of malicious burning, by the oaths of twelve knights of the hundred: if there were no knights, by the oaths of twelve free and lawful men, and by the oaths of four out of every vill in the hundred" should be tried by the ordeal.[43] If he failed in the ordeal, he lost a hand and foot and was banished.   If he was acquitted by the water ordeal he still suffered banishment if accused of certain crimes.[44]

This statute divided the kingdom into six circuits and provided for holding an eyre in each county of the circuit of the justices not more than once in every seven years.

The treatise of Glanville on the laws of England was written in the period 1180 to 1190, and is of great interest by reason of the light it throws upon this institution and the administration of justice relating to the pleas of the crown.   The old Saxon custom of *weregild* lost its force with the coming of the Normal appeal and wager of battle, and, in the time of Glanville, when an appeal was once properly brought which concluded against the king's peace, the parties could not settle the dispute between them or be reconciled to each other except by the king's license.[45]   Like the custom of *weregild,* the appeal was a personal action, and in those appeals which were cognizable in the king's courts, the king had an interest by virtue of the breach of the peace, but this right was only exercised when the battle was not waged.[45*] When the appellee emerged victorious from the battle, he was wholly acquitted of the charge even against the king, for by his victory he purged his innocence against them all.[46]

In the time when Glanville wrote, there were two methods of

---

42 Lesser Hist. Jury System 140.

43 The Older Modes of Trial (Prof. J. B. Thayer) 5 Harv. L. Rev. 64; Lesser Hist. Jury System 140.

44 Reeves Hist. Eng. Law, Vol. 1, p. 193.

45 Glanville (Beame's Translation—Legal Classic Series) 282.

45* Britton (Legal Classic Series) 86.

46 Bracton-de legibus, (Sir Travers Twiss ed.) Vol. II, 417.

instituting prosecutions, viz., by appeal at the suit of the person injured or his proper kinsman; and the accusation by
the public voice, that is, the presentment by the accusing body
that the defendant was suspected of certain offences.[47]   If the
appeal was properly brought, the trial by battle was usually
awarded.   Whether the appellee had the privilege of electing
to do battle or submit to the ordeal, as in the latter part of the
reign of King John he might elect between the battle and the
country, does not appear.   It is certain, however, that he was
not entitled to demand the battle in all cases.   If the appellor
was upward of sixty years of age or was adjudged to have received a mayhem, he seems to have had the privilege of declin-
ing battle, and the defendant was then compelled to purge himself by the ordeal.[48]   If the appellor was a woman and was
entitled to make the appeal, the defendant was obliged to either
abide by her proof or submit to the ordeal.[49]   If the appeal
failed, or before battle was awarded the appellor withdrew, the
accusing body was asked if it suspected the man of any offence,
and if it did he was obliged to clear himself by the ordeal, as
though the presentment had been made against him upon suspicion in the first instance.[50]

Up to this time (A. D. 1190) we have no evidence of the
petit jury being used in criminal cases,[51] and the fact that Glanville fails to make any reference to any mode of trial other than
the ordeal upon presentments of the accusing body, and the
battle upon appeals, may safely be taken as conclusive that the
time had not yet arrived when a defendant was permitted to
have the country pass upon questions affecting his life or his
liberty.   The accusing inquest seems, however, to have a somewhat wider scope than heretofore appears, for Glanville speaks
of it as having authority to make inquisitions concerning nui-

---

47 Glanville (Beames Translation—Legal Classic Series) 278; 1 Reeves
Hist. Eng. Law 195.

48 Glanville (Beames Translation—Legal Classic Series) 282.

49 Id. 287.

50 Bracton-de legibus, Vol. II, p. 447, 448.

51 Hallam's Middle Ages, Vol. II, p. 176, 177; Palgrave English Commonwealth 269.

sances and certain other matters.[52]   In A. D. 1194, the fifth
year of Richard I, the jurisdiction of the itinerant justices was
further increased and certain capitula or articles of inquiry
were delivered to them, which they were to make known to
the accusing body, and to each article which concerned the hundred, this body was obliged to make answer.[53]   The four men
of each vill or township mentioned in the Assize of Clarendon
and the Assize of Northampton are not referred to in these instructions to the justices, which one writer thinks would seem
to indicate that the four men formed no part of the accusing
body.[54]

With the year A. D. 1201, and the third of the reign of King
John, we have the court rolls of the eyres which the itinerant
justices held in the several hundreds of their respective dis-
tricts, which the efforts of the Selden Society[55] are bringing to
light, and many doubtful points by means thereof, are being
cleared up.   From these records we are enabled to obtain some
idea of the instances in which this accusing body would exercise its right of presentment.   They seem to have presented
where they had knowledge of, or suspected a person of an
offence;[56] where a person was accused,[57] probably by some one
appearing before them and there charging a person with an
offence; where an appeal had been held to be null;[58] where an
appeal had been made by a woman;[59] and apparently in all
cases where appeals had been made concluding against the
king's peace.[60]   The inquest was required to answer fully concerning each article of the capitula;[61] and if they failed in
this, they were accused of concealing the truth and were in the

---

52 Glanville (Beames Translation—Legal Classic Series) 194.

53 Bracton-de legibus, Vol. II, p. 241; 1 Reeves Hist. Eng. Law 201.

54 The Grand Jury, etc., in Ireland (Wm. G. Huband) 11.

55 Select Pleas of the Crown.

56 Id. Cases No. 5, 6, 12, 57.

57 Id. Cases No. 10, 181.

58 Id. Case No. 13; Bracton-de legibus, Vol. II, p. 449.

59 Select Pleas of the Crown, cases No. 68, 153.

60 Id. Cases No. 15, 21.

61 2 Reeves Hist. Eng. Law 3; Bracton-de legibus, (Sir Travers Twiss
ed.)   Vol. II, 241.

king's mercy and liable to be fined and imprisoned.[62]   In such case, therefore, it is very reasonable to suppose they would present all persons whom they suspected or knew had violated any of the articles with which they were charged, irrespective of the fact that some of those whom they presented may have been regularly appealed.   The inquest was not restrained in any manner from making such presentments, nor does it appear that they were required to make presentment of such cases except where the appeal had failed.   When we also consider that the eyre was held in the county only once in every seven years, it would be manifestly impossible for the freeholders of each hundred to remember who had been appealed within their hundred during the period, so that they might not present in such cases.   Further than this, the manner of proceeding before the justices upon the appeals would seem to make it necessary in the interest of justice, that the inquest should also present those offences where appeals had been made.

In order to properly make his appeal, the appellor was required to raise the hue and cry, go to the king's sergeants, thence to the coroners of the county where his complaint was enrolled word for word, and lastly to the county court, where his complaint was similarly enrolled.[63]   Then when the cause came before the justices, the appellor was heard and the appellee answered, after which the coroner's rolls were read, and if they or the majority of them agreed with the appellor and there were no good exceptions, then the appellee could choose how he would be tried.[64]   If the coroners' rolls disagreed, but were

62 Bracton-de legibus, Vol. 11, p. 239.   A very curious analogy to this will be found in the laws of the State of Connecticut.   By Gen. St. tit. 20, C. 12, Sec. 23, it is provided that a sworn grand juror shall forfeit $2, if he "shall neglect to make seasonable complaint of any crime or misdemeanor committed within the town where he lives, which shall come to his knowledge."   In Watson v. Hall, 46 Conn., 204, it was held that this must be construed to give him discretion as to whether the offence is too trivial for a criminal prosecution, and he is not liable, if in good faith, he omits to complain.

63 Bracton-de legibus (Sir Travers Twiss ed.) Vol. II, p. 425.

64 Id. p. 431.   This discloses a change in the law subsequent to the time when Glanville's Treatise was written, as the appellee was apparently at that time not permitted to choose the method of trial.   Supra. 10.

evenly divided, then the sheriff's roll was read, and accordingly as this showed, the trial was or was not awarded. If it happened that an appellor did not prosecute his appeal, there seems to have been no provision in the law for making known to the justices such complaint as contained in the rolls, yet it might well happen that the appellee was then confined in prison. It would consequently appear that if the inquest did not present the appellee where an appeal had been made, not only might a felony go unpunished, but an injury be done to the king in the concealment by the inquest of the breach of his peace.[65] How, then, the accusing body could discriminate between appeals that were prosecuted, and those where the appellor defaulted, accusations and rumors, and present in all cases except where the appeal was prosecuted, particularly when they were organized, sworn, charged and went about the performance of their duties before the court was ready to hear the criminal pleas, cannot easily be perceived. It would seem more probable that they presented in all cases where they had either actual knowledge or public fame upon which to base their presentment, irrespective of the fact that an appeal was then pending.

Two instances of this are disclosed by the Selden Society[66] in their researches into the record rolls of the courts held by the itinerant justices in the reign of King John, in both of which the inquest made presentments of offences in which appeals had been made, and in both cases the inquest was adjudged in the king's mercy because the appeals were found to have concluded against the sheriff's peace and therefore were improperly presented in the king's court. This view we see supported by the proceedings in the modern case of Ashford vs. Thornton.[67] In this case the defendant was indicted for murder, tried and acquitted. The brother of the murdered woman then brought an appeal and the appellee elected to wage his battle, which the appellor declined. The attorney general

---

65 Bracton-de legibus, (Sir Travers Twiss ed.) Vol. II, p. 449.

66 Select Pleas of the Crown, Cases No. 15, 21.

67 Ashford v. Thornton 1 B. & Ald 405. This was the last time an appeal was brought in England, the wager of battle being abolished in 1810 by Statute 59, Geo. III, C. 46.

thereupon caused the defendant to be immediately arraigned upon an indictment which had been found in the meantime for the felony at the king's suit, to which at once the defendant pleaded his former acquittal upon the indictment for murder, and the plea was adjudged sufficient.

The rolls of the courts held by the itinerant justices[68] reveal a practice which adds further burdens to the already difficult task of tracing the development of the accusing body. Where the inquest presented anyone either upon suspicion or accusation who had not been appealed, the presentment of the inquest does not appear to have been regarded as sufficiently conclusive in all cases to award the ordeal. In such cases, the justices asked the four neighboring townships if they suspected the defendant, and if they did, then he was obliged to purge himself by the ordeal.[69] What the office of the four townships actually was, how they came to exercise this office, and in what instances they exercised it are purely matters of conjecture. Where an appeal was declared null or for some other cause failed and the inquest ignored the breach of the king's peace, the verdict of the inquest seems to have been conclusive,[70] and the four townships were not called upon, and this also seems to be true in many cases where the inquest presented upon suspicion or accusation.[71]

Glanville makes no reference to the four townships, and his silence is singular if the townships were called upon to officially act. It is also to be noted that he makes no reference to, or comment upon, the four freemen out of every vill in the hundred referred to in the Assize of Clarendon. If the statute had reference to criminal proceedings, this new appendage of the inquest was such a departure from the ancient law as to be the subject of comment. That this comment was not made, leaves but two conclusions to be drawn, either that it is a mistaken idea in holding this provision of the statute to relate to the

---

68 Select Pleas of the Crown (Selden Society).

69 Id. Cases No. 5, 6, 10, 12, 57, 181.

70 Id. Case No. 13. This case is probably the first recorded instance of an "ignoramus." And see Case No. 153.

71 Select Pleas of the Crown, Cases No. 157, 170.

accusing inquest, or that it remained a dead letter until after Glanville's period.

Whether or not the "four freemen out of every vill" and the "four townships" were identical, can only be a subject for conjecture. It remains, however, that the only jurist who wrote in the period A. D. 1166-1200, mentions neither, and the rolls of the courts held by the itinerant justices beginning with A. D. 1201, make reference only to the "four townships" being inquired of. Whatever may have been the purpose of this provision of the Assize of Clarendon, there seems to be no mention of the four freemen until Bracton's treatise was written, and then but little light is shed upon the capacity in which they were required to act. Bracton, however, shows that they formed no part of the inquest which presented the defendant.

The court rolls disclose that the four townships did not act until after the inquest had presented on suspicion. In discussing a presentment on suspicion Glanville states that the defendant was immediately thereafter to be taken into custody. He then continues: "The truth of the fact shall then be inquired into by means of many and various inquisitions and interrogations made in the presence of the justices, and that by taking into consideration the probable circumstances of the facts, and weighing each conjecture which tends in favor of the accused, or makes against him; because he must purge himself by the ordeal, or entirely absolve himself from the crime imputed to him."[72]

If this paragraph could be taken as referring to the four townships, then they were only asked when the justice had a doubt concerning the presentment of the inquest; but that it does not would seem more likely in view of the fact that Glanville does not mention them. That it does not have reference to the four freemen out of every vill in the hundred may be regarded as equally conclusive by his omission to mention them, and particularly so in view of the fact that he was an itinerant justice from 1176 to 1180, a time when he must necessarily have been brought in close contact with them if they were called upon to act, and subsequently wrote his famous

72 (Beames Translation—Legal Classic Series), p. 278.

treatise.[73]   That they were not brought into existence by the instructions of 1194 is equally well settled, for they are not referred to therein.[74]   That they were not called upon in all cases has already been seen.[75]   So far as the cases show, their power did not extend beyond confirming what the inquest had already presented, and they apparently could not nullify its presentment.   It would therefore seem that no provision of law made their use obligatory, otherwise they must have acted in all cases; and when they were called upon to act, they were limited to a concurrence with what the inquest had presented, and if they did not concur, their verdict had no effect upon the result.   The townships appear never to have acted until the inquest made its presentment.[76]

They did not act with the accusing jurors as a trial jury after the defendant had been presented, otherwise he was obliged to submit to two trials—the petit jury as thus composed, and the ordeal, and then too, the trial by jury in criminal cases had not yet come into use.[77]   It is therefore probable that it was optional with the justices whether or not they would inquire of the four townships, and they did this only to satisfy themselves whether the ill repute of the defendant was believed by others than the accusing body.

Mr. Forsyth[78] makes this comment upon the relation which the accusing body bore to the four townships: "We here see that the neighboring townships were associated with the jury in the inquest; and this was by no means an unusual practice. But they were not considered part of the jury, but seem rather to have assisted in the character of witnesses, and to have constituted part of the fama publica."

We have still to consider the methods of trial in force at this

73 This is doubted by eminent authors who attribute it to Hubert Walter, who was clerk to Glanville at the time he was Chief Justiciar.—See Pollock & Maitland Hist. Eng. Law, Vol. I, p. 164.

74 The Grand Jury, etc., in Ireland (Wm. G. Huband), p. 11.

75 Supra 14.

76 See generally the cases in Select Pleas of the Crown.

77 Lesser Hist. Jury System 142.

78 Trial by Jury, p. 166.

time in order to fully comprehend the duty of the inquest in this period.

The trial by battle was in force upon appeals properly brought, but the exceptions which might be taken to the appeal were becoming more numerous. The right of the appellee to decline battle and put himself upon the country is not mentioned by Glanville, nor does there seem to be a recorded instance of it until the early years of King John's reign.

The first instances where the accused was allowed to put himself upon the country, appear to have been the result of an application to the favor of the king and the payment to him of a sum of money for the issuance of a writ awarding an inquest.[79] These cases were, however, rare, and what few cases appear in the books give but little information concerning the instances in which the king would grant such a writ.[80] If wager of battle was declined and the king petitioned for a writ awarding an inquest, if granted, there was apparently no accusation made by the accusing body against such defendant for the breach of the king's peace; the verdict of the trying inquest being alone given and was conclusive.

It was provided by Article 36 of the Magna Charta of King John that writs awarding an inquest should no longer be sold, but be of right.[81] It may, however, be doubted whether this provision was intended to apply to writs thus sold awarding an inquest in criminal cases.[82] It is more probable that it was intended to apply to writs awarding an assize, for the statutes of Clarendon and Northampton had made provision for such an assize in determining property rights. So far as the inquisition to determine title to real property was concerned, this had

---

79 Lesser Hist. Jury System 142, 144; Forsyth Trial by Jury 166.

80 Select Pleas of the Crown.

81 Magna Charta of King John, Article 36, provided: "Nihil detur vel capiatur de cetero pro brevi inquisitionis de vita vel membris, sed gratis concedatur et non negatur." Stubbs Select Charters, p. 301. In the confirmation of the Great Charter by Henry III, in 1216, Article 36 of King John's Charter becomes Article 29: Stubbs Select Charters, p. 342.

82 But rather a contrary view is expressed by Professor J. B. Thayer in The Jury and its Development, 5 Harv. L. Rev. 265, although no reasons are given for the opinion he expresses.

2

become a fixed method of procedure which almost universally superseded the determination of such issue by the wager of battle. In criminal proceedings, however, the inquest was wholly foreign to their institutions and something seemingly to be shunned rather than encouraged.

The ordeal which in Glanville's time was generally awarded when the battle could not be waged, was in full vigor during this period up to the year 1215, when by the action of the Fourth Lateran Council of Innocent III, by which the clergy were expressly forbidden to participate in the ceremonies of the ordeal, the practice came to an end thereby opening the way for the trial by the country.[83]

It is said by Professor Thayer[84] that "the Assize of Clarendon, in 1166, with its apparatus of an accusing jury and a trial by ordeal is thought to have done away in the king's courts with compurgation as a mode of trial for crime; and now the Lateran Council, in forbidding ecclesiastics to take part in trial by ordeal, was deemed to have forbidden that mode of trial, as well in England as in all other countries where the authority of the Council was recognized. The judges would naturally turn to the inquest."

It is reasonable to suppose that the inquest would be adopted as the learned writer above quoted says, for the inquest was the only mode of trial remaining by which suspected persons might be tried.[85] But this the judges could not do unless authorized by the king. The next eyre was held in the years 1218-19, and the judges had started on their journey when the order of the king in council was sent to them in the following words: "When you started on your eyre it was as yet undetermined what should be done with persons accused of crime, the Church having forbidden the ordeal. For the present we must rely very much on your discretion to act wisely, according to the special circumstances of each case." The judges were

83 Lesser Hist. Jury System 142, Note 24; Hallam's Middle Ages, Note to Chapter VIII; Stubb's Select Charters, p. 142.

84 The Jury and its Development, 5 Harv L. Rev. 265.

85 While trial by battle was still in use, it could only be used where an appeal had been properly brought.

then given certain general instructions: Persons charged with the graver crimes, who might do harm if allowed to abjure the realm, are to be imprisoned, without endangering life or limb. Those charged with less crimes, who would have been tried by the ordeal may abjure the realm. In the case of small crimes there must be pledges to keep the peace.[86]

This is one of the most important and interesting periods of English history, for at this time the signing of the Great Charter occurs, establishing the liberties of the people, and the system which was to be most potent in assuring these liberties according to the guaranties of the Charter, supplanted a custom that was brutal in the extreme.

Bracton,[87] who wrote clearly and at great length, in the reign of Henry III, sets forth with precision the various methods of prosecuting offenders against the law. He points out that where there was a certain accuser he might make his appeal or might sue, that is, make his accusation before the inquest; that when the appeal had fallen, the king might sue on behalf of his peace; and finally the presentment which the inquest might make of persons not accused or appealed, but suspected by the inquest to be guilty by reason of public fame.[88] This is a lucid summing up of the methods then pursued, as has been heretofore shown, and may reasonably be assumed to have been the method in vogue at least since the Assize of Clarendon, and from possibly an earlier date. The workings of the system are described carefully and with much attention to detail.[89] When the justices proposed holding an eyre in any county "a general summons issues to appear before the justices itinerant and should issue at least fifteen days prior to their coming."

When the justices come the writs authorizing them to hold an *iter* are read, after which one of the older and more discreet of them sets forth the cause of their coming and what is the utility of their itineration, and what is the advantage if peace be observed. After this they go to a secret place and call four

86 Maitland Glou. Pleas XXXVIII.
87 de legibus (Sir Travers Twiss ed).
88 Bracton-de legibus, Vol. II, p. 451.
89 Id. Vol. II, p. 235, et. seq.

or six of the greater men, the *busones,* of the county to them and consult with them in turn and explain that the king has provided that all knights and others of the age of fifteen and upwards ought to swear that they will not harbor outlaws, etc., and will arrest, if possible, those whom they regard as suspected, without waiting for the mandate of the justices. Afterward the sergeants and bailiffs of the hundred are convoked and the inhabitants of the hundred are enrolled in order. The sergeants each shall pledge his faith "that he will choose from each hundred four knights who shall come forthwith before justices to perform the precept of the lord the king, and who shall forthwith swear that they will choose twelve knights or free and legal men if knights cannot be found, who have no suit against any one and are not sued themselves, nor have any evil fame for breaking the peace, or for the death of a man or other misdeed," and the names of the twelve are placed in a schedule and delivered to the justices. Then the principal one shall make this oath: "Hear this ye justices that I will speak the truth concerning this which ye shall ask me on the part of the lord the king, and I will do faithfully that which you shall enjoin me on the part of the lord the king, and I will not for any one omit to do so according to my ability, so may God help me and these Holy Gospels of God.'[90] And afterward they shall each of them swear separately and by himself: 'The like oath which A. the first juror has here sworn, I will keep on my part so may God help me and these Holy etc."[91]

When this has been done the justices read to the accusing body the various articles, to which the inquest shall make true answers and have their verdict there by a certain day. It is said quietly to them that if they know of anyone in the hundred of evil repute, they shall seize him if possible, otherwise his name is to be secretly conveyed to the justices, that the sheriff may seize him and bring him before the justices.

"And the amercers (jurors) shall pledge their fealty to do this faithfully, that they will aggrieve no one through enmity nor show deference to any one through love, and that they will

---

90 Bracton-de legibus, Vol. II, p. 239, (Sir Travers Twiss ed.).
91 Bracton-de legibus, (Sir Travers Twiss ed.) Vol. II, p. 241.

conceal those things which they have heard."[92]   This would appear to be the first reference we have to the inquest observing a pledge of secrecy, that feature of the grand jury which has aroused the strongest criticism.   The purpose of this provision would, however, seem to have been to prevent the escape of offenders who were presented by the inquest.   The proceedings were not as they are at the present time to be kept secret from every one, for the justices had the power if they suspected the inquest, to inquire of each member separately or of the inquest generally, the causes which induced such action.[93]

We find that Bracton mentions but two kinds of trial in criminal cases, the battle and the country.   It remains to consider how these trials were awarded in relation to the method of instituting the proceedings against the offender.   If an appeal was made, after all exceptions to it had been disposed of, the appellee was entitled to choose the wager of battle or put himself upon the country, but if he chose the country he could not afterward retract and offer to defend himself by his body.[94] If the appellor was a woman, the appellee was compelled to put himself upon the country or be adjudged guilty; and if a man over the age of sixty years, or who had a mayhem, the appellee was obliged to put himself upon the country, unless the appellor was willing to wage battle, but with these exceptions it was optional with the appellee to choose the battle or the country, but he could only choose the battle if the appeal was of a felony.

Where the initial step in the prosecution was the presentment by the accusing body, or where the appeal failed and the defendant was presented by the inquest, then he had no alternative but to place himself upon the country.

Whether when a defendant placed himself upon the country, he placed himself upon the same jurors who accused him, has been a subject of wide discussion, and able authors express contrary opinions upon this point.   Mr. Forsyth[95] says they "for

92 Bracton-de legibus, (Sir Travers Twiss ed.) p. 243.
93 Id. p. 453.
94 Id. p. 403.
95 Trial by Jury 164; but see Id. p. 170.

a long time seem to have united the two functions of a grand jury to accuse, and a petit jury to try the accused." Mr. Reeves[96] considers that the defendant put himself upon the same jury which indicted him and then the jury "under the direction of the justices . . . . were to reconsider their verdict and upon such review of the matter they were to give their verdict finally." Mr. Crabb[97] gives utterance to the same thought, but states that if the defendant "had suspicion of any of the jurors he might have them removed." Mr. Ingersoll[98] considers it doubtful that in Bracton's time the jury which tried offenders was composed of the same persons who had indicted him. Bracton[99] describes the method of proceeding with the trial jury in the following language:

"In order that the proceeding to a judgment may be more safe and that danger and suspicion may be removed, let the justice say to the person indicted, that if he has reason to suspect any one of the twelve jurors he may remove him for just grounds. And let the same thing be said of the townspeople, that, if there have been any capital enmities between any of them and the person indicted, on account of covetousness to possess his land, as aforesaid, they are all to be removed upon just suspicion, so that the inquisition may be free from all suspicion. Twelve jurors therefore being present and four townspeople, each of the townspeople or all together, each holding up his hand shall swear in these words:[100]

"Hear this, ye justices, that we will speak the truth concerning those things, which ye shall require from us on the part of the lord the king, and for nothing will we omit to speak the truth, so God us help," &c.

This statement of the action of the petit jury, made when the institution was in its infancy, discloses several interesting facts. We see without question that an inquest had indicted the defendant before this body was required to determine the

96 2 Hist. Eng. Law 33.

97 Hist. Eng. Law 162.

98 Essay on Law of Grand Juries (E. Ingersoll, Philadelphia, 1849).

99 de legibus, (Sir Travers Twiss ed.) Vol. II, p. 455.

100 Bracton-de legibus, (Sir Travers ed.) Vol. II, p. 457.

issue. We see now for the first time the four townspeople mentioned in the Assize of Clarendon, who apparently form a part of the trial jury. For while the accusing body consisted of but twelve jurors, the trying jury was not so limited, and instances will be seen where the trial jury consisted of twenty-four.[101] If, when the oath was taken by the four townspeople, the twelve jurors were not then sworn, as may well be deduced from Bracton's statement,[102] then it would seem probable that the jurors were the same persons who had indicted the defendant, for they must have been sworn at some prior stage of this particular proceeding. If, however, by this paragraph, Bracton means to convey the idea that the entire sixteen were sworn at one time, then it might well be that the members of the trying jury differed from the accusing body. In either event the make up of the trying jury was changed by adding the four townspeople, while if it was the original accusing jury, charged with the trial of the defendant after they had indicted him, it might be still further and materially changed by challenges for cause.[103]

The theory that the entire sixteen were sworn at one time is strengthened by noting the difference in the oath taken by those acting as the accusing body and those who are to try the truth of the accusation.[104] The trial jurors merely swear that they will speak the truth as to the things required of them. This was in strict accord with their original character as witnesses of the facts of which they spoke the truth. The oath of the accusing juror was much more comprehensive, and required not only that the juror should speak the truth, but that he should do the things enjoined upon him on the part of the king and "not for any one omit to do so."

There is still another and what is perhaps the strongest argu-

---

101 Post 24, 25.

102 Supra. 22.

103 Bracton-de legibus, (Sir Travers Twiss ed.) Vol. II, p. 455. That a petit juror was a member of the grand jury which found the indictment, was made ground of challenge by 25 Edw. III, Stat. 5, Chap. 5. See Robert's Digest of British Statutes, p. xxx, also p. 346.

104 Compare the two oaths Supra. 20 and 22.

ment that can be made against the trial jury being the same
jury which accused.   The accusing body was composed of
twelve only, who presented all offenders.[105]   In order that
they might present, it was not necessary that all the jurors
should be cognizant of the facts as will appear by the following
statement by Bracton.   Speaking of indicting upon common
fame he says,[106] "some one will probably say, or the greater
part of the jurats, that they have learnt those things which they
set forth in their verdict from one of the associate jurats." It is
therefore very clear that the accusing body could indict upon
the knowledge of one of their number.   It is equally plain, and
in this all writers apparently agree, that the trial jury was a
jury of witnesses who had personal knowledge of the facts.[107]
If the twelve of the trial jury did not agree, then the ancient
doctrine of "afforciament," that is, the adding of jurors who
were cognizant of the facts until twelve could be found who
agreed upon a verdict was employed.[108]   This was not done
with the accusing body.   It would consequently seem that the
jury which tried was, in most cases, a different body from that
which accused, for the accusing body found all indictments
with no change in its make up, while the trial jury had not only
four townspeople added to it, but the jurors themselves were
subject to the defendant's challenge for cause.   The record
rolls[109] of the itinerant justices show two instances of a separate jury trying the offenders after they were indicted.   The
first was an appeal by a woman for the murder of her husband,
and she having remarried and no appeal being made by her husband, it was adjudged that the country should inquire concerning the truth.   "And the twelve jurors say that he is guilty of
that death, and twenty-four knights (other than the twelve)
chosen for this purpose say the same."[110]   In the second case

---

105 Supra. 6, 7, 9.

106 Bracton-de legibus, (Sir Travers Twiss ed.) Vol. II, p. 455.

107 Forsyth—Trial by Jury, 104; Lesser Hist. Jury System 104, 113;
Hallam's Middle Ages, note to Chapter VIII.

108 Forsyth—Trial by Jury, 105; Lesser Hist. Jury System 113.

109 Select Pleas of the Crown (Selden Society), Cases No. 153, 157.

110 Id. Case No. 153.

the defendant was taken on an indictment for theft, and it was adjudged the truth should be inquired of by the country. "And twenty-four knights chosen for the purpose, say the same as the said twelve jurors."[111] We consequently see that at a period forty years before Bracton's work was written, the use of two juries had been instituted, and within a period of thirty years after Bracton, the two juries were separate and distinct in cases involving life at least.[112]

In the three decades following the writing of Bracton's treatise, the accusing body suffered marked changes which are revealed by the pages of Britton. The number still continued at twelve, the method of summoning and organizing them was the same, but they now took this oath: "that they will lawful presentment make of such chapters as shall be delivered to them in writing and in this they will not fail for any love, hatred, fear, reward, or promise, and that they will conceal the secrets, so help them God and the Saints."[113] The presentments were made in writing and indented, the inquest keeping one part, the other being delivered to the justices.[114] An indictor could not serve upon the petit jury in offences punishable with death, if challenged by the defendant.[115] The inquest was required to present those whose duty it was to keep in repair bridges, causeways, and highways, for neglect of duty;[116] to inquire into the defects of gaols and the nature thereof, who ought to repair them, and who was responsible for any escapes which had occurred;[117] if any sheriff had kept in gaol those whom he should have brought before the justices;[118] and of all cases where the sheriff placed on the panel persons holding under "twenty shillings to be on inquests and juries in the county."[119]

The inquest now corresponded, in general, with the modern

111 Select Pleas of the Crown (Selden Society) Case No. 157.
112 Britton (Legal Classic Series) 25.
113 Britton (Legal Classic Series) 17.
114 Id. p. 19.
115 Id. p. 25.
116 Id. p. 65.
117 Id. p. 72.
118 Id. p. 74.
119 Id. p. 75.

inquest except in point of number. We find this change taking place in the time of Edward the Third, when the sheriff of the county, in addition to the twelve returned by the bailiffs for each hundred, returned a panel of twenty-four knights to inquire at large for the county, and this body was termed *"le graunde inquest,"* not for the purpose of distinguishing it as the accusing body, but to distinguish it from the hundred inquests. This grand inquest seems to have its foundation solely in the action of the sheriff in returning such a panel,[120] for it was authorized by no statute, and apparently had no existence in prior custom. It, however, was destined to be permanent by reason of its jurisdiction over the entire county and the fact that its number of twenty-four was less unwieldy than the twelves of the many hundreds in the county.

Consequently while the influence of *"le graunde inquest"* grew, that of the hundred inquests declined, until finally they ceased to present offenders and filled the office of petit jurors only.[121] While we therefore see that the beginning of the "grand jury" as known to us, occurs in time within the mind of man, it is plain that this was but the new branch of a tree already firmly rooted among English institutions. It was distinctly a growth produced by the necessities of the times to which its origin relates, and would no more have been a deliberate creation of a Parliament of the fourteenth century than it would of the legislature to-day. Nor did this change, which was apparently without warrant of law, materially alter the ancient institution. The necessity that twelve should concur remained, and to-day in England and all of the states which have not by statute provided otherwise, twelve jurors are all that need be present upon the grand jury, but all must concur.[122] The increase in the number of jurors having occurred in a period when unanimity was requisite, if the increased number was authorized by law, undoubtedly the same principle, which required twelve jurors or twelve or even thirty-six com-

---

120 King *v.* Fitch, Cro. Chas. 414. In this case it is said that "it is usual to have more than twelve *at the sheriff's pleasure,"* on an inquest of office.

121 3 Reeves Hist. Eng. Law 133.

122 Post 45, 46, 147.

purgators (in such instances as compurgation had been allowed) to concur, must necessarily have required the twenty-four on the grand inquest to do likewise. That this was not required makes it quite probable that all over twelve were unlawfully upon the panel.[123]

With the coming of the grand inquest to inquire at large for the county, and the disappearance of the accusing bodies of the hundreds, we practically complete what may be termed the period of formation in the development of the grand jury. So far as we have considered it, we have found it to be an arm of the government, acting as a public prosecutor for the purpose of ferreting out all crime, the members of the inquest being at all times bound to inform the court either singly or collectively their reasons for arriving at their verdict and the evidence upon which it was based.[124] The seed, however, had been sown in Bracton's time, which was destined to change the grand jury from a mere instrument of the crown to a strong independent power which stood steadfast between the crown and the people in the defence of the liberty of the citizen.

In enjoining secrecy upon the inquest in Bracton's time, and in making it a part of the grand juror's oath as shown by Britton,[125] it was perhaps the idea of the crown that such a regulation would prevent knowledge of the action of the inquest from being conveyed to the defendant to allow his escape. That it was for no other purpose will be seen by the fact that the justices might still fully interrogate the jurors as to how they arrived at their verdict.[126] The power of interrogation does not appear to have been exercised by the justices in all cases, but only in such instances as the jury presented upon suspicion and the defendant must purge himself by the ordeal, although this practice continued after the ordeal was abolished. When the separate trial jury became finally established, there no longer existed any necessity for the justices to inquire of the presenting jury, for the ordeal no longer existed, while the

123 Supra. 26.
124 Supra. 21. And see Forsyth Trial by Jury 171.
125 Britton (Legal Classic Series) 18.
126 Bracton-de legibus, (Sir Travers Twiss ed.) Vol. II, p. 455.

truth of the matter was fully inquired of by the country. Further than this, it was more logical that the justices should make inquiry of the trial jurors whose competency rested upon their knowledge of the truth rather than the presentors, whose accusation neither determined the truth nor falsity of the charge and was not conclusive as in Glanville's time.   When the grand inquest came to present for the county, their personal knowledge of the facts, in most cases, became more limited, and the practice at this time of requiring the grand inquest to divulge upon what ground their presentment was based, had probably fallen into disuse.

It was in this period that the independence of the grand jury became established.   No longer required to make known to the court the evidence upon which they acted, meeting in secret and sworn to keep their proceedings secret by an oath which contained no reservation in favor of the government, selected from the gentlemen of the best figure in the county,[127] and without regard to their knowledge of any particular offence, the three centuries that followed the return of a panel of twenty-four knights, witnessed its freedom of action from all restraint by the court.   The independence which the institution had attained was soon to be put to the severest tests, but protected by the cloak of secrecy and free from the control of the court as to their findings, they successfully thwarted the unjust designs of the government.

It was in the reign of Charles the Second that we find the two most celebrated instances of the fearless action of the grand jury in defending the liberty of the subject, although subjected to the strongest possible pressure from the crown. In 1681 a bill of indictment for high treason against Stephen College, the Protestant joiner, was submitted to a grand jury of the City of London.   Lord Chief Justice North compelled the grand jury to hear the evidence in open court and of the witnesses produced it was said, "It is certainly true that never men swore more firmly in court than they did."   The grand jury demanded that the witnesses be sent to them that they might examine them privately and apart, which the court per-

127 4 Bl. Com. 302.

mitted to be done. After considering the matter for several hours the grand jury ignored the bill. Upon being asked by the Lord Chief Justice whether they would give a reason for this verdict, they replied that they had given their verdict according to their consciences and would stand by it.[128] The foreman of this grand jury, Mr. Wilmore, was afterwards apprehended upon a false charge, examined before the Council, sent to the tower, and afterward forced to flee beyond the seas.[129]

In the same year an attempt was made to indict the Earl of Shaftesbury for high treason.[130] As in College's case, the grand jury desired to hear the evidence in private, but the king's counsel insisted that the evidence be heard in open court and Lord Chief Justice Pemberton assented. After hearing the evidence the grand jury desired that they might examine the witnesses apart in their chamber and the court granted the request. After again hearing the witnesses and considering their verdict they returned the bill "ignoramus," upon which "the people fell a hollowing and a shouting." This case is perhaps pointed out more often than any other as an instance of the independent action of the grand jury, and while it is not sought to minimize the action of the grand jurors, for their stand was a bold one in view of the strong pressure which was brought to bear upon them by the crown, still the side lights when thrown upon it disclose other facts which may have been potent in shaping the return of this body.[131] The Earl of Shaftesbury was a very powerful nobleman, with influential friends and adherents in the king's service, but his greatest strength, perhaps, lay in the regard in which he was held by the people. The sheriff who returned the grand jurors before whom the case was laid, was an open adherent of Shaftesbury,

128 Growth of the Grand Jury System, (J. Kinghorn), 6 Law Mag. & Rev. (4th S.) 375. Note to College's Trial, 8 How. State Tr. 549.

129 Growth of the Grand Jury System, (J. Kinghorn) 6 Law Mag. & Rev. (4th S.) 373.

130 8 How. St. Tr. 774.

131 For an interesting discussion of this ignoramus see Hallam's Const. Hist. England, Vol. II, p. 202 et seq.

and it is reasonable to assume that the panel was composed wholly of those whose sympathies were inclined toward the Earl.[132]   It is not strange, therefore, that the proceeding by the crown should meet with an ignominious defeat.

It was by reason of the failure of the crown to coerce grand juries to its oppressive purpose, that the king's officials sought a method whereby justice might be dispensed with results more agreeable to their royal master.   The statute of 3 Henry VIII, C. 12, provided that the judges and justices should have power to reform the panel by taking out the names of improper persons and putting in others according to their discretion, and the sheriff was then bound to return the panel as reformed.   This statute was enacted by reason of the abuse by the sheriffs of their power in the selection and returning of grand jurors resulting in packing the panels with those who would carry out the nefarious designs of the sheriff and those with whom he might be acting.[133]

This statute, Sir Robert Sawyer, the attorney general, sought to employ to carry out the wishes of the crown.   The Court of Sessions endeavored to compel the sheriffs to return the panels as they directed, but the sheriffs refused.   The king thereupon ordered that all the judges should attend on a certain day at the Old Bailey.   Here the same proceeding was desired to be had, but the sheriffs demurred and desired to consult counsel.   The court, however, urged that as all the judges were agreed as to such being the law, there could be no necessity for them to consult counsel, and thereupon the sheriffs re-

---

132 Earl of Shaftesbury's Case, 8 How. St. Tr. 775. The following excerpt from the report of the proceedings shows the attitude of the sheriff toward the Earl:

Sheriff P. I desire the witnesses may be kept out of court, and called one by one.

L. C. J. It is a thing certainly, the king's counsel will not be afraid of doing; but sheriffs do not use to move anything of this nature in court, and therefore 'tis not your duty, Mr. Sheriff, to meddle with it.

Sheriff P. It was my duty last time my lord, and appointed.

Att. Gen. (Sir Robert Sawyer). You were acquainted 'twas not your duty last time, and you appear against the king.

133 4 Reeves Hist. Eng. Law 298.

turned the panel as directed.[134]   Whatever change this may
have produced in the success of state prosecutions, was in any
event destined to be short lived, for the reign of Charles the
Second ended four years later, his successor, James the Second, fled to France in 1688, and William of Orange ascended
the throne and a more liberal policy of state has since ensued.

One of the last known instances of the court attempting to
coerce a grand jury occurred in 1783, in Pennsylvania.   Mr.
Oswald, the printer of the *Independent Gazette,* criticised the
conduct of the Supreme Court.   The justices thereof, Chief
Justice McKean and Judge Bryan ordered him to be indicted
for libel, but the grand jury ignored the bill.   The judges severely reproved them in open court in an attempt to overawe
the inquest and sent them back to reconsider the bill, but the
jury refused to return an indictment.[135]

When the settlement of America was begun by Englishmen,
they brought with them all the civil rights which they enjoyed
in their native land, and with them came the grand jury.[136]

134 North's Examen Part 3, Chap. 8.   Growth of the Grand Jury System, (J. Kinghorn), 6 Law Mag. & Rev. (4th S.) 376.

135 Francis Hopkinson's Works, Vol. 1, p. 194.   In Mississippi in 1902,
in the case of Blau *v.* State, 34 So. 153, will be found an instance where
the Court successfully coerced the grand jury into finding a true bill.   A
motion to quash was overruled.   On appeal the judgment was reversed
upon the ground of the improper influence exercised over the grand jury in
the finding of the indictment.

136 Lesser Hist. Jury System 128.   Details of the earliest use of the
grand jury in the American Colonies are few and very unsatisfactory.   In
the New Haven colony, theocratic notions caused the inhabitants to dis-
pense with trial by jury because no precedent for it could be found in the
laws of Moses.   Fiske—Beginnings of New England 314.   In Boston in
1644, a certain Captain Keayne was tried for larceny by a jury and acquitted: Id. 129; while in Plymouth in 1651, a grand jury presented one
Holmes for holding a disorderly meeting; Id. 218.   In Pennsylvania,
the early cases in which reference to a grand jury is made,
have been collected by Hon. Samuel W. Pennypacker, in an address
entitled Pennsylvania Colonial Cases.   The first case cited is that of the
Proprietor *v.* Charles Pickering, and arose in August, 1683: Pennsylvania
Colonial Cases, p. 32.   The case of Proprietor *v.* Mattson was founded upon
an indictment by the grand jury charging the defendant with witchcraft:
Id. p. 35.   Two presentments by the grand jury in 1685 called attention to

The institutions which they brought, naturally flourished in a land so far away from the mother country, and consequently removed from the attacks which were subsequently made by the crown upon the liberties of the people. For nearly one hundred years the colonies were allowed to exercise to the fullest extent a greater degree of civil rights than at any time had been permitted to the subject in England. The only restraint placed upon them was by the appointment of royal governors, but even then there were no state prosecutions like those being carried on in the mother country. Free from restraints which were there placed upon them, it was most natural that the grand jury should exercise their great power in a manner most calculated to insure the liberty and freedom of thought of the people. In New York in 1735, an attempt was made to indict John Peter Zenger, the editor and proprietor of a newspaper called the *Weekly Journal,* for libel because of the manner in which he held up to scorn the deeds of the royal governor, but the grand jury ignored the bill. He was then proceeded against by an information filed by the attorney general for the province, and after a trial in which he was defended by the Philadelphia lawyer, Andrew Hamilton, was triumphantly acquitted.[137]

The Constitution of the United States, as adopted by the states, contained no guaranty of presentment or indictment by a grand jury, but this omission was remedied by the passing of the first ten amendments, substantially a bill of rights, of which Article V provides: "No person shall be held to answer for a capital or otherwise infamous crime, unless on a presentment or indictment of a grand jury, except in cases arising in the

various public evils and suggested certain public improvements: Id. p. 71-72. In the case of Peter and Bridgett Cock *v.* John Rambo, the indictment, which was found in 1685, is reproduced entire. This indictment seems to have been read to the grand jury in open court at the request of counsel for the prosecution. The finding thereon was "Wee find this bill. John King, foreman." Id. p. 79. In 1703, in Pennsylvania, a grand jury presented a number of individuals for various offences: Watson's Annals of Philadelphia, Vol. I, p. 308; Fiske—The Dutch and Quaker Colonies in America, Vol. II, p. 382.

137 The Dutch and Quaker Colonies (John Fiske), Vol. II, pp. 290-299.

land or naval forces,[138] or in the militia when in actual service in time of war or public danger;" . . . .

This provision applies solely to offences against the United States and triable in the United States Courts,[139] and has reference not only to those offences which at common law were capital or infamous, but to such as might thereafter be made capital or infamous by legislation of Congress.[140] It has been held not to affect prosecutions brought by means of an information filed by the United States District Attorney in cases where the offence does not constitute a capital or otherwise infamous crime.[141] In this respect the Constitution of the United States assures to the citizen the same protection to his liberty which the laws of England afford to the subjects of the king.

The Fourteenth Amendment does not require the states to prosecute crimes by means of indictment or prohibit them from proceeding by information. The provision "due process of law" refers only to the prosecution of offences by regular judicial proceedings.[142]

It has, therefore, become usual both in England and the United States to proceed by information where the law gives that right, and has frequently been employed in cases where a bill has been submitted to, and ignored by, a grand jury.

The Constitution of Pennsylvania affords a still greater pro-

---

138 See Ex Parte Wildman, 29 Fed. Cas. 1232.

139 Hurtado v. California, 110 U. S. 516; Bollyn v. Nebraska, 176 U. S. 83; Twitchell v. Com. 7 Wall (U. S.) 321; Noles v. State, 24 Ala. 672; State v. Wells, 46 Iowa, 662; State v. Barnett, 3 Kan. 250; State v. Jackson, 21 La. Ann. 574; Jackson v. Wood, 2 Cow. (N. Y.), 819; Prescott v. State, 19 Ohio, 184; State v. Shumpert, 1 S. C., 85; Pitner v. State, 23 Tex. App. 366; State v. Keyes, 8 Vt., 57; State v. Nordstrom, 7 Wash., 506; State v. Baldwin, 15 Wash., 15. The powers of local government exercised by the Cherokee Nation are local powers, not created by the Constitution, and hence are not operated upon by Amendment V thereof, requiring a presentment by a grand jury in the case of a capital or other infamous crime; Talton v. Mayes, 163 U. S., 376.

140 U. S. v. Brady, 3 Cr. Law Mag. 69.

141 Mackin v. U. S., 117 U. S. 328; Ex Parte Wilson, 114 U. S. 417.

142 Hurtado v. California, 110 U. S. 516; Kalloch v. Superior Court, 56 Calif. 229; Rowan v. State, 30 Wis. 129.

tection to the liberty of the citizen.   Section 10 of the Declaration of Rights provides: "No person shall for any indictable offence, be proceeded against criminally, by information, except in cases arising in the land or naval forces or in the militia when in actual service in time of war or public danger, or by leave of the court for oppression or misdemeanor in office."

As all offences are indictable offences in Pennsylvania, the filing of an information has been very rarely employed, by reason of the limited class of cases to which it can be applied.   The nature of this proceeding received judicial construction in an early Pennsylvania case[143] decided by Mr. Justice Shippen, who delivered the following opinion: "The present is the first instance, that we recollect, of an application of this kind in Pennsylvania; and on opening the case, it struck us to be within the 10th section of the ninth article of the constitution, which declares that no person shall for any indictable offense, be proceeded against criminally by information, except in cases that are not involved in the present motion.   But, on consideration, it is evident that the constitution refers to informations, as a form of prosecution, to punish an offender, without the intervention of a grand jury; whereas an information, in the nature of a writ of quo warranto, is applied to the mere purpose of trying a civil right and ousting the wrongful possessor of an office."   .   .   .   .

Under the same statute the court made absolute a rule for an information where the proceeding was against a justice of the peace who was charged with a misdemeanor in office in taking insufficient bail.[144]   But where a prosecutor appeared to be proceeding from vexatious motives, the court discharged the rule for an information.[145]

The grand jury of the present time is a wholly different institution from that originated by the Anglo-Saxons.   The ancient institution was designed to aid the government in detecting and punishing crime; the tyranny of kings made it an instrument to defeat the government.   Now it occupies the ano-

---

143 Res. *v*. Wray, 3 Dall. (Pa.) 490.
144 Res. *v*. Burns, 1 Yeates (Pa.) 370.
145 Res. *v*. Prior, 1 Yeates (Pa.) 206.

malous position of a public accuser, while at the same time it stands as a defender of the liberty of the people.

It remains to consider whether or not the grand jury is worthy to be retained among the institutions of a free government in this progressive age.   The institution has been attacked with great vehemence by writers of acknowledged ability, both English and American, but at the same time it has been defended with equal vigor by men no less able.   That the institution and its workings are open to criticism no one will question, but that the defects which are pointed out by its critics are of such a nature as to justify its abolition cannot be so readily conceded.

The attacks upon it are based principally on three grounds:

1. That it is now a useless institution.
2. Its irresponsibility.
3. Its secrecy of action.

It is well said by an English opponent of the institution,[146] "ten centuries of usage give a very striking respectability to any institution; and grand juries existed before the feudal law and have survived its extinction.   They are perhaps the oldest of existing institutions; but if they are to continue, they must rest on their continuing utility, not on their antiquity, for future toleration."

It is urged with great earnestness and the argument contains much merit that the system which has been in force the past three hundred years of giving a defendant a preliminary hearing before a magistrate, makes the work of the grand jury in this class of cases superfluous.[147]   In many instances this argument would seem to be well founded, since the finding of a true bill by the grand jury in cases returned to the district attorney by the committing magistrates would be but a ratification of the action of the magistrate, but it is not true in all cases.   There are many cases of a trifling nature which are returned by the committing magistrates and when brought before the grand jury the indictments are ignored.   In counties where the volume of business is small, it would be of little con-

146 Grand Juries 29 L. T. 21.
147 Bentham—Rationale of Judicial Evidence, Vol. II, p. 312.

sequence if the grand jury found true bills even in these cases, but in counties where the volume of business is large, and this is particularly true of the great cities which frequently are co-extensive with the boundaries of the county, it then becomes of vital importance that there should be a tribunal to sift from the great mass of cases those which are too trifling in their nature to require further prosecution.   And this is a duty which could not well devolve upon a single officer, for unless testimony was heard by him there would be no feasable way to determine which cases should be prosecuted and which should be ignored. If evidence is therefore to be heard, it is wiser that it be heard and considered by a body impartially selected from the people, than by a single officer whose training would incline him to find those grounds upon which the prosecution might be sustained.

While in ignoring bills of indictment it frequently happens that defendants are set free who undoubtedly merit punishment, it is idle to charge that this is a defect in the system or a reason why it should be abolished, for the same result is of frequent occurrence where defendants are tried before petit juries, when the evidence is heard in open court.   If, when the grand jurors hear only the evidence in favor of a prosecutor, given by witnesses summoned by the district attorney, and examined by him before the grand jury, they are unable to return a true bill, how can it reasonably be asserted that a petit jury, where the entire twelve must concur, would have found the defendant guilty when the grand jury, which usually exceeds this number, are unable to muster twelve who concur in finding the bill. To charge a grand jury with failure to act in furtherance of justice, under such circumstances, is an unwarranted imputation upon the judgment of intelligent men and is only made by writers who give the subject a superficial consideration.[148] That because the minority view the evidence in a different

148 Hon. Daniel Davis, Attorney General of Massachusetts, speaking of his own experience says: "But the experience of thirty years furnishes an answer most honorable to the intelligence and integrity of that body of citizens from which the grand jury are selected; and that is, that they almost universally decide correctly:" Precedents of Indictments, p. 21.

light from the majority is to say the majority have come to the wrong conclusion, is a proposition not recognized in this country. The defendant, no matter what the evidence against him may be, is presumed to be innocent until proven guilty, and if the prosecuting officer, with all the power he possesses within the sealed doors of the grand jury room, is unable to convince twelve out of those present, of the guilt of the defendant, he cannot well say that he could do more before the petit jury, where the defendant has the additional advantages of counsel and witnesses in his defence, and a trial judge who may be called upon to rule out incompetent and irrelevant evidence. There are undoubtedly many cases in which true bills are found where incompetent and irrelevant evidence has been given before the grand jury and formed the inducement to their action.

The fact that sometimes they indict innocent persons is to be deplored, but as an argument in favor of the abolition of the institution is without merit. The right still remains for such defendant to establish his innocence before a petit jury, where he is aided by his counsel and may have witnesses in his behalf. If, in such cases, the prosecution was by information filed by the district attorney upon the return of the committing magistrate, there would be no possible chance of the innocent defendant escaping trial. Primarily the object of the grand jury is not to protect the innocent, for all accused persons are presumed innocent until the contrary be shown, but is to accuse those persons, who, upon the evidence submitted by the prosecutor, if uncontradicted, would cause the grand jurors to believe the defendant guilty of the offence charged.[149] When, therefore, the evidence is of such a nature as to justify the return of an indictment by the grand jury, it is only proper that whether innocent or guilty, the accused should be put upon his trial.

It is true that the grand jury ordinarily do but little more than review the judgment of the committing magistrate, and for this reason the institution is said to be useless. But it is eminently fitting that such a body should exist to review the judgment of such magistrates. It is absurd to contend that

149 Post 105, 141, 142.

in a government such as ours, composed of a system of checks and balances, a committing magistrate is an individual whose discretion does not require review.   They are chosen as a rule from men who have but little knowledge of the law and whose principal qualification is the political service rendered to their party and not the personal fitness of the individual for the office.   In a large number of cases the warrant will be issued by a magistrate, known either to the prosecutor or his counsel, who invariably is selected because of the acquaintanceship. That a defendant who is committed or held in bail under such circumstances should be entitled to have the judgment of the magistrate reviewed by a tribunal sufficiently large and without personal interest in the case, is but a reasonable requirement. Not that the magistrate may have acted improperly or violated the terms of his oath, but that prosecutions which are or may have been begun under such conditions, shall be declared by an impartial body to be well founded in fact before a defendant shall be obliged to answer.

An English writer[150] discusses the subject in this language: "The criminal who has been committed on the well considered opinion of the responsible magistrate is set at large by the influence of the random impressions of twenty-three irresponsible gentlemen.   Such an enlargement is in itself a slander or a serious charge against the committing magistrate, and logically ought to be almost conclusive evidence of his unfitness to act either from malice or incapacity."

The English system of committing magistrates is of a somewhat different nature from that of Pennsylvania.   They have there what are known as stipendiary magistrates, that is, men who are paid fixed salaries for their services, but are required either to be learned in the law or to be accompanied by a duly articled clerk.[151]   If the logic of the writer above quoted is to be pursued to a conclusion, it means when the appellate court reverses the court below that that is conclusive evidence of the unfitness of such judge to fill his high office, notwithstanding

150 Grand Juries 29 L. T. 21.
151 Id.

he has adjudged correctly in the great majority of cases which have come before him.

If it be said the cases are not analogous in that the grand jurors are laymen who review the decision of a magistrate learned in the law, it may be answered that the laymen review not the law, but the facts of the case, and as to those facts all the legal learning which the magistrate may possess will not make him a better judge of the truth of the facts or the credibility of the witnesses.   As to the facts, he is but one layman against twenty-three, and all experience has taught that the latter body are far more apt to arrive at a correct conclusion. The same author who contends that the judgment of the stipendiary magistrate is superior to that of the twenty-three grand jurors would probably repel the assertion that the judge who presides at the trial is more likely to arrive at a correct conclusion upon disputed facts than the twelve jurors sworn to pass upon them, yet the two cases are precisely analogous. Upon all questions of fact, the composite make-up of the twelve or the twenty-three vests in such body a knowledge which no one man can possess and is more productive of correct findings. It is given neither to one man nor to any body of men to invariably arrive at correct conclusions, but because they at times may err, it affords no ground for saying that by reason of such error they are either ignorant, malicious or incompetent.

Upon this point an English writer[152] pertinently remarks, "Moreover the stipendiary magistrates we have are not all such oracles of wisdom that we should conclude that the grand jury must always be wrong and the magistrate right upon the question of whether there is a prima facie case."

It is thought by one writer that the grand jury is a useless institution because it no longer occupies its original position, and by reason of this fact should be abolished.[153]   Were we to

152 Grand Juries, 67 L. T. 381.

153 On Grand Juries, (E. E. Meek) 85 Law Times 395.   The absurdity of this argument is brought to our attention in the case of Hurtado v. California, 110 U. S. 516, in which it was contended that the words "due process of law" as used in the Fourteenth Amendment to the Constitution of the United States was the equivalent of the phrase "law of the land" in the twenty-ninth chapter of Magna Charta and had acquired

apply this reasoning to the various branches of the law at the present day, to our courts, our institutions, and our procedure, nearly all must be swept away, for but little of it retains its original position.   Things have changed with the progress of the centuries and it is the height of absurdity to contend that because the grand jury is no longer a power in the hands of unscrupulous persons to oppress those who hindered or interfered with their improper designs as it was in times past, it no longer occupies its original position and should be cast aside.

That the grand jury is an irresponsible body is admitted and it is this want of responsibility which the opponents of the institution seize eagerly upon in their endeavor to show why the institution should be abolished.   An American writer[154] thus expresses his views: "The principal objection which can be urged against the grand jury, as now constituted, is the absolute personal irresponsibility of the individual juror attendant upon the performance of his duties.   He is a law unto himself; no power can regulate him and no power can control him.   He can be called before no earthly tribunal, except his own conscience, to account for his action.   He can pursue an enemy for personal motives of revenge; he can favor a friend or political associate; he can advance and maintain before the jury by argument ideas that he would never father in any other place; he can shirk responsibility by voting to turn the guilty loose, pleading for mercy for the confessed criminal and the next moment

a fixed, definite, and technical meaning; and by reason of this amendment a State could not proceed against a defendant for felony except upon an indictment found by a grand jury. Mr. Justice Matthews who delivered the opinion of the Court meets this argument in this language: "But to hold that such a characteristic is essential to due process of law would be to deny every quality of the law but its age, and to render it incapable of progress or improvement. It would be to stamp upon our jurisprudence the unchangeableness attributed to the laws of the Medes and Persians.

"This would be all the more singular and surprising in this quick and active age when we consider that, owing to the progressive development of legal ideas and institutions in England, the words of Magna Charta stood for very different things at the time of the separation of the American colonies from what they represented originally."

154 The Abolition of the Grand Jury, (C. E. Chiperfield) 5 Am. Law 487.

cast his vote to indict the innocent, but friendless accused; ignoring in order to do so his oath and every distinction between hearsay and competent evidence. The state's attorney is powerless to protest against or prevent these insane antics upon the juror's part, and the court is as equally unable to prevent the denial of justice."

Undoubtedly it is within the power of a grand juror to act in the manner thus described, and that this is sometimes done will hardly be questioned. That, however, it is of such universal occurrence as to seriously affect the administration of justice and demand the abolition of the institution is not the fact. To contend that it is, is to say that on every grand jury there are at least twelve men so lost to all sense of truth, honor and justice and so utterly oblivious to the requirements of their oath, that they will perjure themselves in order to do the will of a fellow juror.

We have only to turn back to early English history to see how the grand jury was so used for improper purposes that the statute of 3 Henry VIII, C. 12, was enacted, giving to the judges and justices the right to reform the panels of grand jurors returned by the sheriff, and then compelling the sheriff to make return of the panel so reformed. It is recited by the preamble of the above statute,[155] "That many oppressions had been, by the untrue demeanor of sheriffs and their ministers, done to great numbers of the king's subjects, by means of returning at sessions holden for the bodies of shires, the names of such persons, as for the singular advantage of the said sheriffs and their ministers; by reason whereof many substantial persons (the king's true subjects) had been wrongfully indicted of divers felonies and other misbehaviour by their covin and falsehood; and also sometimes by labor of the said sheriffs, divers great felonies had been concealed, and not presented by the said persons, by the said sheriffs and their ministers partially returned, to the intent to compel the offenders to make fines, and give rewards to the said sheriffs and their ministers."

Lord Coke[156] also directs attention to this evil and points

---

155 Hawk. Pl. C. Book 2, Ch. 25, Sec. 32.
156 Co. Inst., Vol. III, p. 33.

out the statutory remedy. In Scarlet's case,[157] one Robert
Scarlet had unlawfully procured himself to be placed upon a
panel of grand jurors and caused indictments to be found
against innocent persons. The court suspected that something was wrong, and inquired of the inquest as to the evidence
upon which the bills had been found, which disclosed the
agency of Scarlet and brought punishment upon him.

At the present day it cannot justly be said that the grand
jury is wholly irresponsible. It is true that they have great
freedom of action and the reasons which induce their action
cannot be inquired into.[158]   But if they have acted from improper motives or been improperly influenced, and this could
not be made to appear upon a motion to quash the indictment,
it is still within the power of the district attorney with leave
of court, to enter a nolle pros or submit the bill, without trial,
to a petit jury and have a verdict of not guilty rendered
thereon.   On the other hand, if the grand jury improperly re-
ject a bill, it is still competent for the district attorney to lay
the matter before a subsequent grand jury, which may act
otherwise.[159]   The ability of the grand jurors to work harm by
the abuse of their power is, therefore, more fancied than real.

Nor can there be said to be any more merit in the complaint
that the secrecy surrounding the grand jury is an evil which
should be done away with.   They deliberate in secret, but the
petit jury does likewise, and no one would contend for a moment that a petit jury should deliberate in public.   What reason can then be advanced why a grand jury should deliberate
in public?   Nor would the hearing of the testimony in public
be of any advantage unless counsel for the defence were permitted to cross-examine the witnesses produced, which would
necessitate a judge being present, and such a course as this
would neither be desirable nor productive of good.   If the
closed doors of the grand jury room are an incentive to perjury, the witness must also perjure himself before the petit
jury to make his false testimony effective.   And as only the
witnesses for the prosecution are heard, it is very unlikely that

157 12 Co. 98.
158 Post 119, 166.
159 Post 112, 152.

a defendant would be set free by reason of the prosecution's witnesses committing perjury in his behalf.

The partisan feeling of the opponents and the defenders of the grand jury usually leads them into violent and unwarranted condemnation or rash and extravagant praise.   Chief Justice Shaw,[160] of the Supreme Court of Massachusetts, in a charge to a grand jury in 1832, admirably set forth the conservative view of this institution.   "In a free and popular government," he said, "it is of the utmost importance to the peace and harmony of society, not only that the administration of justice and the punishment of crimes should in fact be impartial, but that it should be so conducted as to inspire a general confidence, and that it will and must be so.   To accomplish this, nothing could be better contrived than a selection of a body, considerably numerous, by lot, from amongst those, who previously and without regard to time, person, or occasion, have been selected from among their fellow citizens, as persons deemed worthy of this high trust by their moral worth, and general respectability of character.   And although under peculiar states of excitement, and in particular instances, in making this original selection, party spirit, or sectarian zeal may exert their influence, yet it can hardly be expected that this will happen so frequently or so extensively, as seriously to affect the character or influence the deliberations of grand juries.   Should this ever occur, to an extent sufficient to weaken the confidence now reposed in their entire impartiality, and thus destroy or impair the utility of this noble institution, it would be an event, than which none should be more earnestly deprecated by every lover of impartial justice, and every friend of free government.

"Were the important function of accusation placed in the hands of any individual officer, however elevated, it would be difficult to avoid the suspicion of partiality or favoritism, a disposition to screen the guilty or persecute the innocent.   But the grand jury, by the mode of its selection, by its number and character, and the temporary exercise of its powers, is placed beyond the reach or the suspicion of fear or favor of being overawed by power or seduced by persuasion."

160 Charge to Grand Jury, 8 Am. Jurist 216.

In some of the Western States the grand jury has either been abolished, or the constitution has been altered to permit this to be done.[161]   In California, where the district attorney files an information in all cases of felony and misdemeanor, the statutes make provision for a grand jury and confer upon it greater inquisitorial power than has ever been conceded to it in those states which proceed with it according to the common law.[162]

The conservatism of the Eastern States has caused the retention of the grand jury among their institutions.   Whether the policy of those states which have abolished it is a wise one or not cannot yet be determined.   This can only be learned after the system which has supplanted it has stood the test through the coming years and emerged unscathed and with honor from great crises.   But when it is proposed to turn aside from a course which has been followed for centuries to new and untried methods, the warning of Judge King[163] applies with great force: "Any and every innovation in the ancient and settled usages of the common law, calculated in any respect to weaken the barriers thrown around the liberty and security of the citizens, should be viewed with jealousy, and trusted with caution."

161 See Constitutions of Colorado, 1876, Art. II, Sec. 23; Illinois, 1870, Art. II, Sec. 8; Indiana, 1851, Art. VII, Sec. 17; Nebraska, 1875, Art. I, Sec. 10. See Thompson & Merriam on Juries, Sec. 471-2. In Michigan, How. Ann. St., Sec. 9554, dispenses with grand juries unless summoned by the order of the judge. See People v. Reigel, 78 N. W., 1017. As to Montana, see State v. King, 24 Pac., 265. Grand Juries abolished in Kansas by Act of Feb. 12, 1864, Sec. 7, and see Rice v. State, 3 Kan. 141. In Minnesota the people, by a large majority vote, have adopted a constitutional amendment abolishing the grand jury. The Literary Digest, Vol. 30, p. 50.

162 See Grand Juries in the United States, 7 Law Journal, 729. Penal Code Calif., Sec. 915-929. The Constitution of California, Art. 1, Sec. 8, provides: "Offences heretofore required to be prosecuted by indictment, shall be prosecuted by information, after examination and commitment by a magistrate, or by indictment, with or without such examination and commitment, as may be prescribed by law. A grand jury shall be drawn and summoned at least once a year in each county."

163 Case of Lloyd and Carpenter, 3 Clark (Pa.) 188.

PART II

The grand jury is a body composed of not less than twelve[1] and not more than twenty-three persons;[2] and in the Federal courts it is provided by Act of Congress that the number shall not be less than sixteen nor more than twenty-three.[3] Twenty-four, however, are summoned, but never more than twenty-three are sworn, lest there be two full juries, one of whom is for finding a true bill, the other for ignoring it.[4] Where twenty-four were sworn the indictment was quashed,[5] and this decision is undoubtedly in accord with the reason of the rule.

If twenty-four are sworn and serve upon the panel, then the reason of the rule that there shall not be two full juries is violated, and while the jurors may be interrogated as to whether

---

1 Ostrander *v.* State, 18 Iowa, 435; State *v.* Green, 66 Mo., 631; State *v.* Clayton, 11 Rich. Law (S. C.) 581; Pybos *v.* State, 3 Humph. (Tenn.) 49; State *v.* Kopp, 34 Kan., 522; State *v.* Brainerd, 56 Vt., 532; State *v.* Perry, 29 S. E., 384. The record must show that the grand jury consisted of twelve men or the judgment will be reversed. Carpenter *v.* State, 4 How. (Miss.) 163.

2 4 Bl. Com. 302. In Utah the statute provides that a grand jury must consist of twenty-four. Brannigan *v.* People, 3 Utah, 488.

3 R. S. U. S. Sec. 808; 1 Whart. Cr. Laws, Sec. 463a. In Reynolds *v.* U. S., 98 U. S. 145, it was held that Sec. 808 of the Revised Statutes applied only to circuit and district courts of the United States; territorial courts being governed by the territorial laws then in force.

4 1 Whart. Cr. Law, Sec. 465, (7th ed.).

5 People *v.* King, 2 Caines (N. Y.) 98; Com. *v.* Salter, 2 Pears. (Pa.) 461; Com. *v.* Leisenring, Id. 466; In Com. *v.* Dietrich, 7 Pa. Supr. Ct. Rep. 515, a presentment of the grand jury was signed by the twenty-four grand jurors, but this question was not raised until after a trial on the merits. In his opinion, Rice, P. J., says, "Its action was none the less valid because it was preceded by the unanimous presentment of a former grand jury." See King *v.* Marsh, 1 N. & P. 187.

twelve concurred in finding the bill, they will not be permitted to make known how many either voted for or against it.[6] The law's requirement of secrecy concerning the manner in which the grand jury acts, therefore makes it imperative that the reason of the rule be adhered to strictly. If more than the number prescribed by law are sworn on the grand jury, even though all be regularly drawn, summoned and returned, it cannot legally act.[7] All on the panel in excess of the legal number are not bound by the oath and their presence in the grand jury room destroys its secrecy of action, and will vitiate the indictment. If more than the legal number of grand jurors are drawn, summoned, empaneled and sworn, but only the legal number actually serve, the defendant will in no manner be prejudiced thereby and an indictment found by such grand jury will be sustained.[8]

While the presence of more than the maximum number of grand jurors will invalidate an indictment, the presence of less than the minimum number will not always work this result[9] unless there should be present less than the legal number required to find an indictment. The general rule seems to be that where the statute specifies a certain number shall constitute the grand jury and less than this number be empaneled, the grand jury is illegally constituted; but if the legal number be empaneled and afterward some of the grand jurors absent themselves, an indictment will be valid if found by the number of grand jurors required to concur in its finding.[10]

---

6 Post 118, 121, 166.

7 Harding v. State, 22 Ark. 210; People v. Thurston, 5 Calif. 69; Keech v. State, 15 Fla. 591; Downs v. Com. 92 Ky. 605; Com. v. Wood, 2 Cush. (Mass..) 149; Miller v. State, 33 Miss. 356; Box v. State, 34 Miss. 614; People v. King, 2 Caines (N. Y.) 98; Com. v. Salter, 2 Pears (Pa.) 461; Com. v. Leisenring, Id. 466; Lott v. State, 18 Tex. App. 627; Wells v. State, 21 Id. 594; Harrell v. State, 22 Id. 692; Ex Parte Reynolds, 34 S. W. 120; Ex Parte Ogle, 61 S. W. 122; Ogle v. State, 63 S. W. 1009.

8 Turner v. State, 78 Ga. 174; Crimm v. Com., 119 Mass. 326; State v. Watson, 104 N. C. 735; State v. Fee, 19 Wis. 562. And see Wallis v. State, 54 Ark. 611; Leathers v. State, 26 Miss, 73.

9 People v. Simmons, 119 Calif. 1; State v. Perry, 29 S. E. 384. But see State v. Cooley, 75 N. W. 729.

10 Gladden v. State, 12 Fla. 562; Straughan v. State, 16 Ark. 37; In re Wilson, 140 U. S. 575. And see Post 56, 147.

While the decisions upon this point are by no means uniform, the later cases hold that the grand jury having consisted of the prescribed number at the time it was empaneled, and thereby was a lawful body when formed, it remains a lawful body thereafter even though less than the minimum number remain, provided the number required to find a true bill are present at its finding. It must be remembered, however, that this question can only present itself where a statute has been enacted prescribing the minimum number of grand jurors necessary to form a legal grand jury and then providing that a number less than the minimum may find a true bill. This question could not arise with the common law grand jury. There the minimum number to constitute a lawful body is fixed at twelve, and this entire number must concur in order to find a true bill. If less than the minimum in such case be present, a bill found by such lesser number would be void.

The leading case upon this question is In re Wilson[10]* where the United States Supreme Court refused to discharge upon a writ of habeas corpus a defendant who had been indicted by a grand jury consisting of fifteen persons, twelve concurring, where the statute provided that the grand jury should consist of not less than seventeen nor more than twenty-three, and requiring only the concurrence of twelve for the finding of a true bill. Mr. Justice Brewer, who delivered the opinion of the court in this case says:

"By petitioner's argument, if there had been two more grand jurors it would have been a legal body. If the two had been present, and had voted against the indictment, still such opposing votes would not have prevented its finding by the concurrence of the twelve who did in fact vote in its favor. It would seem, therefore, as though the error was not prejudicial to the substantial rights of the petitioner."

The manner of selecting and procuring the attendance of grand jurors is now wholly regulated by statute in the various states. While the statutes differ in the method provided for procuring the attendance of grand jurors, the general practice in many of the states is for the court to issue an order or pre-

10* In re Wilson, 140 U. S. 575.

cept[11] to the proper official[12] directing that a venire issue[13] which commands the persons charged with such duties[14] to draw and summon a panel of grand jurors. The venire should be under the seal of the court,[15] although it has been held not to be void when issued without the seal.[16] If it is improperly tested the writ may be amended.[17]

In some states it is provided by statute that the grand jurors shall be drawn or summoned at a certain time prior to the session of the court. Where this requirement has been neglected or disregarded the indictment in some instances has been

11 This need not be entered of record unless directed by statute: Mesmer v. Com., 26 Gratt. (Va.) 976. A verbal order is sufficient; U. S. v. Reed, 27 Fed Cas. 727. Where an indictment is found by a grand jury summoned by a sheriff without precept, the indictment will be quashed: Nicholls v. State, 5 N. J. Law 539; Chase v. State, 20 N. J. Law 218; State v. Cantrell, 21 Ark. 127. But see Hess v. State, 73 Ind. 537. In McGuire v. People, 2 Parker Cr. Rep. (N. Y.) 148, it was held that if no precept issued the defendant could avail himself of such irregularity after verdict. Where a statute authorized the sheriff to summon grand jurors without precept, but he neglected to have a grand jury in court on the first day of the term, it was held that the judge could issue a precept to the sheriff, directing him to produce a grand jury at a later day; the statute did not take from the court the right to issue its precept: Challenge to Grand Jury, 3 N. J. Law Jour. 153. That the order was not served upon the sheriff is not error, he having regularly summoned a grand jury; People v. Cuitano, 15 Calif. 327.

12 That the venire was issued by a person not legally qualified to act was held not a good objection in arrest of judgment: Peters v. State, 11 Tex. 762.

13 State v. Lightbody, 38 Me. 200. A venire need not issue: Bird v. State, 14 Ga. 43; Boyd v. State, 46 Tenn. (6 Cold.) 1; Robinson v. Com. 88 Va. 900; Combs v. Com., 90 Va. 88.

14 Conner v. State, 25 Ga. 515. That the venire is not addressed to the proper officer will not avail a defendant where the writ was actually received and executed by the proper person: State v. Phillips, 2 Ala. 297.

15 State v. Lightbody, 38 Me. 200; State v. Fleming, 66 Me. 142; People v. McKay, 18 Johns (N. Y.) 212.

16 Maher v. State, 1 Port. (Ala.) 265; Bennett v. State, 1 Martin & Yerger (Tenn.) 133; State v. Bradford, 57 N. H. 188.

17 People v. The Justices, 20 Johns (N. Y.) 310; Davis v. Com. 89 Va. 132. In State v. Bradford, 57 N. H. 188, it was held that the venire need not bear teste of the chief, first or senior justice.

quashed;[18] in others it has been sustained upon the ground that this provision of the statute is but directory and a failure to comply with it will in no manner prejudice the defendant.[19]

A venire which directs the sheriff to summon good and lawful men is sufficient; it need not set forth the qualifications requisite to constitute them good and lawful grand jurors.[20] It should set forth correctly the names of the persons to be summoned; failure to observe this requirement affords good ground upon which a defendant may move to set aside the indictment. It has, however, been held that the omission of a middle name, the insertion of a wrong initial, the omission of an initial, or the mis-spelling of a name will in general be no ground for quashing an indictment, there being no proof that a person other than the one summoned bears the name as set forth in the writ and was the person designated thereby to be summoned as a grand juror.[21]

It is the duty of the officer charged with the execution of the venire to make a return thereto, showing the manner in which the command of the writ was obeyed and the authority by which he acted.[22] Should he fail to do so, an indictment will not be quashed for this reason, but the court will, on its attention being directed to the fact, order such officer to make a return, or sign such return if made and not signed.[23] The court

---

18 State *v.* Lauer, 41 Neb. 226; Thorpe *v.* People, 3 Utah, 441.

19 State *v.* Smith, 67 Me. 328; State *v.* Smith, 38 S. C. 270.

20 State *v.* Alderson, 10 Yerg. (Tenn.) 523. And see Welsh *v.* State, 96 Ala. 92; Stewart *v.* State, 98 Ala. 70.

21 Rampey *v.* State, 83 Ala. 31; State *v.* Armstrong, 167 Mo. 257; State *v.* McNamara, 3 Nev. 70; State *v.* Van Auken, 68 N. W. 454. See Turner *v.* State, 78 Ga., 174. In Nixon *v.* State, 68 Ala. 535, a juror regularly drawn was falsely personated by another person of the same surname, who was sworn as a member of the grand jury and a plea in abatement was sustained.

22 State *v.* Rickey, 9 N. J. Law, 293; Challenge to Grand Jury, 3 N. J. Law Jour. 153; Chase *v.* State, 20 N. J. Law 218; State *v.* Clough, 49 Me. 573. And see State *v.* Powers, 59 S. C. 200. It is not necessary that the return should show that the sheriff served the writ upon the jury commissioners, the record showing that the writ issued and that the commissioners acted in accordance therewith: State *v.* Derrick, 44 S. C. 344.

23 Com. *v.* Chauncey, 2 Ashm. (Pa.) 101; State *v.* Derrick, 44 S. C. 344.

4

has allowed it to be signed after verdict of guilty in a capital case.[24]

In this case it was said by Chief Justice Parker: "Here the return was duly made, except that the officer through inadvertence had omitted to affix his signature; and this he has now done, and we think properly, by the permission of the court. It is true, that in a capital case the court would not permit the prisoner to be prejudiced by an amendment, but they are not bound to shut their eyes to the justice of the case, when an error in matter of form can be rectified without any prejudice to him."

The return may be amended to accord with the facts.[25]

Where it happens that less than the requisite number of persons are present to constitute a legal grand jury, it is ordinarily provided by statute how sufficient jurors shall be procured to bring that body up to the legal number. The court issues an order to the sheriff or other officer charged with the duty of summoning the jurors, directing the number to be returned[26] and whether they shall be summoned from the same or other panels of jurors,[27] from the body of the county[28] or from the bystanders.[29] If the judge should give to the sheriff the names

24 Com. v. Parker, 2 Pick (Mass.) 550.

25 Rampey v. State, 83 Ala. 31; State v. Clough, 49 Me. 573.

26 Kilgore v. State, 74 Ala. 1; Levy v. Wilson, 69 Calif. 105. No precept need issue to summon talesmen as grand jurors: State v. Pierce, 8 Iowa 231.

27 State v. Gurlagh, 76 Iowa 141; State v. Silvers, 82 Iowa 714; State v. Jacobs, 6 Tex. 99.

28 Keech v. State, 15 Fla. 591; Jenkins v. State, 35 Fla. 737; State v. Garhart, 35 Iowa 315; Montgomery v. State, 3 Kan. 263; See Chartz v. Territory, 32 Pac. 166. The court may order that the deficiency be filled either from the list furnished by the county commissioners, by drawing from the box or from the body of the county: Jones v. State, 18 Fla. 889; Dukes v. State, 14 Fla. 499; Newton v. State, 21 Fla. 53. In Finley v. State, 61 Ala. 201; Couch v. State, 63 Ala. 163 and Benson v. State, 68 Ala. 513, it was held that talesmen must be summoned from the qualified citizens of the county and not from the by-standers.

29 State v. Swim, 60 Ark. 587; Winter v. Muscogee Railroad Co., 11 Ga. 438; Nealon v. People, 39 Ill. App. 481; Dorman v. State, 56 Ind. 454; Dowling v. State, 5 Smedes & M. (Miss.) 664; Portis v. State, 23 Miss. 578; Yelm Jim v. Territory, 1 Wash. T. 63; Watt v. Territory, Id. 409.

of persons to be summoned as talesmen, while this is an irregularity, it has been held not sufficient to invalidate an indictment found by a grand jury so constituted [30] In the absence of a statute regulating the summoning of talesmen it has been held that a judge has no authority to issue a venire to supply any deficiency in the number of grand jurors, but that a tales should issue and by-standers be brought in.[31] Substitutes cannot be received for any part of the regular panel.[32]

Before talesmen can lawfully be summoned, the panel must be reduced below the number necessary to indict or form a legal grand jury,[33] and this must be shown affirmatively by the record which must also show that a formal order for summoning talesmen was made by the court. If this be not affirmatively shown by the record, it is an irregularity which may be taken advantage of by motion to quash.[34] A trial on the merits of the issue will cure such irregularity.

A grand juror regularly drawn and summoned, but who does not appear until after the grand jury has been organized, sworn and charged, may in general be allowed to act with that body after the oath has been administered to them.[35] This,

30 State *v.* Copp., 34 Kan. 522. And see State *v.* Keating, 85 Md. 188; Runnels *v.* State, 28 Ark. 121.

31 State *v.* Symonds, 36 Me. 128.

32 Rawls *v.* State, 8 Smedes & M. (Miss.) 599. If a grand juror regularly drawn is falsely personated by another person of the same surname, who is sworn as a member of the grand jury in place of the other, this is good ground for a plea in abatement: Nixon *v.* State, 68 Ala. 535.

33 Cross *v.* State, 63 Ala. 40; Berry *v.* State Id. 126; Blevins *v.* State, 68 Ala. 92; Boyd *v.* State, 98 Ala. 33; State *v.* Garhart, 35 Iowa 315; Jewell *v.* Com., 22 Pa. 94; Harris *v.* State, 13 So. Rep. 15, and see Winter *v.* Muscogee Railroad Co., 11 Ga. 438; Beasley *v.* People, 89 Ill. 571. Talesmen may be added to the grand jury after it has been empanelled: State *v.* Mooney, 10 Iowa 506.

34 Jewell *v.* Com. 22 Pa. 94. In State *v.* Miller, 53 Iowa 84, the court made a verbal order and on appeal Judge Beck says: "The sheriff in this case was orally directed to fill the panel. The order upon which this direction was based, we will presume was entered of record, for doubtless the law so requires and the record before us does not show to the contrary."

35 State *v.* Fowler, 52 Iowa 103; In re Wadlin, 11 Mass. 142; Findley *v.* People, 1 Manning (Mich.) 234. In State *v.* Froiseth, 16 Minn. 313, where a

however, is within the discretion of the court, and the court may refuse to allow him to be sworn if there are sufficient jurors without him.[36]

At common law if the array was quashed, or all of the grand jurors challenged or absent, a tales could not issue, and it was necessary that a new venire should be awarded.[37] But under statutes enacted in the various states, talesmen may be summoned when all of the grand jurors are disqualified.[38] If, for any reason, a grand jury has not been drawn and summoned as required by statute, in some States the judge has the statutory power to enter an order directing the sheriff to summon a panel of grand jurors,[39] and should there be no statute giving such authority, there is an implied power in the court to direct that this be done.[40]

Should the order of the court direct that talesmen be selected from an improper class of persons, it has been held that an indictment found by a grand jury so constituted is invalid; otherwise where the order is regular and incompetent persons are selected by the sheriff in executing the order.[41]

The manner of selecting and procuring the attendance of grand jurors in Pennsylvania is regulated by the Act of April

---

juror appeared after the grand jury had duly entered upon its duties, was sworn but no charge delivered to him or again to the grand jury as a whole, McMillan, J., concludes his opinion with this language: "But it may not be improper to say, that in cases where a sufficient number of grand jurors upon the regular panel appear and are sworn and charged, the admission of others of the regular panel appearing afterwards, is a matter addressed to the discretion of the court, and in such cases when they are admitted, or where additional jurors are summoned after the organization of the jury, to supply any deficiency which may occur, in view at least of the oath prescribed, the charge should be repeated."

36 State v. Froiseth, 16 Minn. 313; Findley v. People, 1 Manning (Mich.) 234.

37 Dowling v. State, 5 Smedes & M. (Miss.) 664.

38 State v. Smith, 88 Iowa, 178.

39 State v. Brooks, 9 Ala. 9; Hester v. State, 103 Ala. 83; Newton v. State, 21 Fla. 53.

40 Straughan v. State, 16 Ark. 37; Wilburn v. State, 21 Ark. 198.

41 Oliver v. State, 66 Ala. 8.

10th, 1867,[42] which provides for two jury commissioners who are elected for three years and cannot succeed themselves, one each being of the majority and minority parties. The jury commissioners and a judge, or a majority of them, meet at the county seat thirty days before the first term of the Court of Common Pleas, and place in the proper jury wheels the number of names designated by the Common Pleas Court at the preceding term. The wheels are then locked, sealed, with the separate seals of the jury commissioners and the sheriff,[43] and remain in the custody of the jury commissioners, while the sheriff has possession of the keys to the wheels.

To procure the drawing of a panel of grand jurors, a writ of venire facias is issued by the clerk of the Court of Quarter Sessions or Oyer and Terminer, upon the precept of the court, commanding the sheriff and jury commissioners to empanel, and the sheriff to summon a grand jury.[44] The panel of grand jurors is drawn from the wheel by at least one jury commissioner and the sheriff, who, before selecting or drawing jurors, take an oath that they will faithfully and impartially perform their duties.[45]

After the names of the jurors are drawn from the wheel they

42 Pamph. Laws 62; Section 8 of this Act was held to be directory; Com. v. Zillafrow, 207 Pa. 274.

43 Com. v. Delamater, 2 Dist. Rep. (Pa.) 562.

44 If separate writs of venire issue from the Courts of Quarter Sessions and Oyer and Terminer, the judges shall order the sheriff to return one and the same panel to both writs. Act April 14, 1834, Sec. 110, P. L. 360.

45. Act April 14, 1834, Sec. 87, P. L. 357; Act April 10, 1867, P. L. 62. In Philadelphia, the proceedings for drawing and summoning grand jurors are regulated by the Acts of March 31, 1843, P. L. 123; April 20, 1858, P. L. 354; April 13, 1859, P. L. 595; and March 13, 1867, P. L. 420. The persons eligible for jury duty are returned by the assessors in each ward. The Supreme Court Justices (when sitting in Philadelphia) and Judges of the Common Pleas Courts with the sheriff, constitute a board to superintend the selection and drawing of jurors. Any two of the judges and the sheriff form a quorum. Before December 10, in each year, the board selects sufficient jurors to serve on grand and petit juries for the ensuing year, the names, etc., of those selected being written on slips of paper and placed in the wheel, which is then locked and kept by the sheriff in his exclusive custody. A list of the names placed in the wheel are certified to each court by the members of the board then present, where it is filed. At

are to be inserted in the venire and such persons are then summoned to appear by the sheriff or his deputies. If a grand juror receives notice and attends the court, it has been held to be of no consequence how he was summoned. His attendance in obedience to the command of the writ cures any defect in the manner of summoning.[46] The sheriff makes his return to the venire, showing the persons summoned as grand jurors, but it has been held that it is not necessary for the sheriff and jury commissioners to make an affidavit to their return that the jurors were drawn and returned according to law.[47]

The grand jury may be summoned to meet prior to the holding of the regular terms of court if the judges of such court deem it expedient, and may be detained for an additional week if the business of the court, in the opinion of the judges, requires it.[48]

Where the panel by reason of the failure of grand jurors to appear, or through challenges or other cause, is reduced below the number necessary to indict, a *tales de circumstantibus* may issue.[49] The number of talesmen who may be summoned by this writ, has not been defined by law, but as the full grand jury consists of twenty-three, it would seem that talesmen might lawfully be summoned until the grand jury contained its full number.[50] In Commonwealth *v.* Morton,[51] the panel was reduced to eleven jurors, and on a tales being issued, two talesmen were brought in, were sworn and acted with the grand

---

least three weeks before the beginning of each term the board draws from the wheel sufficient names to constitute the panels of grand and petit jurors for the several courts, and a list of the names, etc., of such jurors is certified to the respective courts and to the sheriff.

46 Com. *v.* Salter, 2 Pears. (Pa.) 461; Sylvester *v.* State, 72 Ala. 201; Hughes *v.* State, 54 Ind. 95.

47 Com. *v.* Salter, 2 Pears, (Pa.) 461.

48 Penna. Act March 18, 1875, Sec. 1, P. L. 28; Com. *v.* Smith, 4 Pa. Sup. Ct. Rep. 1. See State *v.* Davis, 126 N. C. 1007; State *v.* Battle, 126 N. C. 1036.

49 Penna. Act March 31, 1860, Sec. 41, P. L. 439; Com. *v.* Morton, 34 L. I. (Pa.) 438.

50 Post 56. And see note 57.

51 34 L. I. (Pa.) 438.

jury in the finding of indictments.   This proceeding was sustained by Judge Allison.

In the Federal courts, the selection and drawing of grand jurors is regulated by the Act of June 30, 1879,[52] which provides that grand jurors shall be drawn from a box containing at the time of each drawing, the names of not less than three hundred persons, the names having been placed in the box by the clerk of the court and a commissioner, appointed by the judge of such court, and being a citizen of good standing, residing in the district and a well known member of the political party opposing that of which the clerk is a member.   The clerk and the commissioner shall each place one name in the box alternately until the necessary number of names has been placed therein.[53]   The right is reserved to the court to order the grand jurors to be drawn from the wheels used by the State authorities in drawing jurors to serve in the highest court of the state.[54]

When the grand jurors have been drawn, a venire issues from the clerk's office to the marshal, directing him to summon twenty-four persons to serve as grand jurors.   The names of the persons thus drawn from the box are inserted in the venire and are thereupon summoned by the marshal.   If it happens that less than sixteen appear, or having appeared the number is depleted by challenge or other cause to less than the legal requirement, in such case the court orders the marshal to summon, either immediately or for a day fixed, a sufficient number of persons to complete the grand jury, and these persons are taken from the body of the district and not from the by-standers.[55]

---

52 This act is mandatory, but an intention to carry out its provisions in good faith is all that is required: U. S. *v.* Ambrose, 3 Fed. Rep. 283. See U. S. *v.* Greene, 113 Fed. Rep. 683, where many points arising under this act were decided.

53 U. S. *v.* Rondeau, 16 Fed. Rep. 109.

54 Act June 30, 1879, 21 Stat. L. 43; R. S. U. S. Sec. 800-801; U S. *v.* Reed, 27 Fed. Cas. 727; U. S. *v.* Richardson, 28 Fed. Rep. 61.   The clause of Sec. 801, R. S. U. S., relating to Pennsylvania was repealed by Act June 30, 1879.

55 R. S. U. S. Sec. 808.

This statute, like the Pennsylvania statute,[56] does not define whether the number to be summoned shall make the panel sixteen or twenty-three. This, however, would seem to be largely within the discretion of the court,[57] for there being no limitation of the number to be summoned, no objection can well be made where the additional jurors do not increase the panel beyond the legal number. While it is thus necessary that sixteen should be present to constitute a legal grand jury, it is only necessary that twelve should concur in order to find a true bill or make a valid presentment.[58]

Where less than seventeen and more than twelve were present and a true bill was found, the defendant tried on the merits, convicted and sentenced, it was held by the United States Supreme Court upon habeas corpus proceeedings based upon an alleged illegal detention that this was not such a defect as would vitiate the entire proceeding, even although the defendant had no knowledge of it until after sentence had been imposed upon him.[59] If, however, exception should be taken to an indictment found by a grand jury so constituted, either by plea in abatement or motion to quash, the objection should be sustained, for the indictment thus found is the finding of a grand jury not constituted in the manner provided by law.[60] This defect will be cured, however, by the plea of the general issue.

Where in the venire for a panel of grand jurors the court directed that they should be summoned from a certain part of the district,[61] as may be done under authority of the Revised

---

56 Act March 31, 1860, Sec. 41, P. L. 439.

57 In U. S. v. Eagan, 30 Fed. Rep. 608, Judge Thayer says, "Undoubtedly the court may determine of how many persons up to twenty-three the grand jury shall consist."

58 1 Whart. Cr. Law, Sec. 463a, (7th ed.).

59 In re Wilson, 140 U. S. 575, and see State v. Swift, 14 La. Ann. 827; Contra Doyle v. State, 17 Ohio 222.

60 State v. Hawkins, 10 Ark. 71; Doyle v. State, 17 Ohio 222; Barron v. People, 73 Ill. 256; Norris House v. State, 3 G. Greene (Iowa) 513; State v. Cooley, 75 N. W. 729, and see Brannigan v. People, 3 Utah 488.

61 U. S. v. Ayres, 46 Fed. Rep. 651; People v. Reigel, 78 N. W. 1017. See Williams v. State, 61 Ala. 33. In Finley v. State, 61 Ala. 201, Ulmer v.

Statutes of the United States, Section 802, it was held that this was not in conflict with the Sixth Amendment to the Constitution of the United States which provides: "In all criminal prosecutions, the accused shall enjoy the right to a speedy and public trial, by an impartial jury of the state and district wherein the crime shall have been committed. . . . "

In England[62] grand jurors are selected and summoned in accordance with the provisions of the statute 6, Geo. IV, c. 50 as amended. The clerk of the peace causes warrants, precepts and returns to be printed in the form set out in the schedule annexed to the statute. These precepts are then sent by the clerk to the church wardens and overseers of every parish and the overseers of every township, who are required to prepare an alphabetical list of every man residing in their respective parishes or townships who is qualified and liable for grand jury service, with his place of abode, title, quality, calling or business. A copy of such list when prepared is affixed to the principal door of every church and chapel on the first three Sundays of September. The justices of the peace then hold a special session during the last seven days of September of each year, when the lists are produced and names either added or stricken from the list, but no name can either be added or removed unless the justice first gives notice to the party whose name it is proposed to add or remove from the list. The lists are returned to the quarter sessions and kept by the clerk of the peace. The jurors are selected from this list by the sheriff, who thereupon summons them to appear.

Where the provisions of the statute under which grand jurors are selected and drawn are but directory, the court will not quash an indictment upon the ground of irregularity in the selection or drawing when it does not appear that such irregularity will prejudice the defendant.[63]

State, Id. 208, Couch v. State, 63 Ala. 163, and Benson v. State, 68 Ala. 513, will be found instances where the writ directed the sheriff to summon a grand jury from only a portion of the persons from whom the statute provided it should be drawn, and a grand jury thus constituted was held not a legal grand jury.

62 Chitty's English Statutes, Vol 6, Tit. Juries.

63 Bales v. State, 63 Ala. 30; State v. Carney, 20 Iowa 82; Johnson v.

In the selection and drawing of grand jurors the absence of any particular officer designated to participate in the proceedings will not ordinarily invalidate the selection and drawing thus made, a majority of those directed to perform such duty being present and legally competent to act.[64]   The duty thus imposed upon any person by statute cannot be delegated by him to another;[65] it is wholly personal and when disregarded may be successfully relied upon by a defendant for setting aside an indictment returned against him.

Where grand jurors have been selected by officers de facto, it has been held that this cannot be availed of by a defendant for the purpose of invalidating the indictment.   The acts of such officers as to third persons are as valid as the acts of officers de jure.[66]

An indictment found by a de facto grand jury has been sustained.[67]

This doctrine was carried to the extreme limit in New York in the case of People v. Petrea,[67]* where the act under which the grand jurors were selected was unconstitutional, but the

State, 33 Miss. 363; State v. Haywood, 73 N. C. 437; State v. Martin, 82 N. C. 672; Com. v. Zillafrow, 207 Pa. 274.

64 Stevenson v. State, 69 Ga. 68; Roby v. State, 74 Ga. 812; Smith v. State, 90 Ga. 133.

65 Levy v. Wilson, 69 Calif. 105; State v. Conway, 35 La. Ann. 350; State v. Taylor, 43 Id. 1131; Preuit v. People, 5 Neb. 377; Challenge to grand jury, 3 N. J. Law Jour. 153; State v. McNamara, 3 Nev. 70. A deputy clerk may perform the duty imposed upon the clerk of the Circuit Court to draw from the box the names of the persons to serve as grand jurors: Willingham v. State, 21 Fla. 761. But in Dutell v. State, 4 G. Greene (Iowa) 125, it was held that a deputy sheriff could not legally compare the list of grand jurors where that duty was by statute imposed upon the sheriff: And see State v. Brandt, 41 Iowa 593. Where a new constitution imposed upon a superior judge the duties performed by the county judge, the superior judge succeeds to the duties of the county judge in drawing jurors: People v. Gallagher, 55 Calif. 462.

66 Durrah v. State, 44 Miss. 789; Dolan v. People, 64 N. Y. 485; State v. Krause, 1 Ohio, N. P. 91.

67 State v. Marsh, 13 Kan. 596; People v. Petrea, 92 N. Y. 128; People v. Morgan, 95 N. W. 542.

67* 92 N. Y. 128.

Court of Appeals held that the indictment had been found by a de facto grand jury and was therefore valid.

In discussing the case Andrews, J. says:

"We are of opinion that no constitutional right of the defendant was invaded by holding him to answer to the indictment. The grand jury, although not selected in pursuance of a valid law, were selected under color of law and semblance of legal authority. The defendant, in fact, enjoyed all the protection which he would have had if the jurors had been selected and drawn pursuant to the general statutes. Nothing could well be more unsubstantial than the alleged right asserted by the defendant under the circumstances of the case. He was entitled to have an indictment found by a grand jury before being put upon his trial, an indictment was found by a body, drawn, summoned and sworn as a grand jury before a competent court and composed of good and lawful men. This we think fulfilled the constitutional guaranty. The jury which found the indictment was a de facto jury selected and organized under the forms of law. The defect in its constitution, owing to the invalidity of the law of 1881, affected no substantial right of the defendant. We confine our decision upon this point to the case presented by this record, and hold that an indictment found by a jury of good and lawful men selected and drawn as a grand jury under color of law, and recognized by the court and sworn as a grand jury, is a good indictment by a grand jury within the sense of the Constitution, although the law under which the selection was made, is void."

After grand jurors have been drawn they must be summoned to attend at court. This duty, unless other persons be designated by statute, devolves upon the sheriff and his deputies, and should they for any reason be disqualified, then upon the coroner.[68]

In the conduct of legal proceedings the presumption is that official acts have been performed in the manner prescribed by law. When the sheriff selects and summons grand jurors, he

---

68 State *v.* Williams, 5 Port. (Ala.) 130; Bruner *v.* Superior Court, 92 Calif. 239; Conner *v.* State, 25 Ga. 515; Com. *v.* Graddy, 4 Metcalf (Ky.) 223.

will be presumed to have complied with every requirement of the law in the selection, summoning and return of a panel of legal jurors[69] in the absence of evidence to the contrary. In the case of Wilson *v.* People,[70] Chief Justice Thacher said: "We are not permitted to presume in the silence of the record, that the court adopted an illegal method in convening the grand jury." The burden of proof rests upon anyone who alleges irregularity in the drawing or return of the panel or who alleges that a grand juror is personally disqualified from serving.[71]

The qualifications of grand jurors are in general the same as at the common law. In Bracton's time no persons could be grand jurors unless they were "free and loyal men who have no suit against anyone, and are not sued themselves, nor have evil fame for breaking the peace or for the death of a man or other misdeed," and be of the hundred in which they were chosen.[72] In the Sixteenth Century a grand juror must be a "freeman, and a lawful liege subject, and, consequently neither under an attainder of any treason or felony, nor a villain, nor alien, nor outlawed, whether for a criminal matter, or as some say, in a personal action," all of whom were to be of the same county,[73] and they need not be freeholders.[74] A similar view is expressed by Mr. Chitty,[75] who adds, "this necessity for the grand inquest to consist of men free from all objections existed at common law,"[76] and Lord Coke says,[77] "if the indictment be found by any persons that are out-

---

69 Dowling *v.* State, 5 Smedes & M. (Miss.) 664. The list of grand jurors returned by the sheriff is not evidence that such jurors are returned and qualified according to law: State *v.* Ligon, 7 Port (Ala.) 167. And see State *v.* Congdon, 14 R. I. 267.

70 3 Colo. 325.

71 State *v.* Haynes, 54 Iowa 109; State *v.* McNeill, 93 N. C. 552 CONTRA Beason *v.* State, 34 Miss. 602.

72 Bracton-de legibus (Sir Travers Twiss-ed.) Vol. II, p. 235.

73 2 Hawk. Pl. C. Ch. 25, Sec. 16.

74 Id. Ch. 25, Sec. 19.

75 1 Chitty Cr. Law, 307.

76 Id. 309.

77 3 Inst. 33.

lawed, or not the king's lawful liege people, or not lawfully returned, or denominated by any, viz.: by all or any of these, that then the indictment is void." Perhaps the earliest statute relating to the qualifications of grand jurors was 11 Hen. IV. C. 9, which, after setting forth the classes of persons who were disqualified from acting as grand jurors, provided that if an indictment should be presented by a grand jury containing a single disqualified person, it was wholly void.[78]

Blackstone omits all reference to the qualifications of grand jurors except to say, "they are usually gentlemen of the best figure in the county," and considers they should be freeholders.[79]

In England [79*] at the present day the qualifications of grand jurors are defined with great minuteness. The statute 6, Geo. IV. c. 50, provides that a grand juror shall be between twenty-one and sixty years of age, having in his own name or in trust for him in the same county "ten pounds by the year above reprizes, in lands or tenements, whether of freehold, copyhold, or customary tenure, or of ancient demesne, or in rents issuing out of any such lands or tenements, or in such lands, tenements, and rents taken together, in fee simple, fee tail, or for the life of himself or some other person, or who shall have within the same county twenty pounds by the year above reprizes, in lands or tenements, held by lease or leases for the absolute term of twenty-one years, or some longer term, or for any term of years determinable on any life or lives, or who being a householder shall be rated or assessed to the poor rate, or to the inhabited house duty in the county of Middlesex, on a value of not less than thirty pounds, or in any other county on a value of not less than twenty pounds, or who shall occupy a house containing not less than fifteen windows."

In Pennsylvania there are no statutes defining the qualifica-

---

78 2 Hawk. Pl. C. Ch. 25, Sec. 28; 1 Chitty Cr. Law, 309; and see U. S. v. Hammond, 26 Fed. Cas. 99; Com. v. Smith, 10 Bush (73 Ky.) 476; State v. Jones, 8 Rob. (La.) 616; State v. Parks, 21 La. Ann. 251; State v. Rowland, 36 La. Ann. 193; Barney v. State, 12 Smedes & M. (Miss.) 68; State v. Duncan, 7 Yerg. (Tenn.) 271.

79 4 Bl. Com. 302.

79* Chitty's English Statutes, Vol 6, Tit. Juries.

tions of grand jurors, beyond the provision that only sober, intelligent and judicious persons shall be chosen,[80] and, as the common law is a part of the law of the state, their competency would be determined in accordance therewith, but they are not required to be freeholders. It would also seem that a grand juror, like a petit juror, must stand indifferent between the commonwealth and the accused.[81]

In many states, a grand juror is required to be a freeholder;[82] in others a freeholder or householder.[83] In Tennessee[84] he need not have a freehold in the county in which he is summoned, while in West Virginia,[85] although a grand juror is required to be a freeholder, the court has refused to quash an indictment upon the ground that a member of the grand jury finding the indictment did not possess this qualification.

In Arkansas,[86] and South Carolina,[87] it has been held that grand jurors are not required to be freeholders.

In North Carolina the rule which prevailed in Bracton's time that a grand juror must have no suit against any man nor himself be sued seems to be in force. Thus it has been held there was no error in quashing an indictment on the ground that one of the grand jurors was, at the time it was found, a party to an action pending in the same county,[88] and it is not necessary to show that such juror participated in the

80 Act April 10, 1867, P. L. 62. The Act of April 20, 1858, Sec. 2, P. L. 354, which applies only to Philadelphia, provides that the grand jurors shall be "sober, healthy and discreet citizens."

81 Com. v. Clark, 2 Browne (Pa.) 325; Rolland v. Com., 82 Pa. 306; Com. v. Cosler, 8 Luz. Leg. Reg. (Pa.) 97.

82 Fowler v. State, 100 Ala. 96; State v. Herndon, 5 Blackf. (Ind.) 75; Wills v. State, 69 Ind. 286; State v. Rockafellow, 6 N. J. Law 332; State v. Motley, 7 Rich. Law (S. C.) 327; Moore v. Com. 9 Leigh. (Va.) 639; Com. v. Cunningham, 6 Gratt. (Va.) 695.

83 State v. Brown, 10 Ark. 78; State v. Brooks, 9 Ala. 9; Barney v. State, 12 Smedes & M. (Miss.) 68; Jackson v. State, 11 Tex. 261; Stanley v. State, 16 Tex. 557.

84 State v. Bryant, 10 Yerg. 527.

85 State v. Henderson, 29 W. Va. 147.

86 Palmore v. State, 29 Ark. 248.

87 State v. Williams, 35 S. C. 344.

88 State v. Liles, 77 N. C. 496; State v. Smith, 80 Id. 410. But see State v. Edens, 85 Id. 522.

deliberations and finding of the grand jury.[89]   In Louisiana a grand juror who is charged with any crime or offence cannot legally serve.[90]

In some states a grand juror must be a qualified voter, either for candidates for office, to impose a tax, or regulate the expenditure of money in a town.[91]

Where a statute provided that jurors should be selected only from the persons who had paid their taxes for the preceding year, an indictment found by a grand jury containing three persons who had not paid such taxes was quashed.[92]

In the State of Washington, although it is provided by statute that women shall be qualified electors, they are not competent to serve as grand jurors under a statute providing that grand jurors shall be drawn from the qualified electors.[93]

In the Federal courts the qualifications of grand jurors, except where otherwise provided by the Revised Statutes, are determined according to the law of the state in which such court is located.[94]   Congress, however, has provided that no person shall be summoned as a grand juror in a court of the United States more than once in two years,[95] nor shall any person be a grand juror who has been engaged in rebellion against the United States.[96]

The common law provided that no alien should be a grand

89 State v. Smith, 80 N. C. 410.

90 State v. Thibodeaux, 48 La. Ann. 600.

91 Adams v. State, 28 Fla. 511; State v. Davis, 12 R. I. 492; State v. Congdon, 14 R. I. 267.

92 State v. Durham Fertilizer Co., 111 N. C. 658. But see Cubine v. State, 73 S. W. 396.

93 Harland v. Territory, 13 Pac. 453; Rumsey v. Territory, 21 Pac. 152.

94 R. S. U. S. Sec. 721. U. S. v. Clune, 62 Fed. Rep. 798.

95 R. S. U. S. Sec. 812; U. S. v. Reeves, 27 Fed. Cas. 750. But this can only be taken advantage of by challenge to the jurors before indictment found. It cannot be raised by motion to quash or plea in abatement.

96 R. S. U. S. Sec. 820. This provision was repealed by the Act of Congress, June 30, 1879, 21 Stat. L. 43, but the revision committee apparently by mistake included this provision in the Revised Statutes as Sec. 820, and it was re-enacted by Congress. U. S. v. Gale, 109 U. S. 65; U. S. v. Hammond, 26 Fed. Cas. 99.

juror,[97] and, consequently, an alien accused of an offence has no right to demand that he be indicted by a grand jury *de medietate linguae*,[98] although he may demand that a jury de medietate be summoned for his trial.[99]

Where a person is accused of an offence, he has a right to take advantage of every irregularity in the proceedings on the part of the officers appointed to administer the law, of their personal disqualifications, and of the personal disqualifications of the grand jurors, providing he does so at the proper time. There are three separate stages at which a defendant may object to the manner in which the grand jury has been constituted and the members constituting it.

1. Before the grand jurors are sworn.[100]

2. After they have been sworn, but before the defendant is indicted.[101]

---

97 And see Reich *v.* State, 53 Ga. 73; State *v.* Haynes, 54 Iowa, 109; State *v.* Guillory, 44 La. Ann. 317; Territory *v.* Harding, 6 Mont. 323; Territory *v.* Clayton, 8 Id. 1; Com. *v.* Cherry, 2 Va. Cas. 20. In State *v.* Cole, 17 Wis. 674, the juror was a qualified elector of Wisconsin, but was not a citizen of the United States.

98 2 Hawk. Pl. C. Ch. 43, Sec. 36; 2 Hale, P. C. 271; 1 Chitty Cr. Law 309; Bac. Abr. Juries E. 8; Trials per Pais (Giles Duncombe) Vol. 1, p. 246; 1 Whart. Cr. Law, Sec. 473, (7th ed.).

99 4 Bl. Com. 352; Res. *v.* Mesca, 1 Dall. 73; Roberts Digest of British Statutes, 346. The Act of April 14, 1834, Sec. 149, P. L. 366, provides that no jury de medietate shall be allowed in Pennsylvania. In the District of Columbia a foreigner is not entitled to be tried by a jury de medietate; U. S. *v.* McMahon, 26 Fed. Cas. 1131.

100 If the objection is not raised before the grand jurors are sworn, it cannot thereafter be availed of on a motion to set aside the indictment: Moses *v.* State, 58 Ala. 117; State *v.* Ingalls, 17 Iowa 8; State *v.* Pierce, 90 Id. 506; State *v.* Gibbs, 39 Id. 318; Bellair *v.* State, 6 Blackf. (Ind.) 104; State *v.* Hensley, 7 Blackf. (Ind.) 324; State *v.* Welch, 33 Mo. 33; State *v.* Rickey, 10 N. J. Law 83; Lienberger *v.* State, 21 S. W. 603; State *v.* Ames, 96 N. W. 330. See People *v.* Borgstrom, 178 N. Y. 254. Under Code Sec. 2375 of Miss., objections to the qualifications of grand jurors must be made before they are empaneled; they cannot be made afterward. The Texas code of Cr. Proc. 1895, Sec. 397, contains the same provision: Barber *v.* State, 46 S. W. 233; Carter *v.* State, 46 Id. 236. And see as to Mississippi Head *v.* State, 44 Miss. 731; Dixon *v.* State, 20 So. 839.

101 See generally cases in Note 148, page 73.

3. After the defendant has been indicted.[102]

Where the right of challenge exists it has been held that a refusal by the court to allow a prisoner, criminally charged, to challenge the grand jury, renders the jury incompetent to sit in his case, and the indictment worthless and insufficient,[103] but there is no duty imposed upon the court having jurisdiction of the cause to notify the defendant of this right.[104]

When it is proposed to make objection to the grand jurors before they have been sworn, the objection may be either to the array[105] or to the personal qualifications of any juror.[106]

102 In Alabama by Code Sec. 4445, it is provided that no objection shall be made to any indictment on a ground going to the formation of the grand jury except that the jurors were not drawn in the presence of the proper officers. See Boulo v. State, 51 Ala. 18; Weston v. State, 63 Id. 155; Phillips v. State, 68 Id. 469; Billingslea v. State, Id. 486; Murphy v. State, 86 Ala. 45. In Linehan v. State, 21 So. 497, it was held that this provision was not repealed by the Act of February 28, 1887, regulating the drawing and formation of grand juries. And see Compton v. State, 23 So. 750; Stoneking v. State, 24 So. 47. The Act of February 21, 1887, was repealed by the Act of March 2, 1901: Edson v. State, 32 So. 308.

103 People v. Romero, 18 Calif. 89; State v. Osborne, 61 Iowa 330; State v. Warner, 165 Mo. 399; People v. Wintermute, 46 N. W. 694.

104 People v. Borgstrom, 178 N. Y. 254. In People v. Romero, 18 Calif. 89, Judge Baldwin said in his opinion reversing the judgment of the court below: "If the prisoner were refused the privilege of challenging the grand jury in and by the Court of Sessions, the indictment is insufficient and worthless; it is not, in other words, a legal indictment, because not found by a body competent to act on the case; but to have this effect, the prisoner must have applied for leave or requested permission to appear and challenge the jury. It was not the duty of the Court of Sessions to bring him into court for the purpose of exercising this privilege. It is the prisoner's business to know when the court meets, and if he desires to challenge the jury, to apply, if in custody, to the court, to be brought into court for that purpose; and if he fails to do this, he waives his privilege of excepting to the panel or any member."

105 U. S. v. Gale, 109 U. S. 65; Gibbs v. State, 45 N. J. Law 379; Territory v. Young, 2 N. Mex. 93; Huling v State, 17 Ohio St. 583; Reed v. State, 1 Tex. App. 1; Green v. State, Id. 82; Van Hook v. State, 12 Tex. 252; State v. White, 17 Tex. 242; Cook v. Territory, 4 Pac. 887; Stanley v. U. S. 33 Pac. 1025. In some States it is now provided by statute that no challenge to the panel shall be allowed: State v. Davis, 41 Iowa 311; Carpenter v. People, 64 N. Y. 483; People v. Borgstrom, 178 N. Y. 254; State v. Fitzhugh, 2 Ore. 227. And see People v. Reigel, 78 N. W. 1017.

106 Rolland v. Com., 82 Pa. 306; Delaware River Road, 5 Dist. Rep.

5

The challenge to the array may be made for irregularity in making the original selection;[107] keeping the jury wheels in an improper place or in the custody of an improper person, or in failing to lock and seal the wheels in the manner provided by statute;[108] irregularity in the venire, in drawing and summoning the grand jurors,[109] in the list[110] or in the return.[111]

The array will be quashed if it appear that the persons charged with making the selection of grand jurors failed to take the oath which it was prescribed by statute should be taken before any selection was made.[112] It has also been held a good cause for challenge to the array as being in violation of the rights guaranteed by the Fourteenth Amendment to the Constitution of the United States, where the officers, whose duty it was to select and summon the grand jurors, excluded from the

(Pa.) 694; In re Bridge in Nescopeck, 3 Luz. Leg. Reg. (Pa.) 196; State v. Herndon, 5 Blackf. (Ind.) 75.

107 Wells v. State, 94 Ala. 1; State v. Howard, 10 Iowa 101; Clare v. State, 30 Md. 163; Avirett v. State, 76 Md. 510; Green v. State, 1 Tex. App. 82. See also cases in note 108. CONTRA People v. Jewett, 3 Wend. (N. Y.) 314, where it appeared the jurors selected were in every respect qualified. And see People v. Petrea, 92 N. Y. 128.

108 Brown v. Com., 73 Pa. 321; Id. 76 Pa. 319; Rolland v. Com., 82 Pa. 306; Ins. Co. v. Adams, 110 Pa. 553; Klemmer v. R. R. Co., 163 Pa. 521; Com. v. Delamater, 2 Dist. Rep. (Pa.) 562.

109 U. S. v. Antz, 16 Fed. Rep. 119; Com. v. Salter, 2 Pears. (Pa.) 461; U. S. v. Reed, 27 Fed. Cas. 727; Freel v. State, 21 Ark. 212; Williams v. State 69 Ga. 11; Dixon v. State, 3 Iowa 416; State v. Howard, 10 Id. 101; State v. Beckey, 79 Id. 368; State v. Texada, 19 La. Ann. 436; State v. Underwood, 28 N. C. 96; State v. Duncan, Id. 98; State v. Hart, 15 Tex. App. 202; Whitehead v. Com., 19 Gratt. (Va.) 640; State v. Cameron, 2 Chand. (Wis.) 172. CONTRA People v. Fitzpatrick, 30 Hun. (N. Y.) 493; People v. Hooghkerk, 96 N. Y. 149.

110 Edmonds v. State, 34 Ark. 720.

111 Com. v. Chauncey, 2 Ashm. (Pa.) 101.

112 State v. Bradley, 32 La. Ann. 402; Campbell v. Com., 84 Pa. 187; Kendall v. Com., 19 S. W. 173. And see State v. Flint, 52 La. Ann. 62. An indictment will not be quashed nor will judgment be arrested in a capital case upon the ground that although the jury commissioners had taken the oath of office prescribed by the Constitution before entering upon their duties, it had not been filed in the prothonotary's office as provided by the Constitution: Com. v. Valsalka, 181 Pa. 17.

panel, members of the negro race.[113] That negroes were denied the right to vote, although qualified electors, will not be ground for quashing an indictment where the statute provided that grand jurors should be selected from the qualified electors and the persons prevented from voting were lawfully registered as qualified electors in the registration book from which the selection of grand jurors was made.[114] A white man, however, has no right to complain where negroes are excluded by statute from the grand jury, since the Fourteenth Amendment to the Constitution of the United States has given him no rights which he did not possess before its adoption.[115]

While advantage may be taken of any defects or irregularities in the foregoing instances, the court will not quash the array because the sheriff was not present during the entire time in which the selection of jurors was being made; that the selection was spread over a period of several weeks; that the duty of writing the names was done by a clerk in their presence and by their order; because of mere carelessness in keeping the names before being placed in the wheel, or in the keeping of the wheel after being properly locked and sealed.[116] And it has also been held that the array will not be quashed where the defendant alleges a failure to comply with the provisions of a statute in the drawing and selection of grand jurors but neither alleges nor proves that fraud, corruption or partiality was shown.[117]

The court will not quash an indictment upon the ground that the jury commissioners broke open the jury box (the key being lost) and drew the grand jury therefrom;[118] because names drawn were laid aside in the erroneous belief that such

---

113 Neal *v.* Delaware, 103 U. S. 370; Carter *v.* Texas, 177 U. S. 442; Whitney *v.* State, 59 S. W. 895; Rogers *v.* Alabama, 192 U. S. 226.

114 Dixon *v.* State, 20 So. 839.

115 Com. *v.* Wright, 79 Ky. 22.

116 Com. *v.* Lippard, 6 S. & R. 395. And see Com. *v.* Valsalka, 181 Pa. 17; U. S. *v.* Greene, 113 Fed. Rep. 683.

117 Ex Parte McCoy, 64 Ala. 201; State *v.* Champeau, 52 Vt. 313. And see State *v.* Skinner, 34 Kan. 256; State *v.* Donaldson, 43 Kan. 431.

118. Long *v.* State, 103 Ala. 55.

persons had removed from the county;[119] that the record does not show the taking of the oath by the sheriff and his deputies before summoning the jurors;[120] that the grand jurors were not drawn or summoned at the time prescribed by statute, the provisions of the statute being for the convenience of the jurors and not for the benefit of the defendant;[121] or that the grand jurors were selected from the registries of voters instead of the poll books, the two lists being identical as to names.[122]

The challenge to the panel of grand jurors is made by a motion to quash the array, which motion can only be made where the objection is to irregularity in selecting and empaneling the grand jury based upon some one or more of the grounds heretofore named, and does not extend to the competency of the individual juror.[123] A challenge to the array must be supported by an affidavit setting forth the facts upon which the challenge is based[124] and be substantiated by evidence.[125]

The motion may be made at any time before the defendant pleads to the indictment,[126] although a contrary view was taken

119 State v. Wilcox, 104 N. C. 847.

120 State v. Clifton, 73 Mo. 430.

121 Johnson v. State, 33 Miss. 363; State v. Mellor, 13 R. I. 666.

122 Downs v. State, 78 Md. 128.

123 People v. Southwell, 46 Calif. 141; People v. Goldenson, 76 Id. 328; U. S. v. Blodgett, 35 Ga. 336; Dixon v. State, 3 Iowa 416; Barney v. State, 12 Smedes & M. (Miss.) 68; Chase v. State, 46 Id. 683; People v. Jewett, 3 Wend. (N. Y.) 314; Huling v. State, 17 Ohio St. 583; State v. Jacobs, 6 Tex. 99; Van Hook v. State, 12 Id. 252; State v. White, 17 Tex. 242; Reed v. State, 1 Tex. App. 1; Green v. State, Id. 82; Smith v. State, Id. 133; Cook v. Territory, 4 Pac. 887.

124 McClary v. State, 75 Ind. 260.

125 State v. Gillick, 10 Iowa 98; Hart v. State, 15 Tex. App. 202.

126 1 Whart. Cr. Law 468; Carter v. Texas, 177 U. S. 442; Wilson v. People, 3 Colo, 325; Miller v. State, 69 Ind. 284; Pointer v. State, 89 Ind. 255; State v. Belvel, 89 Iowa 405; State v. Kouhns, 103 Id. 720; State v. Herndon, 5 Blackf. (Ind.) 75; State v. Texada, 19 La. Ann. 436; State v. Hoffpauer, 21 Id. 609; State v. Watson, 31 Id. 379; State v. Thomas, 19 Minn. 484; Clare v. State, 30 Md. 163; State v. Welch, 33 Mo. 33; People v. Robinson, 2 Parker Cr. Rep. (N. Y.) 235; State v Sears, 61 N. C. 146; Com. v. Freeman, 166 Pa. 332; Com. v. Shew, 8 Pa. Dist. Rep. 484; State v. Jeffcoat, 26 S. C. 114; Thomason v. State, 2 Tex. App. 550. Under Texas

in United States v. Butler,[127] where it was held that a challenge to the array of the grand jury cannot be made after it is organized and enters upon its duties, but this ruling has been somewhat modified.[128] In the Federal courts the law now is, that if the defendant was arrested and held in bail, or in any other manner had knowledge that proceedings would be instituted against him before the session of the grand jury at which he was indicted, then he must move to quash the array and make his challenge to the polls before the grand jury is sworn; but if he was indicted without knowledge that the grand jury either was or intended taking any action against him, then he might, before pleading to the indictment, file a plea in abatement, or move to quash the indictment for the same reasons as would have supported a motion to quash the array or challenges to the polls for statutory or common law disqualifications,[129] but not for favor. The courts of some of the states have adopted a similar rule.[130]

Where a challenge is made to the array but the objection is to only a portion of the grand jurors, it will be overruled and the defendant left to challenge the individual jurors for cause.[131]

Code, the proper time to object to the array is before the grand jurors have been interrogated as to their qualifications: Reed v. State, 1 Tex. App. 1; Grant v. State, 2 Id. 163. An objection to the manner of empaneling cannot be made after indictment found: Carter v. State, 46 S. W. 236.

127 25 Fed. Cas. 213. And see People v. Moice, 15 Calif. 329; People v. Arnold, Id. 476; State v. Howard, 10 Iowa 101.

128 U. S. v. Gale, 109 U. S. 65.

129 Carter v. Texas, 177 U. S. 442; Wolfson v. U. S., 101 Fed. Rep. 430; U. S. v. Reeves, 27 Fed. Cas. 750; U. S. v. Jones, 31 Fed. Rep. 725; U. S. v. Hammond, 26 Fed. Cas. 99; U. S. v. Blodgett, 30 Fed. Cas. 1157; Agnew v. U. S., 165 U. S. 36; U. S. v. Palmer, 27 Fed. Cas. 410.

130 People v. Beatty, 14 Calif. 566; People v. Hidden, 32 Id. 445; People v. Geiger, 49 Id. 643; Turner v. State, 78 Ga. 174; Musick v. People, 40 Ill. 268; Mershon v. State, 51 Ind. 14; Dixon v. State, 3 Iowa 416; State v. Hinkle, 6 Id. 380; State v. Ostrander, 18 Id. 435; State v. Reid, 20 Id. 413; State v. Gibbs, 39 Id. 318; State v. Ruthven, 58 Id. 121; Logan v. State, 50 Miss. 269; Patrick v. State, 16 Neb. 330; Territory v. Clayton, 19 Pac. 293.

131 U. S. v. Richardson, 28 Fed. Rep. 61; U. S. v. Rondeau, 16 Fed. Rep. 109; People v. Simmons, 119 Calif. 1; McElhanon v. People, 92 Ill. 369;

The right to determine the time and manner of making objections to the qualifications of grand jurors is vested in the legislature, and while it has the power to enact laws designating the time and specifying how such objection shall be made, it has no power to wholly take away the right of objecting.[132]

It is necessary in order to make a challenge, either to the array or to the polls of the grand jury, that the person proposing to make the challenge shall show that he is under prosecution.[133]. In Iowa[134] it was decided that the challenge could not be made where a defendant was held to await the action of a subsequent grand jury, and the grand jury then sitting, of its own motion examined into the offence and returned an indictment. At first sight this ruling would appear to deprive the defendant of a substantial right, but a close inspection of the decision shows that no allegation was made by defendant that the grand jury which found the indictment was not a legal body nor did the defendant allege the disqualification of any member thereof. He was therefore indicted by a body unobjectionable in every respect which acted on its own motion and not on the return of the magistrate.

The state's attorney cannot challenge the panel[135] although he may challenge the individual jurors for favor or for cause.[136] Where a challenge is made by the state, whether

State v. Furco, 51 La. Ann. 1082; Foust v. Com., 33 Pa. 338; Rolland v. Com., 82 Pa. 306; Bowen v. State, 24 So. 551.

132 Palmore v. State, 29 Ark. 248. And see People v. Glen, 173 N. Y. 395, where the court in discussing the effect of the words *but in no other* except the two instances specified in Sec. 313 of the Code of Criminal Procedure says: "That the legislature has the undoubted right to regulate mere matters of procedure in all actions and proceedings, both criminal and civil, is too well established to require either discussion or citation of authority. But it is equally clear that no legislative enactment can be permitted to deprive the citizen of any of his constitutional rights."

133 2 Hawk. Pl. C. c. 25, Sec. 16; 1 Chitty Cr. L. 309; Hudson v. State, 1 Blackf. (Ind.) 317; Thayer v. People, 2 Doug. (Mich.) 417. And see State v. Davis, 22 Minn. 423.

134 State v. Chambers, 87 Iowa 1.

135 Keitler v. State, 4 G. Greene (Iowa) 291.

136 Challenge to Grand Jury, 3 N. J. Law Jour. 153. But see CONTRA as

authorized or not, and is afterward withdrawn, this cannot be assigned as error by a defendant.[137]

The defendant must express a desire to challenge; if he fail to demand at the proper time the privilege of exercising this right he cannot afterward complain.[138] If a time is designated by statute when the challenge shall be made, if the defendant does not avail himself of his right at that time he will be held to have waived the privilege. It is no ground for subsequently pleading in abatement or moving to quash, that he was, at the time designated for challenging the grand jurors, confined in prison, friendless, without counsel or funds, or that he was not apprised of his right to challenge. He is presumed to know the law and abide by it; if he should not, his misfortune will afford him no redress.[139] The challenge may be made by an attorney as *amicus curiae* or as representing accused persons awaiting the action of the grand jury.[140] It may be made by a defendant at a later time than that fixed by statute where he was confined in the jail of another county and thereby deprived of exercising his right to challenge at the proper time.[141] If the defendant declines to challenge when the opportunity is offered, he thereby waives his right[142] and cannot afterward question the validity of the indictment upon any

---

to Iowa, where in the case of Keitler *v.* State, 4 G. Greene 291, Greene, J., said: "While the Code expressly confers the right of challenge upon the defendant, it is entirely silent as to the state or private prosecutor, and hence it must be inferred that the object of the law was to limit this right exclusively to defendants."

137 State *v.* Gut, 13 Minn. 341.

138 Ross *v.* State, 1 Blackf. (Ind.) 390; Maher *v.* State, 3 Minn. 444; State *v.* Hinckley, 4 Id. 345; State *v.* Hoyt, 13 Id. 132; Kemp *v.* State, 11 Tex. App. 174; Brown *v.* State, 32 Tex. Cr. Rep. 119; Webb *v.* State, 40 S. W. 989; Barber *v.* State, 46 S. W. 233; Barkmann *v.* State, 52 S. W. 69. See Reed *v.* State, 1 Tex. App. 1; State *v.* Taylor, 171 Mo. 465; Territory *v.* Ingersoll, 3 Mont. 454.

139 Maher *v.* State, 3 Minn. 444; State *v.* Hinckley, 4 Id. 345; State *v.* Taylor, 171 Mo. 465; Kemp *v.* State, 11 Tex. App. 174; Barber *v.* State, 46 S. W. 233; Barkmann *v.* State, 52 S. W. 69.

140 Challenge to Grand Jury, 3 N. J. Law Jour. 153.

141 Russell *v.* State, 33 Ala. 366.

142 People *v.* Phelan, 123 Calif. 551.

ground going to the competency of the grand jurors and which could have been raised by challenge.

The exclusion of a grand juror on a challenge, or for cause, extends only to the particular case in which he was challenged.[143]

In some of the states, statutes have been enacted exempting certain classes of persons from jury service. In many instances exempt persons have served upon grand juries and this has led to attacks upon the indictments found by such grand juries upon the theory that the exempt person was not a legal juror. A distinction, however, is to be noted between disqualifications and exemptions; the former vitiate the proceedings if attacked before issue joined; the latter are privileges which may be waived by the persons entitled to the benefit thereof and an indictment will not be quashed because an exempt person served as a grand juror.[144]

Under a Florida statute providing that persons "under sixty years shall be liable to serve and are hereby made competent jurors," a person over that age was held not a competent juror.[145] In other states having similar statutes the weight of authority is to the contrary.[146]

143 State v. Hughes, 1 Ala. 655. And see People v. Manahan, 32 Calif. 68.

144 State v. Brooks, 9 Ala. 9; State v. Adams, 20 Iowa 486; Slagel v. Com., 5 Ky. Law. Rep. 545; State v. Stunkle, 41 Kan. 456; State v. Quimby, 51 Me. 395; State v. Wright, 53 Me. 328; Owens v. State, 25 Tex. App. 552. And see the cases cited in note 146.

145 Kitrol v. State, 9 Fla. 9. The decision in this case was rested wholly upon the words of the statute, Forward, J., saying: "Had the statute ended where it says *shall be liable to serve,* then we might with propriety say, the statute leaves it a question of privilege with the juror; but the statute goes further; it declares that such persons are *competent* jurors, &c. It follows that if such persons are competent, others not possessed of such qualifications are not competent.

"It was evidently the intention of the legislature to secure, for the protection of the citizen whose rights might be affected, a grand jury composed of members possessing certain qualifications, *defined by the law.* In giving this statute such a construction we carry out that intention. We are therefore of the opinion that a person *over sixty years* of age is not, under the statute, a *competent* grand juror."

146 Spigener v. State, 62 Ala. 383; Loeb v. State, 75 Ga. 258; Carter v.

Section 1671 R. S. U. S. provides: "All artificers and workmen employed in the armories and arsenals of the United States shall be exempted, during the time of service, from service as jurors in any court."

Objections to the personal qualifications of a grand juror may be divided into two classes.[147]

1. Those where the disqualification is imposed by statute or by the common law, to which exception may be taken at any time before the defendant pleads to the indictment[148]

2. Those where the juror does not stand indifferent between the state and the accused and may be challenged for favor,[149] but in this case unless the right of challenge is exercised before the indictment is found it cannot thereafter be exercised.

With the exception of the provisions of the United States Revised Statutes that no person shall be a grand juror who has been engaged in rebellion against the United States,[150] which has been held to be an absolute disqualification;[151] or a person who has served as a grand juror within two years[152]

State, Id. 747; Jackson v. State, 76 Ga. 551; Davidson v. People, 90 Ill. 221; State v. Miller, 2 Blackf. (Ind.) 35; Booth v. Com., 16 Gratt. (Va.) 519; State v. Edgerton, 69 N. W. 280.

147 U. S. v. Williams, 28 Fed. Cas. 666.

148 Crowley v. United States, 194 U. S. 461; State v. Herndon, 5 Blackf. (Ind.) 75; State v. Griffice, 74 N. C. 316; McTigue v. State, 63 Tenn. 313. In the following cases it was held that the objection must be made before indictment found: State v. Hamlin, 47 Conn. 95; State v. Felter, 25 Iowa 67; State v. Harris, 38 Id. 242; Com. v. Smith, 9 Mass. 107; Lacey v. State, 31 Tex. Cr. Rep. 78; People v. Jewett, 3 Wend. (N. Y.) 314. This ruling, however, was criticized in Newman v. State, 14 Wis. 393, Judge Cole saying: "We think these cases are unsound in reason and principle; and that the current of authorities is the other way."

149 Rolland v. Com., 82 Pa. 306; Com. v. Cosler, 8 Luz. Leg. Reg. 97: Com. v. Craig, 19 Pa. Sup. Ct. 81; U. S. v. Jones, 31 Fed. Rep. 725; U. S. v. White, 28 Fed. Cas. 572; State v. Ames, 96 N. W. 330.

150 R. S. U. S. Sec. 820.

151 U. S. v. Hammond, 26 Fed. Cas. 99.

152 R. S. U. S. Sec. 812. For a similar ruling under Rev. St. 5164 of Ohio see Roth v. State, 3 Ohio Cir. Ct. Rep. 59, where upon issue joined on plea in abatement the court excluded defendant's evidence showing that a grand juror had previously served within two years from the time at

which has been held to be a disqualification which can only be taken advantage of by challenge,[153] the grand jurors in the Federal courts may be challenged for the same causes as a grand juror serving in the highest court of the state within which such Federal court may be located.[154]

In the case of Crowley v. United States,[155] it was held that a disqualification of a grand juror imposed by statute is a matter of substance and cannot be regarded as a mere defect or imperfection within the meaning of Section 1025 R. S. U. S.

The challenge to grand jurors for favor was a common law right,[156] but if not exercised before an indictment is found, the right is wholly gone,[157] notwithstanding a defendant may have had no knowledge that he was charged with any offence. It was perhaps first used in the United States on the trial of Aaron Burr for treason in 1807.

In that case, "the grand jury being reduced to sixteen, Colonel Burr claimed the right to challenge for favor. This challenge he admitted was not a peremptory challenge and good cause must be shown to support it."[158]

The authors of a well known work upon juries comment

---

which the indictment was found. The Circuit Court on appeal held this to be error and reversed the judgment of the lower court. See State v. Elson, 45 Ohio St. 648; State v. Ward, 60 Vt. 142.

153 U. S. v. Reeves, 27 Fed. Cas. 750. In Roth v. State, 3 Ohio Cir. Ct. Rep. 59, the appellate court sustained the objection to the indictment that a grand juror had served as a petit juror within two years in violation of the Ohio statute. The point that the question should have been raised by challenge and that it could not be raised by plea in abatement does not seem to have been considered in this case. CONTRA U. S. v. Clark, 46 Fed. Rep. 633; State v. Brown, 28 Ore. 147.

154 U. S. v. Reed, 27 Fed. Cas. 727; U. S. v. Clune, 62 Fed. Rep. 798.

155 194 U. S. 461. In this case Mr. Justice Harlan discusses in an admirable manner the question as to when a plea in abatement may be filed.

156 But see contra Sheridan's Trial, 31 How. St. Tr. 567.

157 The challenge must be made before the grand jury is sworn: State v. Ames, 96 N. W. 330. In the case of State v. Hamlin, 47 Conn. 95, it was doubted whether the members of a grand jury could be challenged for favor before they were sworn.

158 U. S. v. Aaron Burr, 25 Fed. Cas. 55.

upon challenges to grand jurors in the following language,[159] "If it is to be conceded that the right of challenging grand jurors existed at common law, it would seem clear that consistency requires that this right should embrace all kinds of challenge, namely: to the array, for cause, and peremptory. Perhaps the best evidence that a challenge of any sort to grand jurors is anomalous, is found in the fact that no court was ever sufficiently bold to allow peremptory challenges to grand jurors."

Their criticism, however, will be seen to be without merit when we consider that the grand jury in criminal cases is of much greater antiquity than the petit jury,[160] the qualifications of which were clearly defined. If any person was returned thereon who was not qualified, the only manner in which the disqualification could be made known and taken advantage of, was by an objection made before the justices. A defendant could not peremptorily challenge a grand juror in the majority of cases since he would have no notice that they were considering an accusation against him until presentment was actually made. In the time of Bracton and Britton peremptory challenges were wholly unknown, while both writers describe with great care the objections which may be made to the competency of the jurors.

In 1811 on Sheridan's Trial,[161] Mr. Justice Osborne refused to permit grand jurors to be challenged, holding that "In the case of a grand juror, the objection is to be relied upon, in the form of a plea. Therefore, I think that there does not exist by the common law, the right to challenge a grand juror." Since that time this has been the uniform English practice.

That the right to challenge grand jurors for cause or for favor has been but seldom used, cannot be made an argument against its existence. It is firmly established in the common law and can only be destroyed by legislative enactment.

If a grand juror is disqualified when drawn and summoned

---

159 Thompson & Merriam on Juries, Sec. 513.
160 Supra. 10.
161 31 How. St. Tr. 567.

but becomes qualified before service as such, an indictment found by the grand jury of which he is a member will be sustained;[162] but where a grand juror though competent when drawn and summoned was incompetent when a true bill was found, the indictment was quashed.[163]

A grand juror may be challenged for favor who has conscientious scruples against capital punishment,[164] for while the grand jury is usually not sworn in any particular cause, it may be necessary for them to consider a bill charging a capital offence. A similar ruling was made in the case of United States v. Reynolds where a grand juror had conscientious scruples against indicting persons charged with the crime of polygamy.[165] In this case it was said: "A person who upon his conscience could not find indictments under a law, would not make a good juryman to enforce that law. And if all members or a majority of a grand jury had like scruples, that ancient and venerable body would not only become useless, but also an absolute hindrance to the enforcement of the law. A party having these conscientious scruples would, if sworn upon the grand jury, have to commit moral perjury. He upon oath, admits that his conscience forbids his aiding in the enforcement of a specific law, yet as a grand juryman he swears to go counter thereto, and enforce the law."

A challenge may be made where a grand juror has formed and expressed an opinion as to the guilt or innocence of the accused[166] but this only applies where such grand juror is not

162 Collins v. State, 31 Fla. 574; and see State v. Perry, 29 S. E. 384.
163 State v. Wilcox, 104 N. C. 847.
164 Jones v. State, 2 Blackf. (Ind.) 475; Gross v. State, 2 Ind. 329.
165 U. S. v. Reynolds, 1 Utah 226.
166 Com. v. Clarke, 2 Browne (Pa.) 325; U. S. v. White, 28 Fed. Cas. 572; U. S. v. Aaron Burr, 25 Fed. Cas. 55; U. S. v. Jones, 31 Fed. Rep. 725; U. S. v. Clune, 62 Fed. Rep. 798; State v. Hamlin, 47 Conn. 95; State v. Hinkle, 6 Iowa 380; State v. Gillick, 7 Id. 287; State v. Osborne, 61 Id. 330; State v. Shelton, 64 Id. 333; State v. Billings, 77 Id. 417; People v. Jewett, 3 Wend. (N. Y.) 314; In re Annexation to Borough of Plymouth, 167 Pa. 612. Contra State v. Clarissa, 11 Ala. 57; People v. District Court, 29 Colo. 83; Musick v. People, 40 Ill. 268; Com. v. Woodward, 157 Mass. 516. In Betts v. State, 66 Ga. 508, in delivering the opinion of the court, Speer, J., said: "To hold that a grand juror was subject to challenge *propter*

the prosecutor;[167] or where he has any personal or financial interest in the result of the finding of the grand jury;[168] or that he is an alien;[169] or not a qualified elector[170] or free-holder[171] or householder.[172] But it has been held not to be a ground for challenge that a grand juror belonged to a particular political party and was a strong partisan;[173] that he had previously issued a warrant for the arrest of the defendant and had expressed an opinion as to his guilt,[174] that a grand juror was a tax payer and acted on a grand jury which found an indictment against the township supervisors for neglecting to re-

affectum would lead to endless embarrassments in criminal proceedings. We presume it rarely occurs that a crime, especially of great magnitude, does not elicit an expression of opinion from that class of citizens who make up the grand jury; to allow this expression to disqualify and vacate an indictment would entail endless delay and embarrassment in the prosecution of crime, and too often secure immunity to the criminal."

The Supreme Court of Georgia, however, appears to have weakened in this view in the next year, since in the cases of Williams v. State, 69 Ga. 11 and Lee v. State, Id. 705, the court intimated that if a defendant could except to a grand juror at all on the ground that he had formed and expressed an opinion, it should be done before a true bill was found.

167 The prosecutor is disqualified by statute to act as a grand juror: State v. Holcomb, 86 Mo. 371; State v. Williamson, 106 Mo. 162; State v. Millain, 3 Nev. 409; People v. Smith, 76 N. W. 124.

168 Rolland v. Com., 82 Pa. 306; Delaware River Road, 5 Dist. Rep. (Pa.) 694; In re Bridge in Nescopeck, 3 Luz. Leg. Reg. (Pa.) 410; In re County Bridge, 3 Luz. Leg. Reg. (Pa.) 196; Fisher v. State, 93 Ga. 309. But see State v. Brainerd, 56 Vt. 532.

169 Supra. 63, 64, note 97.

170 Supra. 63.

171 State v. Bleekley, 18 Mo. 428. Supra. 62.

172 Supra. 62.

173 U. S. v. Eagan, 30 Fed. Rep. 608.

174 U. S. v. Belvin, 46 Fed. Rep. 381; U. S. v. Williams, 28 Fed. Cas. 666; In re Tucker, 8 Mass. 286. CONTRA People v. Smith, 76 N. W. 124. In 1 Whart. Cr. Law, Sec. 469, the ruling as set forth in the text is severely criticised. But while it is true that if the accuser corruptly causes himself to be placed upon the grand jury a challenge should be sustained and the panel purged, yet if he was returned without his agency or instigation, the challenge should not be sustained, for as a lawful member of that body a presentment could be made upon knowledge which he might communicate to them.

pair a township road;[175] that he was the magistrate who committed the defendant;[176] that he was a civil officer[177] or special police officer,[178] or that he was a member of an association the object of which was to detect crime;[179] that he has subscribed funds for the suppression of crime;[180] or that his name was absent from the last assessment roll of the county from which he is summoned.[181]

Where the prosecutor is returned upon the grand jury without his agency or instigation the better opinion is that the challenge for favor should not be sustained for as a lawful member of that body a presentment could be made upon knowledge which he might communicate to them as to this particular offence.

Where a grand juror admits that he has formed an opinion as to the guilt or innocence of the accused but declares that his opinion would not preclude him from passing on the question impartially as presented by the evidence,[182] or where the evidence of the alleged forming and expressing of opinion is not clear, a challenge will not be sustained.[183]

If a case be submitted to the grand jury which considered a former bill against the same defendant, the question at once arises whether or not they are competent to again pass upon the question by reason of their expressed opinion as to the guilt of the accused in finding the former indictment. There are but few decisions upon this point and the better view seems to be that the grand jurors may be challenged upon the ground

175 Com. v. Bradney, 126 Pa. 199; Penna. Act April 16, 1840, Sec. 6, P. L. 411; and see State v. Newfane, 12 Vt. 422.

176 U. S. v. Palmer, 27 Fed. Cas. 410; State v. Chairs, 68 Tenn. 196.

177 Com. v. Rudd, 3 Ky. Law Rep. 328; Com. v. Pritchett, 74 Ky. 277; Owens v. State, 25 Tex. App. 552; Com. v. Strother, 1 Va. Cas. 186.

178 Com. v. Hayden, 163 Mass. 453.

179 Musick v. People, 40 Ill. 268. See Com. v. Craig, 19 Pa. Superior Ct. 81.

180 Koch v. State, 32 Ohio St. 353.

181 U. S. v. Benson, 31 Fed. Rep. 896; State v. Harris, 97 N. W. 1093.

182 State v. Hinkle, 6 Iowa 380; State v. Shelton, 64 Id. 333; State v. Billings, 77 Id. 417.

183 State v. Billings, 77 Iowa 417.

that they have formed and expressed an opinion upon the matter to come before them.[184]

The reason for this is best expressed in the language used by Stockton, J., in the case of State v. Gillick:[185] "The juror challenged was as much disqualified from taking any part in the consideration of the charge against the defendant, by reason of the opinion formed by him from the evidence given under oath in the grand jury room, and by his action thereon, as if that opinion had been formed from rumor, or had been induced by malice or ill-will. It is the preconceived opinion, that renders a grand jury incompetent, and not the sources from which that opinion is formed or derived. A juror who has formed or expressed an opinion, is set aside, because he is supposed not to be indifferent to the result of the matter to be tried. Such an opinion, in the presumption of law, is not less

---

184 In State v. Osborne, 61 Iowa, 330, this question arose under Section 4261 of the Code and was considered at length by Beck, J., who says: "In the absence of any statute so providing, the prisoner ought to be permitted to exercise the right to challenge the jurors at any time before they consider the case, upon information gained that they are lawfully subject to challenge on account of matters arising after a prior challenge had been made. A different rule would defeat the very purpose of the statute, namely, to secure a fair and unprejudiced grand jury, to whom the charge shall be submitted. In the case before us, after the first indictment was set aside, the rights of the prisoner were no other or different from what they were when the first challenge was made. He had a right to an unprejudiced grand jury. The proceedings resulting in the first indictment stood for nothing.. The prisoner should have been permitted to fully exercise his right to challenge the jurors. There was ground for believing, nay, for *knowing*, that the jurors had formed and expressed an opinion of the prisoner's guilt, for they had heard the evidence, and upon their oaths returned an indictment against him. But, it is said, they gained the knowledge of the facts, and expressed their opinion of his guilt, acting as grand jurors. This does not change the case. Suppose one of the grand jurors had been upon a coroner's jury, or had been upon a jury before whom an accomplice had been tried and convicted. In each case the juror would have gained knowledge of the facts, and expressed an opinion of the prisoner's guilt, under circumstances substantially the same as existed in this case. It will not be claimed that he would not be the subject of challenge. It is also said that no prejudice resulted from refusing defendant the right to make the challenge, as he was convicted, and thus shown to be guilty; and that we must presume another grand jury would have found an in-

the effect of partiality and prejudice operating on the mind of the juror, than it is the efficient agent to produce such partiality and prejudice on his mind, perhaps without his consciousness."

Upon this principle a plea in abatement has been sustained where it was made to appear that one of the grand jurors who found the indictment had served on a petit jury which formerly convicted the defendant of the same offence.[186]   A precisely opposite view was taken in a case where one of the grand jurors had been a member of the coroner's jury which found that the deceased was murdered by the accused.[187]

An indictment will not be set aside upon the ground that a grand juror was related to the prosecutor by blood or marriage,[188] although defendant could have availed himself of this fact by challenge before indictment found.[189]

dictment against him. The facts stated may all be admitted, but we cannot exercise a presumption of a prisoner's guilt in order to sustain proceedings resulting in his conviction. Such a rule would in effect declare that a verdict cures all violations of law and irregularities in criminal trials. In People v. Hansted, 135 Calif. 149. it was said by McFarland, J.: "It is clear that grand jurors who have examined the charge against one accused of a crime, and found and presented an indictment against him for such crime, thus officially declaring their conviction upon the evidence before them that he is probably guilty, are disqualified from again passing upon a second charge against him for the same offence." But see People v. Northey, 77 Calif. 618.

185 7 Iowa 287. Compare with the language of the court in People v. Northey, 77 Calif. 618.

186 U. S. v. Jones, 31 Fed. Rep. 725. And see People v. Landis, 139 Calif. 426. The case of State v. Cole, 19 Wis. 129, raises this question and presents a contrary ruling, but no reason is given for the ruling and the judgment was reversed on other grounds. And see State v. Wilcox, 104 N. C. 847, where the court held that the grand juror was competent and was bound by his oath to communicate to his fellow jurors the knowledge he had acquired while serving upon the petit jury.

187 Betts v. State, 66 Ga. 508; Lee v. State, 69 Ga. 705. It is interesting to note that the ruling in both of these cases is at variance with the illustration used by Judge Beck in his opinion in the case of State v. Osborne, 61 Iowa 330. Supra. page 79. Note 184.

188 State v. Russell, 90 Iowa 569; State v. Sharp, 110 N. C. 604; State v. Easter, 30 Ohio St. 542; Simpson v. State, 34 S. E. 204. And see State v. McNinch, 12 S. C. 89; Shope v. State, 32 S. E. 140.

189 Lascelles v. State, 90 Ga. 347.

In Tennessee,[189]* Section 5085 of the Code, provides that if any member of the grand jury is connected by blood or marriage with the person charged, he shall not be present or take part in the consideration of the charge. A defendant pleaded in abatement that one of the grand jurors was related to him within the prohibited degree by affinity and the plea was sustained and the indictment quashed. The appellate court, however, reversed the judgment of the court below and in its opinion said: "But the provision is merely directory, as the next section, which provides for supplying the vacancy during the investigation, clearly shows. No doubt, either the state or the defendant might make the objection, and it is the duty of the juror to conform to the requirement. But if, through inadvertence, a relation or connection of the person charged does actually participate in the finding, it is not seen how his relationship could have prejudiced such person."

That one of the grand jurors making presentment of an indictment for not making and opening a road through a town was a taxable inhabitant of the town, cannot be used as an objection to the validity of the indictment by the town as a defendant, since his interest would be favorable to the defendant.[190]

A person is not disqualified from serving as a grand juror by reason of his absence from his domicile, there being no intention to change the domicile;[191] but should he remove after being summoned but before serving as a grand juror, he thereby becomes incompetent to act.[192]

A grand juror is not disqualified because of his religious belief.[193]

When a challenge was made for favor it has been held to be against public policy to permit the grand juror to be examined upon his *voir dire* to establish the favor, but the court

---

189* State *v.* Maddox, 1 Lea (Tenn.) 671.

190 State *v.* Newfane, 12 Vt. 422. See Com. *v.* Ryan, 5 Mass. 90; Com. *v.* Brown, 147 Mass. 585.

191 State *v.* Alexander, 35 La. Ann. 1100; Harless *v.* U. S., 1 Morris (Iowa) 169; State *v.* Carlson, 62 Pac. 1016.

192 State *v.* Wilcox, 104 N. C. 847; and see State *v.* Kouhns, 103 Iowa 720.

193 Com. *v.* Smith, 9 Mass. 107; State *v.* Wilson, 2 McCord, (S. C.) 393.

6

was willing that it should be proved by other evidence.[194]   "A due regard for public policy as well as for the interests of justice and the nature of the inquiry, forbids that grand jurors should be polled and tried in this manner.   If the prisoner have evidence to purge the panel, let him produce it."[195] .

That this was the law was recognized by Colonel Burr[196] upon his trial, who, after announcing his intention to challenge for favor said to the Chief Justice (Marshall) : "It would, of course, be necessary to appoint triers to decide, and before whom the party and the witnesses to prove or disprove the favor must appear."   The same method of determining a challenge for favor was pursued in Pennsylvania.[197]

While peremptory challenges to grand jurors are not allowed,[199] a practice bordering closely upon this was permitted

---

194 Brown v. Com., 76 Pa. 319. And see Territory v. Hart, 14 Pac. 768. The Act of Congress of March 22, 1882, relating to the Territory of Utah provided that in prosecutions for bigamy, polygamy or unlawful cohabitation under any statute of the United States it should be cause for challenge that a proposed juror was himself living in the practice of bigamy, polygamy or unlawful cohabitation with more than one woman, and allowing the juror to be examined upon his oath as to such matters. This was held to apply to grand jurors in Clawson v. U. S., 114 U. S. 477. In the case of State v. Hughes, 1 Ala. 655, the court refused to allow counsel for defendant to ask grand jurors before they were sworn "whether they had formed and expressed an opinion as to the guilt or innocence of the prisoner"

195 Brown v. Com. 76 Pa. 319. In Com. v. Craig, 19 Pa. Superior Ct. 81, upon motion to quash upon the ground of favor, the court permitted the examination of the grand juror whom it was alleged did not stand indifferent. The grand jurors were examined on their voir dire: State v. Billings, 77 Iowa 417; Jones v. State, 2 Blackf. (Ind.) 475.

196 U. S. v. Aaron Burr, 25 Fed. Cas. 56.

197 Com. v. Clarke, 2 Browne (Pa.) 323.

199 Jones v. State, 2 Blackf. (Ind.) 475. In this case Stevens, J. said: "There is no statute or sanctioned practice in this state, authorizing a prisoner to peremptorily challenge grand jurors; and it is believed that no such practice exists in England. The common law requires grand jurors to be good and lawful freeholders, and the English statutes require several additional qualifications; and Chitty in his treatise on criminal law, when speaking of these qualifications of grand jurors, says that a prisoner, who is at the time under a prosecution for an offence about to be submitted to the consideration of a grand jury, may challenge any of the

upon Lewis' trial[200] where the attorney for the Crown took exception to some of the grand jurors and stood them aside, the court permitting it, although it had previously in another case refused to permit such a proceeding. A somewhat similar proceeding was taken in a case in a United States court,[201] the court of its own motion excusing certain of the grand jurors and substituting other qualified persons in their stead. No objection was made to this procedure by counsel for defendant although they were then present, but the question being afterward raised the court sustained its action.

This action, however, is open to severe criticism and such a practice should not be permitted to continue. If upheld, it places within the power of the court the ability to so mold the grand jury that it may be deprived of its independence of action.[202] The statutes and the common law prescribe the way in which a grand jury shall be constituted and what shall disqualify any person from acting as a grand juror, and it would seem that where there is no statute giving the court the power on its own motion to remove persons who are duly qualified in order to substitute others, such an act is done without warrant of law, and a grand jury thus made up is illegally constituted.

The general tendency, however, is to preserve to grand

grand jurors, who lacks any of these qualifications required by the common and statute laws. Chitty refers to Hawkins' Pleas of the Crown, where it is said that a challenge to grand jurors is very properly limited to persons who are, at the time, under a prosecution for an offence about to be submitted to a grand jury. By these authorities it is clear, that in England, these challenges are limited to one certain class of cases, and then only for cause."

200 7 How. St. Tr. 249.

201 U. S. v. Jones, 69 Fed Rep. 973. And see also Territory v. Barth, 15 Pac. 673; People v. Hidden, 32 Calif. 445; State v. Drogmond, 55 Mo. 87. In State v. Bowman, 73 Iowa 110, where the grand jury was empaneled in the absence of several persons drawn to serve as jurors, they failing to be present by reason of the judge stating to them that they would not be wanted and an indictment was found in their absence, the court held that the grand jury was illegally constituted and the indictment was quashed. And see Baker v. State, 23 Miss. 243.

202 O'Byrne v. State, 51 Ala. 25; Finley v. State, 61 Ala. 201; Keitler v. State, 4 G. Greene (Iowa) 291; Portis v. State, 23 Miss. 578.

jurors the right to act unless in some manner they are not competent. Thus where a district attorney in good faith but through a misunderstanding excluded a legally competent grand juror, who had been duly sworn, from the grand jury room during the consideration of a certain case by the grand jury, the court sharply criticised the action of the district attorney.[203]

In England the rule is now firmly established that the court cannot lawfully order a grand juror to withdraw himself from the panel in a particular case,[204] and inasmuch as all objections to the qualifications of a grand juror must be taken by plea in abatement[205] this rule would seem to apply even although the juror was not competent.

It is ordinarily within the province of the court to excuse a grand juror upon application and showing sufficient reason why he should not serve.[206] And where the record does not show the reason for excusing such person, it will be presumed that the excuse was sufficient.[207] The court may of its own motion dismiss a grand juror for cause[208] and may fill the vacancy with a qualified juror[209] or a talesman.[210] The

---

203 Com. v. Bradney, 126 Pa. 199.

204 Bac. Abr. Indict. C. In Vermont, in the case of In re Baldwin, 2 Tyler 473, the Supreme Court held that they had no power to order a grand juror to withdraw from the panel in any particular case, although it was one of a complaint against himself.

205 Supra. 75.

206 Denning v. State, 22 Ark. 131; People v. Hidden, 32 Calif. 445; Mills v. State, 76 Md. 274; Portis v. State, 23 Miss. 578; State v. Bradford, 57 N. H. 188; State v. Ward, 60 Vt. 142; State v. Schieler, 37 Pac. 272. But see CONTRA Smith v. State, 19 Tex. App. 95; Watts v. State, 22 Id. 572; Drake v. State, 25 Id. 293; Trevinio v. State, 27 Id. 372.

207 Burrell v. State, 129 Ind. 290; Cotton v. State, 31 Miss. 504, and see Wallis v. State, 54 Ark. 611.

208 In re Ellis, 8 Fed Cas. 548; People v. Leonard, 106 Calif. 302; State v. Bradford, 57 N. H. 188; State v. Jacobs, 6 Tex. 99; Com. v. Burton, 4 Leigh. (Va.) 645; State v. Brooks, 48 La. Ann. 1519; Territory v. Barth, 15 Pac. 673. CONTRA Keitler v. State, 4 G. Greene (Iowa) 291.

209 Denning v. State, 22 Ark. 131; State v. Reisz, 48 La. Ann. 1446; Mill v. State, 76 Md. 274; State v .Wilson, 85 Mo. 134; State v. Thomas, 61 Ohio St. 444; Jetton v. State, 19 Tenn. 192; People v. Lee, 2 Utah 441; Com. v. Burton, 4 Leigh (Va.) 645. In Peters v. State, 98 Ala. 38; the court directed

grand jury as thus constituted is a legal body, although the foreman be not again appointed nor the oath re-administered to him or to the other members as a body.[211]

In Arkansas where more than sixteen persons were selected and summoned and the record showed that only sixteen were empaneled, it was held that it would be presumed that the grand jurors in excess of the legal number were excused from serving.[212]

After the grand jury has been sworn, but before indictment found, a defendant may still either challenge the array or the polls[213] (except in states where the statute otherwise provides) for the same causes and with the same effect as if the right of challenge had been exercised before the oath was administered,[214] reasonable excuse being shown in the Federal courts for failure to act before the grand jury was fully organized.[215]

After the defendant has been indicted he may except to the array or to the individual jurors for any cause which would disqualify except for favor.[216] In the Federal courts this

the sheriff to add two new members to the jury without first making an order discharging two who were incapacitated by illness from serving and it was held that the grand jury was illegally constituted. And see Ramsey v. State, 21 So. 209; Portis v. State, 23 Miss. 578.

210 Germolgez v. State, 99 Ala. 216; State v. Fowler, 52 Iowa 103; State v. Ward, 60 Vt. 142.

211 State v. Thomas, 61 Ohio St. 444.

212 Wallis v. State, 54 Ark. 611.

213 People v. Colmere, 23 Calif. 632; State v. Hamlin, 47 Conn. 95; U. S. v. Blodgett, 35 Ga. 336; Hudson v. State, 1 Blackf. (Ind.) 317; Ross v. State, Id. 390; Jones v. State, 2 Id. 475; Mershon v. State, 51 Ind. 14; Com. v. Smith, 9 Mass. 107; Com. v. Clark, 2 Browne (Pa.) 323; Lacy v. State, 31 Tex. Cr. Rep. 78; Territory v. Hart, 14 Pac. 768. See State v. Clarissa, 11 Ala. 57.

214 State v. Hamlin, 47 Conn. 95.

215 U. S. v. Blodgett, 30 Fed. Cas. 1157; Agnew v. U. S., 165 U. S. 36.

216 Fenalty v. State, 12 Ark. 630; Barney v. State, 12 Smedes & M. (Miss.) 68; State v. Larkin, 11 Nev. 314; Rolland v. Com., 82 Pa. 306. Contra Lee v. State, 45 Miss. 114. In Com. v. Smith, 9 Mass. 107, it was held that after indictment filed, no objection of irregularity in the empaneling of the grand jury would be received as a plea to such indictment. In Boyington v. State, 2 Port (Ala.) 100, it was held too late to except to the qualifications of a grand juror after indictment filed and accepted in court.

right is limited to those cases where the defendant shows good cause why he could not raise the objection either before the grand jury was sworn or before it found the indictment.[217] The objection, however, cannot be raised by challenge either to the array or to the polls but must be raised by a motion to quash the indictment, and in the Federal courts may also be raised by a plea in abatement,[218] or by leave of court a defendant may file two or more pleas in abatement.[219] It cannot be raised by demurrer unless the defect appears upon the face of the indictment.[220]

The accused cannot afterward plead in abatement the same grounds or facts upon which he has challenged the array of the grand jury.[221]

The courts do not look with favor, at the present time, upon objections to the grand jury which are based merely upon the ground of irregularity in its organization, the defendant having suffered no prejudice thereby,[222] and the Federal courts are averse to quashing an indictment upon such a ground and will not do so unless the defendant take advantage of such irregularity at each stage of the proceedings.[223]

217 Carter v. Texas, 177 U. S. 442; Wolfson v. U. S., 101 Fed. Rep. 430; U. S. v. Reeves, 27 Fed. Cas. 750; U. S. v. Jones, 31 Fed. Rep. 725; Agnew v. U. S., 165 U. S. 36.

218 Carter v. Texas, 177 U. S. 442; U. S. v. Reeves, 27 Fed. Cas. 750; U. S. v. Gale, 109 U S. 65; Agnew v. U. S., 165 U. S. 36. And see Mershon v. State, 51 Ind. 14; State v. Seaborn, 15 N. C. 305; State v. Ward, 60 Vt. 142. In Lee v. State, 45 Miss. 114, it was held that the competency or qualifications of the grand jury cannot be questioned by plea in abatement, the empaneling being conclusive as to these facts. And see Durrah v. State, 44 Miss. 789; Head v. State; Id. 731. See also Supra. 64. Note 100.

219 U. S. v. Richardson, 28 Fed. Rep. 61.

220 State v. Brandon, 28 Ark. 410; Williams v. State, 60 Ga. 88; Jackson v. State, 64 Ga. 344; State v. Hart, 29 Iowa 268; State v. Vincent, 91 Md. 718; Com. v. Church, 1 Pa. 105; Com. v. Smith, 27 S. W. 810; Fisher v. U. S., 31 Pac. 195.

221 Meiers v. State, 56 Ind. 336; McClary v. State, 75 Ind. 260.

222 Woodward v. State, 33 Fla. 508; State v. Glascow, 59 Md. 209; Cox v. People, 80 N. Y. 500.

223 Wolfson v. U. S., 101 Fed. Rep. 430; U. S. v. Eagan, 30 Fed. Rep. 608.

Where the defendant before pleading to the indictment does not object to the array or to the polls of the grand jury, he will be held to have waived his right and cannot afterward raise the objection upon a motion in arrest of judgment,[224] and it is too late to move to quash the array after the defendant has been arraigned, pleaded "not guilty" and four jurymen have been selected.[225]

It has been held that the presence of one disqualified person upon the panel of grand jurors will vitiate the indictment found by it,[226] but this is subject to the qualification that the defendant had no opportunity to challenge the disqualified juror before indictment found, and raises the objection either by motion to quash or by plea in abatement before pleading to the indictment. After a trial on the merits, the objection cannot be raised on a motion in arrest of judgment.[227]

---

224 State v. Clarissa, 11 Ala. 57; Horton v. State, 47 Id. 58; Sanders v. State, 55 Id. 183; Shropshire v. State, 12 Ark. 190; Fenalty v. State, Id. 630; Stewart v. State, 13 Id. 720; Dixon v. State, 29 Id. 165; Wright v. State, 42 Id. 94; Carpenter v. State, 62 Id. 286; People v. Hidden, 32 Calif. 445; Terrell v. State, 9 Ga. 58; Miller v. State, 69 Ind. 284; State v. Wash. 33 La. Ann. 896; State v. Griffin, 38 Id. 502; McQuillen v. State, 8 Smedes & M. (Miss.) 587; State v. Borroum, 25 Miss. 203; Green v. State, 28 Id. 687; State v. Smallwood, 68 Mo. 192; State v. Clifton, 73 Mo. 430; State v. Rand, 33 N. H. 216; People v. Robinson, 2 Parker Cr. Rep. (N. Y.) 235; People v. Griffin, 2 Barb. (N. Y.) 427; State v. Martin, 2 Ired. (N. C.) 101; State v. Seaborn, 15 N. C. 305; Com. v. Chauncey, 2 Ashm. (Pa.) 90; State v. Motley, 7 S. C. 327; State v. Washington, 28 Tenn. 626; Ellis v. State, 92 Id. 85; Robinson v. Com. 88 Va. 900; Territory v. Armijo, 37 Pac. 1117; Territory v. Barrett, 42 Pac. 66; Barber v. State, 46 S. W. 233. The same ruling was made in Dyer v. State, 79 Tenn. 509, even though a plea in abatement had been filed before general issue pleaded and was not acted upon.

225 Com. v. Freeman, 166 Pa. 332. And see Com. v. Shew, 8 Pa. Dist. Rep. 484.

226 U. S. v. Hammond, 26 Fed. Cas. 99; Com. v. Smith, 73 Ky. 476; State v. Rowland, 36 La. Ann. 193; Barney v. State, 12 Smedes & M. (Miss.) 68; State v. Duncan, 7 Yerg. (Tenn.) 271.

227 Johnson v. State, 62 Ga. 179; State v. Carver, 49 Me. 588; Clare v. State, 30 Md. 163; Territory v. Romero, 2 N. Mex. 474; State v. Lamon, 10 N. C. 175; State v. Martin, 24 Id. 101; State v. Haywood, 94 N. C. 847; State v. Vogel, 22 Wis. 471. But see State v. Parks, 21 La. Ann. 251; State v. Rowland, 36 Id. 193.

While the right is thus reserved in general to a defendant to take advantage of irregularities in the organization of the grand jury, such irregularity cannot be availed of by a person who attacks the grand jury in a collateral proceeding.[228] It has therefore been held that in a proceeding to punish a witness for defying the authority of the grand jury, he cannot in such collateral proceeding question its regularity;[229] and similarly, a person cannot refuse to testify before a grand jury upon the ground that it was not empaneled in accordance with the law.[230]

When the grand jurors have appeared in court in answer to the summons, they are then empaneled.[231] This has been judicially determined to mean the final act of the court ascertaining who should be sworn immediately preceding the administration of the oath to the grand jurors.[232] In the absence of any statutory provision prescribing the time when the grand jury shall be organized, it would seem that it may be empaneled at any time during the term for which it was summoned.[233] If, however, the grand jury is not formed in accordance with such statute then the indictments are void.[234]

228 State v. Noyes, 87 Wis. 340.

229 In re Gannon, 69 Calif. 541. But see In re Lester, 77 Ga. 143.

230 Ex Parte Hammond, 91 Calif. 545.

231 In U. S. v. Wilson, 28 Fed. Cas. 725, it was held that although the Act of Congress, July 20, 1840 (5 Stat. 394) provided for the adoption in the Federal courts of the methods of the highest courts of the respective states "in so far as such mode may be practicable," the Federal court sitting in Ohio had authority in its discretion to adopt the mode of empaneling grand juries practiced in the inferior courts of the State.

232 State v. Ostrander, 18 Iowa 435.

233 Perkins v. State, 92 Ala. 66; Jackson v. State, 102 Ala. 167; Meiers v. State, 56 Ind. 336. Where the statute provided that the grand jury should be empaneled on the first day of the term, this provision was held to be merely directory and that if empaneled on a subsequent day it was legally constituted: State v. Davis, 14 La. Ann. 678; State v. Dillard, 35 Id. 1049.

234 Yelm Jim v. Territory, 1 Wash. T. 63; Stokes v. State, 24 Miss. 621. The court has refused to quash where the formality of drawing the names as provided by statute was disregarded: Workman v. State, 36 Tenn. 425. Where a statute provided a method for the convening of grand jurors it was held that the empaneling of a grand jury summoned prior to its passage was legal: Bell v. State, 42 Ind. 335. And see State v. Wiltsey, 103 Iowa 54.

Where persons summoned as "trial jurors" were empaneled as a grand jury the indictment was set aside.[235]

The record must show the empaneling of the grand jury otherwise the indictment may be set aside,[236] but this need not be repeated in the record of each indictment found.[237] If the indictment recites the empaneling and the record shows its return into court, this will be sufficient,[238] but if the only evidence of the empaneling be the endorsement on the indictment "a true bill" and the foreman's signature, the indictment will be quashed.[239]

In the absence of statutory authority, the same judge cannot organize two successive grand juries with general powers at the same term.[240] If the first grand jury be illegally empaneled, the court may, during the term, discharge it and empanel another according to law.[241] But the second grand jury cannot be legally empaneled while the first grand jury continues to be recognized as a legal body and before it is set aside.[242]

Should a court without authority of law empanel a grand jury, it has been held that all indictments found by the body so constituted are void.[243]

Where a statute is enacted changing the manner of drawing and summoning grand jurors and repealing former statutes, a grand jury drawn while the prior statutes are in force may lawfully be empaneled and act after the repealing statute becomes effective.[244] And where a territory is admitted as a

---

235 People v. Earnest, 45 Calif. 29.

236 Parker v. People, 13 Colo. 155; App v. State, 90 Ind. 73. But see Turns v. Com., 47 Mass. 224.

237 Parker v. People, 13 Colo. 155.

238 Stout v. State, 93 Ind. 150.

239 Parmer v. State, 41 Ala. 416.

240 O'Brien v. State, 91 Ala. 16.

241 Meiers v. State, 56 Ind. 336.

242 State v. Jacobs, 6 Tex. 99. The discharge of the former grand jury will be presumed: State v. Dusenberry, 112 Mo. 277; State v. Overstreet, 128 Id. 470.

243 Ex Parte Farley, 40 Fed. Rep. 66; O'Brynes v. State, 51 Ala. 25; State v. Doherty, 60 Me. 504; Stevens v. State, 3 Ohio St. 453. And see Davis v. State, 46 Ala. 80; Finnegan v. State, 57 Ga. 427.

244 Bell v. State, 42 Ind. 335; State v. May, 50 Ind. 170; State v. Graff,

state, the territorial laws relating to the authority of the grand jury to act and the powers conferred upon it which were in force before its admission, remain in effect after its admission, as to offences committed prior thereto.[245]

After any challenges to the array or to the polls have been disposed of, the foreman is then selected from the persons summoned.[246] In no case should he be illiterate for his duties are important and require knowledge and ability, but an indictment will not be invalidated because the foreman could not write his name.[247]

In England, the United States Courts and in many of the state courts, the foreman is appointed by the court.[248] In some states he is selected by the grand jury from their number;[249] in others they are permitted to make selection subject to the approval of the court,[250] or the court may direct them to choose their foreman.[251] If he should afterward be excluded from the grand jury by reason of disqualification or other cause, the court may appoint his successor,[252] and if he is but temporarily disqualified from serving by reason of sickness, absence or the like, then a foreman *pro tem.* may be named,[253] who lawfully exercises all the powers, and must perform all the duties, which devolve upon the regularly appointed foreman.

The appointment of the foreman should be noted upon the minutes of the court and such entry is sufficient evidence of his

97 Iowa 568; State *v.* Wiltsey, 103 Iowa 54; In re Tillery, 43 Kans. 188; Broyles *v.* State, 55 S. W. 966. CONTRA Clark *v.* U. S., 19 App. D. C. 295.

245 State *v.* Rock, 57 Pac. 532.

246 In State *v.* Texada, 19 La. Ann. 436, it was held that the statute relating to the drawing of grand jurors makes it essential that the foreman should be selected from the whole venire.

247 State *v.* Tinney, 26 La. Ann. 460.

248 The court may appoint a talesman selected from the by-standers as foreman of the grand jury: State *v.* Brandt, 41 Iowa 593.

249 1 Whart. Cr. Law, Sec. 466; Revised Statutes Maine, Ch. 135; Sec. 4; Revised Laws Massachusetts, Ch. 218, Sec. 7; Revised Statutes Florida, Sec. 2809.

250 Blackmore *v.* State, 8 S. W. 940.

251 Lung's Case, 1 Conn. 428.

252 U. S. *v.* Belvin, 46 Fed. Rep. 381.

253 Com. *v.* Noonan, 38 Leg. Int. (Pa.) 184.

appointment;[254] although this has been held not to be material where the indictment was indorsed by the foreman and returned into court.[255]

If the record shows that one person has been appointed foreman and an indictment is returned signed by another as foreman, in the absence of proof to the contrary the court will presume that the foreman named in the record has been regularly discharged and the other appointed in his stead.[256]

An indictment endorsed "a true bill" and returned upon the authority of the whole grand jury was sustained although no foreman had been appointed.[257]

The clerk of the grand jury is usually one of that body, who is selected by his fellow jurors after they have been sworn and have retired to their room. In his absence or inability to act, another juror may be named to act in his stead.

When the foreman of the grand jury has been appointed, but one step more is required to complete its organization and fit it to enter upon the performance of its duties, and that is the administration of the oath.[258] The foreman is first sworn alone and afterward the grand jurors, three at a time come forward and take the oath, and such of them as will not take an oath are allowed to affirm,[259] until all have either been sworn or af-

254 Byrd v. State, 1 How. (Miss.) 247; Woodsides v. State, 2 How. (Miss.) 655.

255 People v. Roberts, 6 Calif. 214. And for a similar ruling see State v. Gouge, 80 Tenn. 132, in the absence of plea in abatement and proof to sustain the allegations thereof.

256 Mohler v. People, 24 Ill. 26; State v. Collins, 65 Tenn. 151.

257 Friar v. State, 3 How. (Miss.) 422; Peter v. State, Id. 433; And see Yates v. People, 38 Ill. 527.

258 The grand jury is not complete and organized for business until sworn: Ridling v. State, 56 Ga. 601. The oath may be administered under the direction of the court by any officer authorized generally to administer oaths: Allen v. State, 77 Ill. 484.

259 Where an indictment is based on the affirmations of some of the grand jurors it will be quashed unless it appears they were legally entitled to serve on their mere affirmation: State v. Harris, 7 N. J. Law 361; and where found on the affirmation of Quakers it must appear that they had conscientious scruples against taking an oath: State v. Fox, 9 N. J. Law 244.

firmed.[260]   This was the common law method of administering the oath and in some jurisdictions has now given place to the custom of swearing the grand jurors as a body after the administration of the oath to the foreman; in others, it is provided by statute that the full oath shall be administered to the first two grand jurors whose names appear upon the list, and then the balance of the panel shall be sworn with the short form of oath.[260*]

The method of administering the oath has been discussed by Chief Justice Johnson in the case of Brown vs. State[261] in the following language:

"The form of oath required to be administered to the grand jurors is of ancient origin, and it is necessary that it should be observed, at least in substance; but the mode or order of administering it is purely a matter of practice, and must of necessity be governed by circumstances. . . . . It is conceived to be entirely a matter of practice as to the number that shall be sworn at a time, and that such practice is regulated alone by considerations of convenience."

The panel need not be complete when the oath is administered, but the full oath must be administered to those who are added after part have been sworn.[262]

If a form of oath be prescribed by statute, it should be substantially complied with.[263]

The minutes of the court must show that the grand jury was sworn;[264] it is not sufficient that the indictment sets forth that

---

260 1 Whart. Cr. Law, Sec. 466.

260* Revised Statutes Maine, Ch. 135, Sec. 2; Revised Laws Massachusetts, Ch. 218, Sec. 5; Wisconsin Statutes, Ch. 116, Sec 2547.

261 10 Ark. 613.

262 Brown v. State, 10 Ark. 607. And see State v. Furco, 51 La. Ann. 1082.

263 Ashburn v. State, 15 Ga. 246. CONTRA West v. State, 6 Tex. App. 485.

264 The minutes of the court are not the exclusive mode of proving that the grand jury had been duly empanelled and sworn: State v. Stuart, 35 La. Ann. 1015.

the grand jurors were duly sworn.[265]   If regularly sworn
but this fact be inadvertently omitted from the record, the
defect may be cured and the record amended *nunc pro tunc*.[266]
The record must show that the foreman was sworn.[267]

265 Abram *v.* State, 25 Miss. 589; Foster *v.* State, 31 Id. 421; Russell *v.*
State, 10 Tex. 288; Pierce *v.* State, 12 Id. 210. In People *v.* Rose, 52 Hun.
(N. Y.) 33, it appeared that the oath was informally administered, but it
was held that the facts thus shown did not impeach the recital of the indictment that the oath was duly administered.

266 Baker *v.* State, 39 Ark. 180; State *v.* Folke, 2 La. Ann. 744.

267 Roe *v.* State, 2 So. 459.

PART III

"The oath of a grand juryman," says Judge Wilson,[1] "is the commission under which he acts." This statement, while undoubtedly a correct exposition of the law as then understood, is in our modern jurisprudence not sufficiently comprehensive, and is subject to the qualification that, coupled with additional statutory powers, and duties within the bounds prescribed by statutes or as defined by the courts, it forms his commission.

The oath as administered to the foreman of the grand jury[1*] is generally in the following language: "You, as foreman of this inquest, for the body of the County of   , do swear,

---

1 Jas. Wilson's Works, Vol. II, p. 365.

1* No statutory form of oath has been adopted by the United States, nor is any form of oath prescribed by statute in the states of New Jersey, Pennsylvania, Maryland, Delaware, North Carolina, South Carolina, Louisiana, and the Territory of Hawaii.

The oath adopted by statute in all other states and territories is given as follows:

MAINE. Revised Statutes, Chapter 135, Sec. 2: "You, as grand jurors of this county of ——, solemnly swear, that you will diligently inquire and true presentment make of all matters and things given you in charge. The state's counsel, your fellows and your own, you shall keep secret. You shall present no man for envy, hatred or malice; nor leave any man unpresented for love, fear, favor, affection or hope of reward; but you shall present things truly as they come to your knowledge, according to the best of your understanding. So help you God."

NEW HAMPSHIRE. Public Statutes, Chapter 253, Sec. 5, with slight changes, prescribes the same oath as used in Maine.

VERMONT. Statutes, Chapter 233, Sec. 5418, prescribes with slight changes the same oath as used in Maine, but concludes with the added words, "According to the laws of this state.''

MASSACHUSETTS. Revised Laws, Chapter 218, Sec. 5, prescribes with slight changes the same oath as used in Maine.

RHODE ISLAND. General Laws, Chapter 227, Sec. 34, provides "diligently

94

(or affirm) that you will diligently inquire, and true presentment make, of such articles, matters, and things as shall be given you in charge or otherwise come to your knowledge, touching the present service; the commonwealth's counsel,

inquire and true presentment make of all such crimes and misdemeanors cognizable by this court as shall come to your knowledge," but otherwise is the same as the oath used in Maine.

CONNECTICUT. General Statutes, Title 54, Chapter 281, Sec. 4795: "You solemnly swear by the name of the ever living God, that you will diligently inquire after, and due presentment make, of all breaches of law that shall come to your knowledge, according to your charge; the secrets of the cause, your own, and your fellows', you will duly observe and keep; you will present no man from envy, hatred, or malice; neither will you leave any man unpresented, from love, fear, or affection, or in hope of reward; but you will present cases truly, as they come to your knowledge, according to the best of your understanding, and according to law; so help you God."

NEW YORK. Code Criminal Procedure, Sec. 245, with slight changes, prescribes the same oath as used in Maine.

VIRGINIA. Code, Tit. 53, Chapter 195, Sec. 3980: "You shall diligently inquire, and true presentment make, of all such matters as may be given you in charge, or come to your knowledge, touching the present service. You shall present no person through prejudice or ill will, nor leave any unpresented through fear or favor, but in all your presentments you shall present the truth, the whole truth, and nothing but the truth, so help you God."

GEORGIA. Penal Code, 1895, Sec. 825, prescribes substantially the form of oath contained in the text with this change, viz: "The state's counsel, your fellows', and your own, you shall keep secret, unless called upon to give evidence thereof in some court of law in this state."

FLORIDA. Revised Statutes, 1892, Sec. 2808, prescribe substantially the same form of oath as used in Georgia.

TEXAS. Code Cr. Proc. 1897, Art. 404, substantially the same as the Maine oath except in this, viz: "The state's counsel, your fellows', and your own you shall keep secret, unless required to disclose the same in the course of a judicial proceeding in which the truth or falsity of evidence given in the grand jury room, in a criminal case, shall be under investigation."

ALABAMA. Code 1896, Sec. 5024, prescribes a form of oath similar to the oath in the text, but makes particular reference to offences "committed or triable within the county."

TENNESSEE. Code, Sec. 5833, prescribes substantially the same oath as used in Alabama.

KENTUCKY. Statutes, Chapter 74, Sec. 2250: "Saving yourselves, you do swear that you will diligently inquire of, and present all treasons, felon

your fellows' and your own you shall keep secret; you shall
present no one for envy, hatred or malice; neither shall you
leave any one unpresented for fear, favor or affection, hope of
reward or gain, but shall present all things truly as they come

ies, misdemeanors, and breaches of the penal laws which shall have been
committed or done within the limits of the jurisdiction of this county, of
which you have knowledge or may receive information."

MISSISSIPPI. Code, Sec. 2372, prescribes substantially the form given
in the text.

WEST VIRGINIA. Code, Chapter, 157, Sec. 5, prescribes substantially
the same form of oath as used in Virginia.

OHIO. Revised Statutes, Sec. 7191, prescribes the form given in the
text, but beginning, "Saving yourself and fellow jurors;" preserving
secrecy "unless called on in a court of justice to make disclosures;" and
concluding, "you shall present the truth, the whole truth and nothing but
the truth, according to the best of your skill and understanding."

INDIANA. Code Crim. Proc., Sec. 1721: "You and each of you, do
solemnly swear that you will diligently inquire, and true presentment make,
of all felonies and misdemeanors, committed or triable, within this county,
of which you shall have or can obtain legal evidence; that you will present
no person through malice, hatred or ill-will, nor leave any unpresented
through fear, favor or affection, or for any reward, or the promise or hope
thereof, but in all your indictments you will present the truth, the whole
truth, and nothing but the truth; and that you will not disclose any evidence given or proceeding had before the grand jury, so help you God."

ILLINOIS. Statutes, Chapter 78, Sec. 18, prescribes substantially the form
set forth in the text.

MICHIGAN. Howell's Ann. Stat., Sec. 9491, prescribes substantially the
same form as used in Maine.

WISCONSIN. Statutes, Chapter 116, Sec. 2547, prescribes substantially
the same oath as used in Maine.

MISSOURI. Revised statutes 1899, Sec. 2489, prescribes a form substantially the same as used in Indiana.

NEBRASKA. Compiled statutes, Sec. 8139, prescribes the same oath as
used in Ohio.

KANSAS. General Statutes 1897, Chapter 102; Sec. 97, prescribes substantially the same oath as used in Indiana.

MINNESOTA. General Statutes, Sec. 5641, prescribes substantially the
same oath as used in Indiana.

ARKANSAS. Statutes, Chapter 49, Sec. 2041, prescribes substantially the
same oath as used in Kentucky.

IDAHO. Penal Code, Sec. 5293: "You, as foreman of the grand jury,
will diligently inquire and true presentment make, of all public offences
against the State of Idaho, committed or triable, within this county, of

to your knowledge, according to the best of your understanding (so help you God.)"

This oath the balance of the grand jurors pledge themselves to observe in these words: "The same oath (or affirmation) which your foreman hath taken, on his part, you and every of

which you shall have or can obtain legal evidence. You will keep your own counsel, and that of your fellows, and of the government, and will not, except when required in the course of judicial proceedings, disclose the testimony of any witness examined before you, nor anything which you or any other grand juror may have said, nor the manner in which you or any other grand juror may have voted on any matter before you. You will present no person through malice, hatred, or ill will, nor leave any unpresented through fear, favor or affection, or for any reward or the promise or hope thereof; but in all your presentments you will present the truth, the whole truth, and nothing but the truth, according to the best of your skill and understanding, so help you God."

NEVADA. Compiled Statutes, Sec. 4158, prescribes a form of oath substantially the same as the oath used in Indiana.

COLORADO. Ann. Statutes, 1891, Chapter 73, Sec. 2617, prescribes substantially the same oath as given in the text.

UTAH. Revised Statutes 1898, Sec. 4708, prescribes substantially the same oath as used in Idaho.

CALIFORNIA. Penal Code, Sec. 903, prescribes substantially the same oath as used in Idaho.

OREGON. Code, Section 1271, prescribes the following form of oath: "You and each of you, as grand jurors for the county of ——, do solemnly swear that you will diligently inquire into, and true presentment or indictment make, of all crimes against this state, committed or triable within this county, that shall come to your knowledge; that the proceedings before you, the counsel of the state, your own counsel, and that of your fellows, you will keep secret; that you will indict no person through envy, hatred, or malice, nor leave any person not indicted through fear, favor, affection, or hope of reward, but that you will indict, according to the truth, upon the evidence before you, and the laws of this state; so help you God."

WASHINGTON. Code, Section 6809 prescribes substantially the same oath as used in Vermont.

WYOMING. Revised Statutes, Sect. 5282: "You, as foreman of this grand inquest, do solemnly swear (or affirm) that you will diligently inquire and true presentment make of all such matters and things as shall be given you in charge, or otherwise come to your knowledge touching the present service. The counsel of the state, your own and your fellows, you shall keep secret unless called on in a court of justice to make disclosures. You shall present no person through malice, hatred or ill will, nor shall you leave any person unpresented through fear, favor or affection, or for

you, shall well and truly observe, on your part (so help you God)."

The grand juror's oath is of great antiquity. When in the time of Ethelred II. the twelve Thanes went out, they "swore upon the relic that was given them in hand that they would accuse no innocent man nor conceal any guilty one."[2] In Bracton's time the oath and pledge bound the grand jurors to

any reward or hope thereof; but in all your presentments you shall present the truth, the whole truth and nothing but the truth, according to the best of your skill and understanding."

MONTANA. Penal Code, Sec. 1761: "You, and each of you, do solemnly swear (or affirm) that you will diligently inquire into and true presentment make, of all public offences against the laws of this state, committed or triable by indictment in this county, of which you have or can obtain legal evidence, you will present no one through hatred, malice or ill will, nor leave any unpresented through fear, favor or affection, or for any reward, or the promise or hope thereof; but in all your presentments you will present the truth, the whole truth and nothing but the truth, according to the best of your skill and understanding, so help you God."

NORTH DAKOTA. Revised Code 1895, Sec. 8004, prescribes substantially the same oath as used in Idaho.

SOUTH DAKOTA. Revised Code Criminal Proc., Sec. 177, prescribes the same oath as used in North Dakota.

IOWA. Code 1897, Sect. 5249: "You, as foreman of the grand jury, shall diligently inquire and true presentment make of all public offences against the people of this state, triable on indictment within this county, of which you have or can obtain legal evidence; you shall present no person through malice, hatred or ill will, nor leave any unpresented through fear, favor or affection, or for any reward or the promise or hope thereof, but in all your presentments you shall present the truth, the whole truth and nothing but the truth, according to the best of your skill and understanding."

ARIZONA. Code Crim. Proc. Sec. 800, prescribes substantially the same oath as used in Idaho.

NEW MEXICO. Compiled Laws 1897, Sec. 967, prescribes substantially the same oath as used in Iowa.

INDIAN TERRITORY. Statutes Cr. Proc., Chapter 20, Sec. 1418: "Saving yourselves and fellow jurors, you do swear that you will diligently inquire of and present all treasons, felonies, misdemeanors and breaches of the penal laws over which you have jurisdicton, of which you have knowledge or may receive information."

OKLAHOMA. Revised Statutes 1903, Sec. 5329, prescribes substantially the same oath as used in Idaho.

2 Wilkin's Leges Angliæ Saxonicæ 117.

similar action.[3]   But while the powers of the grand jury were much broader than they are today, the oath of the grand juror was narrower in its scope.   "I will speak the truth concerning this *which ye shall ask me,*"[4] the grand juror swore, and if the oath was his commission, then the limits of his powers were defined by those things concerning which the king's justice should ask.   The oath proper, as usually referred to, in no wise resembles the present day oath, but at the conclusion of the reading of the capitula by the justices as to which the grand jurors had sworn to speak the truth, they pledged themselves to do faithfully those things which the justices required of them, to aggrieve no one through enmity, nor defer to any one through love, and to conceal what they had heard.[5]   This was undoubtedly, in the nature of a supplemental oath and contains the elements of the oath of the present day.

In the time of Britton[6] but one oath was taken, containing all the elements of the two oaths taken in Bracton's time, and more generally conforming to the oath now administered.   In a book printed in the time of Oliver Cromwell,[7] the oath taken by the foreman of the grand jury is given as follows: "Ye shall truly inquire, and due presentment make of all such things as you are charged withall on the Queen's behalf, the Queen's councell, your owne, and your fellowes, you shall well and truly keepe; and in all other things the truth present, so help you God, and by the contents of this Booke."

It will be noted that this oath, like the one taken by the grand jurors in Bracton's time, places a limitation upon the power of the grand jury.   They are charged to present "all such things as you are charged withall on the Queen's behalf," so that if their oath be regarded as their commission and defining the bounds within which they could lawfully act, they were prevented from making presentment of anything with which they had not been charged.   But in practice no such re-

---

3 Bracton-de legibus, (Sir Travers Twiss éd.) Vol. II, pp. 237-243.
4 Id.
5 Supra. 20, 21.
7 Book of Oaths (London, 1649) 206.
6 Britton (Legal Classic Series) p. 17.

striction was placed upon them.   They were regarded as an arm of the government to bring wrong-doers to justice, and in this respect they exercised the broadest and most unlimited powers.

The view was taken in the early history of the Federal courts that grand juries, on their own motion, institute all proceedings whatsoever.[8]   This view received strong support from Judge Wilson,[9] at that time one of the justices of the United States Supreme Court, who remarks that the grand jurors' oath "assigns no limits, except those marked by diligence itself, to the course of his inquiries: why, then, should it be circumscribed by more contracted boundaries?   Shall diligent inquiry be enjoined?   And shall the means and opportunities of inquiry be prohibited or restrained?"

The same broad view of the right of the grand jury to act was taken by Mr. Bradford, Attorney General of the United States in 1794, in a letter to the secretary of state.[10]   In this he recognized the right of a prosecutor to personally appear before the grand jury with his witnesses and make his complaint directly to them without the necessity of it passing through any intermediate tribunal.[11]   This, however, is not now the law in the Federal courts.[12]

8 1 Whart. Cr. Law, Sec. 453 (7th ed.).

9 Jas. Wilson's Works, Vol. II, p. 365.

10 Opinions of Attorneys General 22.   And see 1 Whart. Cr. Law, Sec. 453 (7th ed.).

11 In State v. Stewart, 45 La. Ann. 1164, decided in 1893, the grand jury were considering a bill against the defendant when a person, without being summoned appeared before the grand jury and gave his version of the case.   A true bill was returned and the defendant sought to quash the indictment upon the ground that the indictment had been found at the instance of this witness.   The court overruled the motion.   In his opinion on appeal by the state on other grounds it was said by McEnery, J.: "It is complained by the defendant that one S. A. Morgan, the leading state witness, went without summons or request before the grand jury and gave his own version of the case against defendant, and instituted this prosecution. The witness had the undoubted right to go before the grand jury voluntarily and disclose his knowledge of facts in the case.   As a good citizen it was his duty to do so.   No one can be excused for withholding knowledge of a crime from the public until he is summoned to give his testimony of

In Pennsylvania, a somewhat narrower view of the power of the grand jury was taken. Judge Addison in his very learned charges to grand juries says: "The matters which, whether given in charge or of their own knowledge, are to be presented by the grand jury, are all offences within the county. To grand juries is committed the preservation of the peace of the county, the care of bringing to light for examination, trial and punishment, all violence, outrage, indecency and terror, everything that may occasion danger, disturbance or dismay to the citizens. Grand juries are watchmen, stationed by the laws to survey the conduct of their fellow-citizens, and inquire where and by whom public authority has been violated, or our constitution or laws infringed." But the grand jury is not to summon witnesses except under the supervision of the court.[13] This effectually limits them to such matters as are within their own knowledge or may be given them in charge by the court or by the district attorney.

The first duty imposed upon the grand jurors by their oath is that they will "diligently inquire and true presentment make." Judge Addison, in his charge to the grand jury at September Sessions, 1792, said, "the accurate interpretation, in its true extent, of the diligent inquiry and true presentment which the grand jury is sworn to make, has not been precisely agreed on by learned men."[14] Four years earlier, however, these words had received a judicial interpretation in Pennsylvania,[15] in a case pending before the grand jury. A grand juror asked what was meant by the words "diligently inquire," to which Chief Justice McKean replied, "The expression meant, diligently to inquire into the circumstances of the charge, the credibility of the witnesses who support it, and from the

its commission." As to this decision it is sufficient to say that it is contrary to the law as laid down by the courts of every other state.

12 Mr. Justice Field's Charge to Grand Jury, 30 Fed. Cas. 992. And see Welch *v.* State, 68 Miss. 341; Wilson *v.* State, 70 Miss. 595; McCullough *v.* Com. 67 Pa. 30.

13 Addison App. 47; Mr. Justice Field's Charge to Grand Jury, 30 Fed. Cas. 992.

14 Addison, App. 38.

15 Res. *v.* Shaffer, 1 Dall. 236.

whole, to judge whether the person accused ought to be put upon his trial.   For (he added) though it would be improper to determine the merits of the cause, it is incumbent upon the grand jury to satisfy their minds, by a *diligent inquiry,* that there is a probable ground for the accusation, before they give it their authority, and call upon the defendant to make a public defense."

In his charge to the grand jury in the Circuit Court for the District of Maryland in 1836, Chief Justice Taney, of the United States Supreme Court, said,[16] "But in our desire to bring the guilty to punishment, we must still take care to guard the innocent from injury; and every one is deemed to be innocent until the contrary appears by sufficient legal proof. You will, therefore, in every case that may come before you, carefully weigh the testimony, and present no one, unless in your deliberate judgment, the evidence before you is sufficient in the absence of any other proof, to justify the conviction of the party accused."

The difference in the extent of the powers of grand jurors in the Federal courts and in the courts of Pennsylvania and other states is reflected in the wider range which the Federal judges give to this clause of the oath. The construction placed upon these words in the Federal courts is probably most fully and clearly expressed by Chief Justice Chase[17] in the following language: "You must not be satisfied by acting upon such cases only as may be brought before you by the district attorney, or by members of your body to whom knowledge of particular offences may have come.   Your authority and your duty go much further.   You may and you should, summon before you, officers of the government, and others whom you may have reason to believe possess information proper for your action, and examine them fully."

But in making diligent inquiry neither the Federal nor the state grand jury is wholly unrestrained.   They may only inquire and present within the extent of their powers as will be

16 30 Fed. Cas. 998.
17 Charge to Grand Jury, 30 Fed. Cas. 980.

hereafter treated of,[18] and according to the well established principles of law. A grand jury may only inquire into offences occurring within its territorial jurisdiction,[19] and not barred by the statute of limitations;[20] but within such jurisdiction they may investigate into every crime known to the law,[21] and which comes before them in one of the methods provided by law. They may investigate a crime committed after they are empaneled.[22]

In making their inquiries, the grand jurors are not permitted to summon witnesses for the defence either upon their own motion[23] or at the request of the defendant or his counsel,[24] nor will the court allow the defendant's witnesses to go before the grand jury,[25] either with or without the consent of the district attorney;[26] nor may any witnesses appear before or send any communication to them, pertaining to a matter then pending before the grand jury, except upon the previous order of the court.[27]   In Connecticut, the extraordinary method is in force of allowing the defendant to be present during the examination of witnesses before the grand jury,[28] but his counsel will not be admitted to their deliberations.[29]

If the grand jurors are not satisfied with the evidence pre-

---

18 Post 106 et. seq.

19 People v. Beatty, 14 Calif. 566; Ward v. State, 2 Mo. 120; State v. Overstreet, 128 Mo. 470; People v. Green, 1 Utah 11; Beal v. State, 15 Ind. 378; Rutzell v. State, 15 Ark. 67.

20 People v. Beatty, 14 Calif. 566; State v. Overstreet, 128 Mo. 470.

21 Territory v. Corbett, 3 Mont. 50.

22 People v. Beatty, 14 Calif. 566; Com. v. Gee, 60 Mass. 174; Allen v. State, 5 Wis. 329. But see Stark v. Bindley, 52 N. E. 804.

23 1 Chitty Cr. Law 317; U. S. v. Terry, 39 Fed. Rep. 355.

24 Res. v. Shaffer, 1 Dall. 236; U. S. v. Lawrence, 26 Fed. Cas. 886.

25 U. S. v. Palmer, 27 Fed. Cas. 410; People v. Goldenson, 76 Calif. 328. But see Lung's Case, 1 Conn. 428; In re Morse, 87 N. Y. Sup. 721.

26 U. S. v. Blodgett, 30 Fed. Cas. 1157. In U. S. v. White, 28 Fed. Cas. 588, the court intimated that witnesses for the defence may be sent to the grand jury with the consent of the district attorney.

27 Mr. Justice Field's Charge to the Grand Jury, 30 Fed. Cas. 992.

28 State v. Fasset, 16 Conn. 457. And see State v. Walcott, 21 Conn. 272; State v. Hamlin, 47 Conn. 95.

29 Lung's Case, 1 Conn. 428.

sented by such witnesses as they have heard, they may ask
that additional testimony be submitted to them.[30] This request should be made to the court, who has the sole power of
ordering that process issue to produce any additional evidence
before the grand jury;[31] but in the United States courts it is
sufficient if application be made to the district attorney, who
may direct that process issue.[32] Ordinarily the grand jury
cannot on their own motion summon witnesses to appear before them,[33] for they usually have neither the right to issue
the necessary process to command their attendance nor the
power to punish if witnesses refuse to appear.

In Tennessee the grand jury is vested by statute with broad
inquisitorial powers in certain cases, and in such instances they
may send for witnesses without an order of court.[34]

In Missouri[35] and Maryland[36] a grand jury is vested with
similar authority. But the powers conferred on grand juries
by such statutes being in derogation of the common law, cannot be extended beyond the express provisions of the statute
itself.[37]

30 1 Chitty Cr. Law 317; Dickinson's Quarter Sessions, (5th ed.) 156-
158.

31 The process is issued by the clerk of the court: O'Hair v. People,
32 Ill. App. 277; Baldwin v.. State, 126 Ind. 24.

32 And see O'Hair v. People, 32 Ill. App. 277; 1 Whart Cr. Law Sec.
490. But see contra Warner v. State 81 Tenn. 52.

33 In re Lester, 77 Ga. 143.

34 State v. Smith, 19 Tenn. 99; Deshazo v. State, 23 Tenn. 275; State v.
Parrish, 27 Tenn. 80; Doebler v. State, 31 Tenn. 473; Robeson v. State, 50
Tenn. 266; State v. Adams, 70 Tenn. 647; State v. Estes, 71 Tenn. 168;
State v. Barnes, 73 Tenn, 398; State v. Staley, 71 Tenn. 565; Glenn v. State,
31 Tenn. 19; Garret v. State, 17 Tenn. 389. But see State v. Lee, 87 Tenn.
114; State v. Lewis, Id. 119, for instances, where the inquisitorial power was
illegally exercised. Where the grand jury is not specially vested with this
authority, the general rule in Tennessee appears to be that the witness
should be summoned to appear before the court to give evidence to the
grand jury: State v. Butler, 16 Tenn. 83.

35 Ward v. State, 2 Mo. 120.

36 Blaney v. State, 74 Md. 153. This authority is not based upon any
statute of Maryland.

37 Deshazo v. State, 23 Tenn. 275; Harrison v. State, 44 Tenn. 195;
Robeson v. State. 50 Tenn. 266; State v. Adams, 70 Tenn. 647.

When they have heard all the evidence which can be produced, they are then prepared to make their presentment. It was formerly thought in England that the grand jury should present "in case there be probable evidence,"[38] but this rule is now altered.[39]   In the Federal courts[40] the rule there prevailing is thus stated by Mr. Justice Field,[41] "To justify the finding of an indictment the grand jury must believe that the accused is guilty.   They should be convinced that the evidence before them, unexplained and uncontradicted, would warrant a conviction by a petit jury."[42]   This is now the law in Pennsylvania,[43] although formerly the English rule obtained.[44]   The same rule is recognized in New York,[45] Massachusettts[46] and Virginia,[47] and has been adopted in California by statute.[48]

In making diligent inquiry and true presentment, the grand jury is restricted to *"such articles, matters and things as shall be given you in charge or otherwise come to your knowledge, touching the present service."*[49]   This clause of the oath is the

---

38 1 Chitty Cr. Law 317; 2 Hale Pl. C. 157; 1 Whart. Cr. Law, Sec. 492. And see Co. Inst. Vol. II, p. 384.

39 1 Chitty Cr. Law 317.

40 In re Grand Jury, 62 Fed. Rep. 840.

41 Charge to Grand Jury, 30 Fed. Cas. 992; and see Chief Justice Shaw's Charge to Grand Jury, 8 Am. Jurist 218.

42 In re Grand Jury, 62 Fed. Rep. 840; People *v.* Hyler, 2 Parker Cr. R. (N. Y.) 570.   And see 4 Bl. Com. 303; Sir John Hawles, 4 State Trials 183; Lord Somers on Grand Juries, etc.   In People *v.* Lindenborn, 52 N. Y. Sup. 101, it was held that the presumption of innocence must be overcome before an indictment can legally be found.   In Com. *v.* Dittus, 17 Lanc. Law Rev. (Pa.) 127, although three respectable witnesses testified to the facts, the grand jury ignored the bill.   Judge Landis criticised their action as being equivalent to the trial of the cause.   As they, however, are the exclusive judges of the credibility of the witnesses, this criticism would seem unwarranted.

43 1 Whart. Cr. Law Sec. 491; 7 Smith's Laws 687; 1 Hopkinson's Works, 194; James Wilson's Works, Vol. II, p. 365.

44 Res. v. Shaffer, 1 Dall. 236; Add. App. 39.

45 People *v.* Hyler, 2 Parker, Cr. R. (N. Y.) 570.

46 Davis Precedents of Indictments, 25.

47 Davis Criminal Law in Va. 426.

48 Penal Code, Sec. 921, People *v.* Tinder, 19 Calif. 539.

49 Supra. 95.

grant of power to the grand jury, but the extent of the powers under this grant have not received a like construction in the various jurisdictions. It has been the tendency in Pennsylvania[50] to restrict this power within the narrowest lines, while the Federal courts, like the English courts, permit a very wide exercise of it. The first view is set forth in a celebrated opinion rendered by Judge King[51] in 1845. After describing how the ordinary mode of instituting prosecutions is by arrest on a warrant based upon an affidavit, with a subsequent binding over of the defendant or holding him in bail to answer at court, and detailing the subsequent steps whereby a bill charging the offence is submitted by the district attorney to the grand jury, and which is either returned a true bill or ignored, he then describes the extraordinary modes of criminal procedure which may be pursued, in the following words:

"The first of these is, where criminal courts of their own motion call the attention of grand juries to and direct the investigation of matters of general public import, which, from their nature and operation in the entire community, justify such intervention. The action of the court on such occasions, rather bear on things than persons; the object being the suppression of general and public evils, affecting in their influence and operation communities rather than individuals and therefore, more properly the subject of general than special complaint. Such as great riots that shake the social fabric, carrying terror and dismay among the citizens; general public nuisances affecting the public health and comfort; multiplied and flagrant vices tending to debauch and corrupt the public morals, and the like. In such cases the courts may properly in aid of inquiries directed by them, summon, swear, and send before the grand jury, such witnesses as they may deem necessary to a full investigation of the evils intimated, in order to enable the grand jury to present the offence and the offenders. But this course is never adopted in case of ordinary crimes, charged against individuals. Because it would involve, to a certain extent, the expression of opinion by antici-

---

50 McCullough *v.* Com. 67 Pa. 30.
51 Case of Lloyd and Carpenter, 3 Clark (Pa.) 188.

pation, on facts subsequently to come before the courts for direct judgment; and because such cases present none of those urgent necessities which authorize a departure from the ordinary course of justice. In directing any of these investigations, the court act under their official responsibilities, and must answer for any step taken, not justified by the proper exercise of a sound judicial discretion.

"Another instance of extraordinary proceedings, is where the attorney general ex-officio prefers an indictment before a grand jury, without a previous binding over or commitment of the accused. That this can be lawfully done is undoubted. And there are occasions where such an exercise of official authority would be just and necessary, such as where the accused has fled the justice of the state, and an indictment found, may be required previous to demanding him from a neighboring state, or where a less prompt mode of proceeding might lead to the escape of a public offender. In these, however, and in all other cases, where this extraordinary authority is exercised by an attorney general, the citizen affected by it is not without his guarantees. Besides, the intelligence, integrity, and independence, which always must be presumed to accompany high public trust, the accused unjustly grieved by such a procedure, has the official responsibility of the officer to look to. If an attorney general should employ oppressively, this high power, given to him only to be used when positive emergencies or the special nature of the case requires its exercise, he might be impeached and removed from office for such an abuse. The court, too, whose process and power is so misapplied, should certainly vindicate itself, by protecting the citizen. In practice, however, the law officer of the commonwealth always exercises this power cautiously; generally under the direction of the court, and never unless convinced that the general public good demands it.

"The third and last of the extraordinary modes of criminal procedure known to our penal code, is that which is originated by the presentment of a grand jury. A presentment, properly speaking, is the notice taken by a grand jury of any offence from their own knowledge or observation, without a bill of indictment being laid before them at the suit of the commonwealth. Like an indictment, however, it must be the act of the whole jury, not less than twelve concurring on it. It is, in fact, as much a criminal accusation as an indictment, except that it emanates from their own knowledge, and not from the public accuser, and except that it wants technical form. It is regarded as instructions for an indictment. That a grand jury may adopt such a course of procedure, without a previous preliminary hearing of the accused, is not to be questioned by this court."

The other view was expressed in an equally able manner by Mr. Justice Field[52] in 1872. "Your oath requires you to diligently inquire and true presentment make, 'of such articles, matters and things as shall be given you in charge, or otherwise come to your knowledge touching the present service.'

"The first designation of subjects of inquiry are those which shall be given you in charge; this means those matters which shall be called to your attention by the court, or submitted to your consideration by the district attorney. The second designation of subjects of inquiry are those which shall otherwise come to your knowledge touching the present service; this means those matters within the sphere of and relating to your duties which shall come to your knowledge, other than those to which your attention has been called by the court or submitted to your consideration by the district attorney.

"But how come to your knowledge?

"Not by rumors and reports,[53] but by knowledge acquired from the evidence before you, or from your own observations. Whilst you are inquiring as to one offence, another and different offence may be proved, or witnesses before you may, in testifying, commit the crime of perjury.

"Some of you, also, may have personal knowledge of the

---

52 Charge to Grand Jury, 30 Fed. Cas. 992.

53 It is of interest to note the change in the law as thus laid down by Mr. Justice Field from that prevailing in the time of Glanville and Bracton. Then the accusing body was generally obliged to present upon rumor alone. See Supra. part 1, generally.

commission of a public offence against the laws of the United States, or of facts which tend to show that such an offence has been committed, or possibly attempts may be made to influence corruptly or improperly your action as grand jurors. If you are personally possessed of such knowledge, you should disclose it to your associates; and if any attempts to influence your action corruptly or improperly are made, you should inform them of it also, and they will act upon the information thus communicated as if presented to them in the first instance by the district attorney.

"But unless knowledge is acquired in one of these ways, it cannot be considered as the basis for any action on your part.

"We, therefore, instruct you that your investigations are to be limited:—

"First. To such matters as may be called to your attention by the court: or

"Second. May be submitted to your consideration by the district attorney: or

"Third. May come to your knowledge in the course of your investigations into the matters brought before you, or from your own observations: or

"Fourth. May come to your knowledge from the disclosures of your associates.

"You will not allow private prosecutors to intrude themselves into your presence, and present accusations. Generally such parties are actuated by private enmity, and seek merely the gratification of their personal malice.

"If they possess any information justifying the accusation of the person against whom they complain, they should impart it to the district attorney, who will seldom fail to act in a proper case. But if the district attorney should refuse to act, they can make their complaint to a committing magistrate, before whom the matter can be investigated, and if sufficient evidence be produced of the commission of a public offence by the accused, he can be held to bail to answer to the action of the grand jury."

It will consequently be seen from the opinions of Judge King and Mr. Justice Field that the powers of the grand jury in Pennsylvania and the Federal courts coincide in these particulars:

1. That they may present such matters as are given them in charge by the district attorney, by means of bills submitted to them based upon the return of the committing magistrate, or with the investigation of which they are specially charged by the court.[54]

2. That they may present such matters as are within the actual knowledge of one of the grand jurors, the facts of which are communicated by him to his fellow jurors.

3. That they may present where the district attorney, upon his official responsibility, submits a bill to the grand jury without a previous commitment or binding over, in cases where the defendant is a fugitive from justice, and when emergencies may require that he should act promptly.

But the Federal grand juries have the additional power of presenting such offences as come to their knowledge while they are investigating other matters, through the testimony of the witnesses appearing before them.[55]   This method of procedure has been held to be unlawful by the Supreme Court of Pennsylvania.[56]

The right of the district attorney to prefer a bill of indictment to the grand jury upon his official responsibility and without leave of court is now firmly established both in the Federal courts[57] and in the courts of Pennsylvania,[58] but this

54 For instances where the grand jury has been directed to investigate into matters specially submitted to them by the court, see Hartranft's Appeal, 85 Pa. 433; Com. v. Green, 126 Pa. 531; Com. v. Hurd, 177 Pa. 481; Charge to Grand Jury, 5 Dist. Rep. (Pa.) 130; Com. v. Kulp, 17 Pa. C. C. Rep. 561; Bucks County Grand Jury, 24 Pa. C. C. Rep. 162; Com. v. Wilson, 2 Chester Co. Rep. (Pa.) 164.

55 Supra. 108, 109.

56 Com. v. Green, 126 Pa. 531; Com. v. McComb, 157 Pa. 611.   And see State v. Love, 4 Humph. (Tenn.) 255; Harrison v. State, 4 Cold (Tenn.) 195.

57 U. S. v. Fuers, 25 Fed. Cas. 1223; U. S. v. Thompkins, 28 Fed. Cas. 89.

58 Rowand v. Com. 82 Pa. 405; Com. v. Clemmer, 190 Pa. 202; Com. v. Beldham, 15 Pa. Superior Ct. 33; Com. v. Brown, 23 Pa. Superior Ct. 470; Com. v. Delemater, 2 Dist. Rep. (Pa.) 562; Com. v. Whitaker, 25 Pa. C. C. 42; Com. v. Reynolds, 2 Kulp (Pa.) 345;

right has invariably been stoutly opposed by defendants, and the exercise of it may well be the subject of criticism in view of the very weak foundation upon which the decisions have been made to rest. The inherent weakness of it is perhaps best observed in the fact that the district attorney rarely exercises the right without first obtaining leave of court,[59] and those decisions which are most frequently quoted as sustaining the right invariably contain the proviso, "with leave of court."

Treating of the right of the attorney general to thus act upon his official responsibility without leave of court, Judge King says,[60] "that this can be lawfully done is undoubted," and his ability and learning make his opinion of great weight. But he cites no authority in support of the doctrine which he states so positively, and in the case of Commonwealth *v.* English,[61] Judge Pratt, while he cites and follows the doctrine thus laid down, admits that the opinion of Judge King upon this point may be considered obiter dictum." In the cases of McCullough *v.* Commonwealth,[62] and Brown *v.* Commonwealth,[63] while the right of the district attorney, with the leave of court, to send in bills of indictment to the grand jury without any prior prosecution has been distinctly affirmed, the right

Com. *v.* Shupp, 6 Kulp (Pa.) 430; Com. *v.* Schall, 6 York Leg. Rec. 24; Com. *v.* English 11 Phila. (Pa.) 439; Com. *v.* Simons, 6 Phila. (Pa.) 167; Com. *v.* Wetherold, 2 Clark (Pa.) 476. Case of Lloyd and Carpenter, 3 Clark (Pa.) 188; Com. *v.* Green, 126 Pa. 531: In this latter case the court granted leave to the district attorney to lay an indictment before the grand jury. In Com. *v.* Jadwin, 2 Law T. (N. S.) 13, a defendant was discharged at the preliminary hearing by the magistrate and the district attorney subsequently laid a bill before the grand jury upon his official responsibility which was returned a true bill. The court quashed the indictment. See also Com. *v.* Moister, 3 Pa. C. C. 539; Com. *v.* Shubel, 4 Pa. C. C. 12.

59 Com. *v.* Sheppard, 20 Pa. Superior Ct. 417.

60 Case of Lloyd and Carpenter, 3 Clark (Pa.) 188 .

61 11 Phila. (Pa.) 439.

62 67 Pa. 30. In this case the indictment was based upon the return of a constable. In Com. *v.* Pfaff, 5 Pa. Dist. Rep. 59, it was held that an indictment based on a constable's return should not be sent to the grand jury without special leave of court.

63 76 Pa. 319.

of this officer to do so without leave of court is nowhere shown.

In the case of Rowand v. Commonwealth,[64] the assignments of error unfortunately failed to raise this point, and raised only questions which were then well settled. The grand jury in this case ignored the bill and the district attorney without leave of court sent a new bill to a subsequent grand jury, which returned a true bill. Judge White in his opinion in the court below upon a motion to quash the indictment said, "I doubt not the power of the court, on cause shown upon affidavit, to direct a bill to be sent back to be reconsidered by the same or a subsequent grand jury. But in the absence of such direction by the court, I doubt the legality, and very much condemn the practice of sending up the same bill (or one just like it, based on the same information) to a subsequent grand jury, after it has been ignored by one grand jury. Ordinarily an ignoramus should be the end of the case. If I were acting on my own judgment I would quash these, *but as I have been informed that the course pursued in these cases has been always sustained by this court, I shall conform to that practice and refuse these motions.*"

Mr. Justice Woodward, who delivered the opinion of the Supreme Court, said, "But principles have been long settled which require that the action of the district attorney in these cases shall be sustained," and he rests this statement upon the dictum of Judge King. He further says, "While, however, the possession of this exceptional power by prosecuting officers cannot be denied, its employment can only be justified by some pressing and adequate necessity, when exercised without such necessity it is the duty of the Quarter Sessions to set the officer's act aside."

If, as the learned judge says, the possession of this exceptional power by prosecuting officers cannot be denied, then surely it must rest upon some clearly defined authority. But he relies upon a statement for which the author thereof, cites

---

64 82 Pa. 405. In New York under Code Cr. Proc., Sec. 270, a bill once ignored by the grand jury cannot again be resubmitted without leave of court: People v. Warren, 109 N. Y. 615.

no authority. This question not having been raised by the assignments of error, the opinion of the court upon this point must consequently be regarded as obiter dictum.

This question was directly involved in a case before Judge Pratt,[65] who states, "After the most careful examination of the text books and reports, I have been able to find but few adjudicated cases on the subject, and no one case reported where this authority has been conceded to the attorney general or to the district attorney, without some qualification; only, perhaps in the case of Brown v. Commonwealth, 26 P. F. Smith, 319." He, however, attempts to show that the powers now claimed for the district attorney are those which were formerly possessed by the attorney general and were the same as those which Blackstone states[66] were possessed by the attorney general for the crown.

An examination of the authority cited shows that the attorney general only exercised this authority by *informations* filed in the Court of King's Bench for "such enormous misdemeanors as peculiarly tend to disturb or endanger his government, or to molest or affront him in the regular discharge of his (the king's) royal functions."[67] But neither Blackstone nor any of the other English authorities concede the right of the attorney general, ex-officio, to lay before the grand jury an indictment. The right of the attorney general or the district attorney to exercise this power of proceeding by information is swept away by the Constitution of Pennsylvania, which provides that no information shall be filed for an indictable offence.[68]

That he may exercise the same power over indictments that at common law he exercised with regard to informations cannot be conceded, when by constitutional provisions he can no longer exercise such power in filing informations and it never existed in connection with indictments and has not been extended to them by statute. In the absence of clear evidence of

---

65 Com. *v.* English, 11 Phila. (Pa.) 439.
66 4 Bl. Com. 309.
67 U. S. *v.* Shepard, 27 Fed. Cas. 1056.
68 Art. I, Sec. 10.

8

this authority to so act, it would appear improper to permit the exercise of this high power except by leave of court.

In Commonwealth v. Sheppard,[69] Rice, P. J., said: "In such cases, that is, where the indictment is sent up by the district attorney without first obtaining the leave of the court, the discretion of the court may be invoked, and is exercisable upon motion to quash. If the court refuses to quash, this, ordinarily, is equivalent to giving its sanction. If the court sustains the motion to quash, this is tantamount to refusing its approval of the action of the district attorney."

Where the district attorney first obtains leave of court to send a bill of indictment to the grand jury without previous arrest and binding over, the court will overrule a motion to quash the indictment.[70] When, however, the initial step in the prosecution is the laying of the district attorney's bill before the grand jury, it is necessary that it should possess some special earmark by which it is to be known as his official act other than merely affixing his signature thereto.[71]

The courts, having thus sustained the right of the district attorney to send a bill of indictment to the grand jury on his official responsibility alone, have had no hesitation in supporting the right of the district attorney to send to the grand jury indictments charging offences which were not included in the original informations made before the magistrate, and his right to so do may now be regarded as settled.[72]

---

69 20 Pa. Superior Ct. 417. And see Com. v. Brown, 23 Pa. Superior Ct. 470.

70 Com. v. Leigh, 38 L. I. (Pa.) 184; Com. v. Taylor, 12 Pa. C. C. Rep. 326; Com. v. Fehr, 2 Northampton Co. Rep. 275; Davidson v. Com. 5 Cen. Rep. 484; Com. v. Bredin, 165 Pa. 224. In Com. v. New Bethlehem Borough, 15 Pa. Superior Ct. 158, Rice, P. J., says: "It is undoubtedly true that the court has discretionary and revisory powers over what are called district attorney bills, and where the sanction of the court to sending up such a bill has been obtained by deception, whether wilful or unintentional, it may revise its action even after the return of an indictment."

71 Com. v. Griscom, 36 Pitts. L. J. (Pa.) 332. But see Com. v. Brown, 23 Pa. Superior Ct. 470.

72 Com. v. Simons, 6 Phila. (Pa.) 167; Harrison v. Com. 123 Pa. 508. See Com. v. Hughes, 11 Pa. Co. Ct. Rep. 470, where an indictment was

In the Federal courts a defendant may be proceeded against by information in cases where the offence is not "a capital or otherwise infamous crime,"[73] but it has been held that the right to file an information is not a prerogative of the prosecutor's office and the district attorney must first obtain leave of court.[74] The court may direct before granting leave that the accused be brought into court to show cause why the information should not be filed against him.[75] This right to proceed by information is in addition to the right to lay an indictment before the grand jury and may be and sometimes is used when the grand jury has ignored a bill.[76] The provisions of the United States Revised Statutes[77] authorizing the prosecution of certain offences either by indictment or by information do not preclude the prosecution by information of such other offences as may be so prosecuted without violating the constitution and United States statutes.[78]

In some of the states provision has likewise been made for the prosecution of offences other than capital or other infamous crimes by information, while in other states even capital crimes may be prosecuted by information.

In the exercise of their power, the grand jury has frequently acted as the defender of the liberty of the press in attempted prosecutions for libel; and have stood as a shield between courageous editors who have boldly endeavored to expose official wrong doing, and the persons who have been stung into action by the exposures thus made. Two instances, however, have occurred in Pennsylvania where the public press has made

quashed upon the ground that it was for a different offense than that set out in the affidavit upon which the prosecution was based.

73 Cons. U. S. Amend. V.

74 U. S. v. Smith, 40 Fed. Rep. 755; and see Walker v. People, 22 Colo. 415; State v. De Serrant, 33 La. Ann. 979.

75 U. S. v. Smith, 40 Fed. Rep. 755; U. S. v. Shepard, 27 Fed. Cas. 1056.

76 Ex Parte Moan, 65 Calif. 216; State v. Ross, 14 La. Ann. 364; State v. Vincent, 36 La. Ann. 770; State v. Whipple, 57 Vt. 637. CONTRA State v. Boswell, 104 Ind. 541; Richards v. State, 22 Neb. 145. A defendant may be prosecuted by information after a nolle pros. is entered on a bill of indictment: Dye v. State, 130 Ind. 87.

77 Sec. 1022.

78 Ex Parte Wilson, 114 U. S. 417.

sharp attacks upon the grand jury. The grand jurors made inquiry of the court as to what redress they had or what action could be taken. Judge Ludlow advised them that as an official body they had no redress and could take no action against the persons responsible for the publication.[79]

The grand juror's oath enjoins upon him "the commonwealth's counsel, your fellows and your own you shall keep secret." We have seen how the pledge of secrecy was enjoined upon the grand jury in the time of Bracton, and how it became a part of their oath prior to the time of Britton. The purpose of enjoining secrecy upon the inquest has been a theme for much discussion and has produced many diverse views. Mr. Christian considers that its purpose was to prevent a defendant from contradicting the testimony produced before the grand jury by subornation of perjury;[80] while others hold that its purpose was to prevent the grand jurors from being overawed by the power and high connections of those whom they should present.[81] Both of these views are attacked vigorously by Mr. Bentham[82] and Mr. Ingersoll,[83] the latter of whom concedes the propriety of the secrecy in the time of Bracton that the offender might not escape, while contending that in the present day aspect of the institution it no longer has any purpose to serve and should be abolished.

While it would seem, without doubt, that its original purpose was that no offender should escape, it could not be insisted upon by the grand jurors as a matter of right. They were originally bound to disclose to the court the grounds upon which the inquest had acted and the part each juror had taken in it. When the right to deliberate and keep the manner in which each juror had voted secret, first became a prerogative of the grand jury, cannot be determined. In Scar-

---

79 Grand Jury v. Public Press, 4 Brews. (Pa.) 313; and see Act June 16, 1836, P. L. 23.

80 4 Bl. Com. 126, Christian's Note. The same reason for the requirement of secrecy is given in the case of Crocker v. State, Meigs (19 Tenn.) 127.

81 Huidekoper v. Cotton, 3 Watts (Pa.) 56.

82 Rationale of Judicial Evidence, Vol. 11, p. 312.

83 An Essay on the Law of Grand Juries (Phila. 1849).

let's case[84] we have what is perhaps the last recorded instance of the court being informed by the grand jurors how any matter had come to their knowledge.   Subsequent to this, we see the crown exercising its alleged right to compel the grand jury to hear the evidence in open court, although it did not attempt to deny them the right to deliberate in the privacy of their own room, nor when they refused to divulge why they had ignored a bill did the court take any steps to compel them to do so.   And the last instance where the grand jury were even obliged to hear the evidence in public seems to have been in Lord Shaftesbury's case,[85] where the grand jury so stoutly asserted their right to hear the evidence only within their own room.

A very remarkable case, savoring of the methods pursued in England in Lord Shaftesbury's case arose in North Caro·lina[86] in 1872.   One Joseph R. Branch was charged with having committed an affray and with assault on one, Spier Whitaker.   The case was heard by the grand jury, the witnesses being Whitaker and one Hardy, and the grand jury offered to return the bill "not a true bill" which the court refused to receive.   The court thereupon directed the grand jurors to be seated in the jury box and in open court examined the same witnesses before them.   The judge then charged that if the testimony was believed, a true bill should be returned.   The grand jury accordingly returned a true bill.   The defendant moved to quash the indictment, which motion was refused and an appeal was then taken to the Supreme Court which reversed the ruling of the lower court.   In his opinion Pearson, C. J., says:

"There is nothing in our law books, and no tradition of the profession to show that such has ever been the practice or the course of the courts in this state; and we are of opinion that the ruling of his honor is an innovation not warranted by the law of the land.

---

84 12 Co. 98.

85 8 How. St. Tr. 774.   Another instance of the grand jury hearing the evidence in public will be found in The Poulterer's Case, 9 Coke 55b.

86 State v. Branch, 68 N. C. 186.

"The power of the judge to require a grand jury to come into open court and have the witnesses for the state examined, is not only opposed to immemorial usage, but is not sustained either by principle or authority."

It was by reason of this requirement of secrecy that in England the view obtained that a grand juror not only could not be compelled to reveal in evidence what had transpired in the grand jury room, but under no circumstances would be allowed to voluntarily do so.[87] This doctrine, however, received its first test in a case mentioned by Mr. Christian,[88] where a member of a grand jury heard a witness testify before a petit jury contrary to what he had testified before the grand inquest. "He immediately communicated the circumstances to the judge, who upon consulting the judge in the other court, was of opinion that public justice in this case required that the evidence which the witness had given before the grand jury should be disclosed; and the witness was committed for perjury to be tried upon the testimony of the gentlemen of the grand jury."[89]

The same view was taken by Mr. Justice Huston in a Pennsylvania case.[90] "That part of the oath," he says, "as well as the whole of the proceeding, was intended to punish the guilty, without risk to those who, in performance of their duty, took a part in the proceeding; but it never was intended to punish the innocent or obstruct the course of justice."

The tendency is to permit grand jurors to testify where it will not be revealed how any member of the jury voted.[91]

87 Grand Jurors as Witnesses (M. W. Hopkins) 21 Cen. L. J. 104.

88 4 Bl. Com. 126, Christian's Note.

89 That a witness who testifies falsely before the grand jury may be indicted for perjury upon the testimony of the grand jurors or by them of their own knowledge, see 1 Chitty Cr. Law 322; U. S. v. Charles, 25 Fed. Cas. 409; R. v. Hughes, 1 Car. & K. 519; People v. Young, 31 Calif. 563; State v. Fassett, 16 Conn. 457; State v. Offutt, 4 Blackf. (Ind.) 355; Com. v. Hill, 11 Cush. (Mass.) 137; Huidekoper v. Cotton, 3 Watts (Pa.) 56; State v. Terry, 30 Mo. 368; Crocker v. State, Meigs (Tenn.) 127; Thomas v. Com. 2 Robinson (Va.) 795.

90 Huidekoper v. Cotton, 3 Watts (Pa.) 56.

91 Grand Jurors as Witnesses (M. W. Hopkins) 21 Cen. L. J. 104.

Thus it has been held that a grand juror may testify as to who was the prosecutor upon a certain bill of indictment;[92] that twelve jurors concurred in the finding;[93] that a witness had testified to a different state of facts when before the grand jury;[94] that the presentment was made upon facts not within the personal knowledge of any of the grand jurors;[95] that for the protection of public or private rights, any person may disclose in evidence what transpired before a grand jury.[96]

In Iowa[97] affidavits of the grand jurors were received on motion to quash the indictment to show that the judge visited the grand jury during its deliberation and directed that an indictment should be returned against a certain person for a certain offence and an indictment was so found under the express instructions of the court.

The court has permitted the record to go in evidence to the jury to prove the time when a witness testified before the grand jury.[98] But a grand juror cannot testify to facts that would impeach the finding of the grand jury[99] or disclose how

---

92 Huidekoper v. Cotton, 3 Watts (Pa.) 56.

93 1 Greenleaf on Evidence Sec. 252; Low's Case, 4 Greenl. (Me.) 439; Territory v. Hart, 7 Mont. 489; State v. Logan, 1 Nev. 509; People v. Shattuck, 6 Abb. (N. Y.) 33; State v. Horton, 63 N. C. 595. But see Gitchell v. People, 146 Ill. 175; Shoop v. People, 45 Ill. App. 110; Hooker v. State, 56 Atl. 390; State v. Baker, 20 Mo. 338.

94 U. S. v. Porter, 27 Fed. Cas. 595. Fotheringham v. Adams Ex. Co., 34 Fed. Rep. 646; Burnham v. Hatfield, 5 Blackf. (Ind.) 21; Perkins v. State, 4 Ind. 222; Kirk v. Garrett, 84 Md. 383; Com. v. Mead, 12 Gray (Mass.) 167; Com. v. Hill, 11 Cush. (Mass.) 137; State v. Broughton, 7 Ired. (N. C.) 96; Gordon v. Com. 92 Pa. 216. And see Rocco v. State, 37 Miss. 357. CONTRA. 1 Greenleaf on Evidence, Sec. 252; Imlay v. Rogers, 2 Halst. (N. J.) 347.

95 Com. v. Green, 126 Pa. 531; Com. v. McComb, 157 Pa. 611; Com. v. Kulp. 5 Pa. Dist. Rep. 468. But see State v. Davis, 41 Iowa, 311.

96 U. S. v. Farrington, 5 Fed. Rep. 343; Burdick v. Hunt, 43 Ind. 381; Hunter v. Randall, 69 Me. 183; Jones v. Turpin, 6 Heisk. (Tenn.) 181.

97 State v. Will, 97 Iowa 58. And see Contra. Hall v. State, 32 So. 750.

98 Virginia v. Gordon, 28 Fed. Cas. 1224.

99 U. S. v. Terry, 39 Fed. Rep. 355; U. S. v. Reed, 27 Fed. Cas, 727; R. v. Marsh, 6 Ad. & El. 236; Spigener v. State, 62 Ala. 383; Ex Parte Sontag, 64 Calif. 525; State v. Hamlin, 47 Conn. 95; Simms v. State, 60 Ga. 145; Gilmore v. People, 87 Ill. App. 128; State v. Gibbs, 39 Iowa 318;

any juror voted or what they said during their investigations.[100]

Where a statute provided "no grand juror shall disclose any evidence given before the grand jury," it was held not a violation of the act to state that a certain person, naming him, had testified before the grand jury, and the subject matter upon which he testified.[101] Nor is it a violation of the grand juror's oath of secrecy to report to the court the fact that a witness refuses to testify.[102] If the grand jurors are not required to take an oath of secrecy, they may be examined as witnesses touching matters which came to their knowledge while acting as grand jurors.[103]

This provision of secrecy not only surrounds the grand jurors, but also includes their clerk if he be not one of their number,[104] and the district attorney.[105] They may or may not be permitted to testify accordingly as a grand juror may or may not testify.[106] But it does not include witnesses who

---

State v. Davis, 41 Iowa 311; State v. Mewherter, 46 Iowa 88; Com. v. Skeggs, 66 Ky. 19; State v. Beebe, 17 Minn. 241; State v. Baker, 20 Mo. 338; State v. Hamilton, 13 Nev. 386; People v. Hulbut, 4 Denio (N. Y.) 133; People v. Briggs, 60 How. Pr. Rep. (N. Y.) 17; Ziegler v. Com. 22 W. N. C. (Pa.) 111; Com. v. Twitchell, 1 Brews. (Pa.) 551; State v. Oxford, 30 Tex. 428.

100 U. S. v. Farrington, 5 Fed. Rep. 343; U. S. v. Kilpatrick, 16 Fed. Rep. 765; Stewart v. State, 24 Ind. 142; State v. Lewis, 38 La. Ann. 680; Com. v. Twitchell, 1 Brews. (Pa.) 551.

101 State v. Brewer, 8 Mo. 373. CONTRA. State v. Baker, 20 Mo. 338; Beam v. Link, 27 Mo. 261. And see Ex Parte Schmidt, 71 Calif. 212; Hinshaw v. State, 47 N. E. 157.

102 People v. Kelly, 21 How. Prac. Rep. (N. Y.) 54; In re Archer, 96 N. W. 442; Heard v. Pierce, 8 Cush. (Mass.) 338.

103 Granger v. Warrington, 8 Ill. 299.

104 Trials per Pais (Giles Duncombe) Vol. II, p. 387; 1 Greenleaf on Evidence, Sec. 252; State v. McPherson, 87 N. W. 421.

105 Com. v. Twitchell, 1 Brews. (Pa.) 551; 1 Greenleaf on Evidence, Sec. 252; McLellan v. Richardson, 13 Me. 82; 1 Bost. Law Rep. 4; Jenkins v. State, 35 Fla. 737. And see State v. Grady, 84 Mo. 220, where the prosecuting attorney was required to testify. The attorney general on plea in abatement cannot stipulate what the evidence was: People v. Thompson, 81 N. W. 344.

106 1 Greenleaf on Evidence, Sec. 252.

testify before the grand jury; they may be compelled to disclose the testimony given by them.[107]

It has been held that it is not a contempt of court for a grand juror to refuse to testify how he voted on the finding of a certain indictment; the court had no authority to require such disclosure[108] and in refusing to answer the juror was acting strictly within his legal rights. In fact had he so testified in response to the question put, he would have been guilty of a violation of his oath.

The remaining portion of the grand juror's oath does not require special consideration. It is clear and unmistakable in its terms and, consequently, has never been made the subject of judicial inquiry.

In addition to the powers vested in them by their oath and the common law, grand jurors have in many instances other duties imposed upon them by statute. In many states grand jurors are required by statute to examine into the condition of jails, asylums and other public institutions; examine the books and accounts of the various public officials in the county, fix the tax rate, and have a general supervision over public improvements.[109]

The Pennsylvania statutes impose upon a grand jury certain duties which relate to matters of the general public good within the county. Thus it is essential that the grand jury should pass upon the proposition to incorporate a borough within the county,[110] and the court will not review a question of fact as to the incorporation of such borough when the grand jury considers the incorporation necessary.[111] No public buildings may be erected within the county unless two successive grand juries have approved of the erection of such buildings,[112] and likewise no county bridge may be erected unless

107 People v. Young, 31 Calif. 563; People v. Northey, 77 Calif. 618: People v. Naughton, 38 How. Prac. Rep. 430.

108 Ex Parte Sontag, 64 Calif. 525.

109 See Thompson and Merriam on Juries, Sec. 473-474.

110 Act April 1, 1834, P. L. 163; Act June 2, 1871, P. L. 283; Act May 26, 1891, P. L. 120.

111 Millville Borough, 10 Pa. C. C. Rep. 321.

112 Act April 15, 1834, P. L. 539; Act June 1, 1883, P. L. 58.

two successive grand juries shall determine that it is necessary.[113]

In Connecticut[114] the town meeting chooses annually not less than two nor more than six grand jurors who are charged to "diligently inquire after and make complaint of all crimes and misdemeanors that shall come to their knowledge, to the court having cognizance of the offence, or to some justice of the peace in the town where the offence is committed," and they have power to require the person who informs them of the offence to make a proper information under oath and ad minister to them the oath of a witness. In Georgia[115] they ar. authorized to act as a board of revision of taxes, and examine statements of the county liabilities and fix the rate of tax necessary to discharge such liabilities. They are also required to ascertain the condition of the county treasury. In Mississippi[116] they are obliged to examine the tax collectors' books and accounts. In Alabama[117] and Tennessee[118] they must investigate the sufficiency of the bonds of all county officers, while in Vermont[119] grand jurors are charged by statute with the duty of arresting persons having liquor for sale contrary to law, and may do so without a warrant; must seize the liquor, and may arrest intoxicated persons who have committed a breach of the peace.

Grand jurors are in general not called to be sworn in any cause,[120] but are sworn to inquire into all crimes which have

113 Act April 29, 1891, P. L. 31; Pequea Creek Bridge, 68 Pa. 427.

114 General Statutes 1875, p. 241, Sec. 1; p. 531, Sec. 2, 3, 4, 5. Smith v. State, 19 Conn. 493.

115 Code 1873, Sec. 3919; Sec. 510; Sec. 3920.

116 Revised Code 1880, Sec. 1675.

117 Code 1876, Sec. 4767-68.

118 Statutes 1871, Sec. 5079.

119 General Statutes 1862, p. 596, Sec. 25; p. 600, Sec. 33.

120 U. S. v. Reeves, 27 Fed. Cas. 750. In Indiana, St. 1825, p. 21, authorizing special sessions of the Circuit Court, does not warrant the finding of an indictment at the special term against any other person than the one for whose trial the court was convened: Wilson v. State, 1 Blackf. (Ind.) 428.

been committed within the county.[121]   If, therefore, when the oath is administered it embraces one or more persons by name whose cases are about to be laid before the grand jury and in respect to which the oath is administered and nothing more, no evidence can be given under it in support of any accusation against others.[122]

[121] Addison, App. 36.

[122] U. S. *v.* Reed, 27 Fed. Cas. 727.   And see Wilson *v.* State, 1 Blackf. (Ind.) 428.   CONTRA. In re County Commissioners, 7 Ohio N. P. 450.

PART IV

When the grand jurors have been duly empaneled and sworn, the court delivers to them a charge ordinarily in relation to their duties and those matters concerning which they may be called upon to investigate.[1] At times the court may thus commit specially to their care, matters of great public importance.[2] Judge Addison, in his charges to grand juries, availed himself of the opportunity in that early stage of our Federal government, to inculcate in the citizens through the medium of the grand jury, a better knowledge of our political institutions, the theory of government, the relations between the government and its subjects, and the subjects with each other. Other eminent jurists have used it as a means of communication with the public. Judge Wilson expressed the same thought when he said:[3] "The grand jury are a great channel of communication, between those who make and administer the laws, and those for whom the laws are made and administered."

In the press of business at the present day, it is rare, in the absence of some event of great public importance which the court deems it necessary the grand jury should consider, for

---

1 While it is the duty of the court to charge the grand jury, it will not invalidate an indictment should this be omitted: Stewart *v.* State, 24 Ind. 142; Com. *v.* Sanborn, 116 Mass. 61; State *v.* Froiseth, 16 Minn. 313; Clair *v.* State, 40 Neb. 534; Cobb *v.* State, Id. 545; State *v.* Edgerton, 69 N. W. 280; State *v.* Furco, 51 La. Ann. 1082. And see State *v.* Will, 97 Iowa 58; State *v.* Turlington, 102 Mo. 642. Nor will a conviction be disturbed: Porterfield *v.* Com. 91 Va. 801.

2 In re Citizens Association, 8 Phila. (Pa.) 478.

3 Jas. Wilson's Works, Vol. II, p. 366.

the court to do more than deliver a brief charge as to the duties of the grand jury.

While it is usual for the court to charge the grand jury only when they first enter upon their duties, it may at any time during their period of service, deliver a supplementary charge or charges to them upon any particular matter, or upon any special matter which the district attorney may be prepared to send before them, or may direct them to investigate any matters of grave importance to the public welfare. This is usually done by the court upon its own motion or at the request of the grand jury and probably would be done upon motion of the district attorney. Whether it will be done upon motion of counsel for a defendant whose case will be considered by the grand jury, has not been settled.[4]

This question first arose in this country upon the trial of Aaron Burr.[5] In the report of the trial the following appears:

"Mr. Burr called up the motion for a supplemental charge to the grand jury, in support of which he had, on yesterday, submitted a series of propositions, with citations of authorities.

"The Chief Justice (Marshall) stated that he had drawn up a supplemental charge, which he had submitted to the attorney for the United States, with a request that it should also be put into the hands of Col. Burr's counsel; that Mr. Hay had, however, informed him that he had been too much occupied to inspect the charge with attention, and deliver it to the opposite counsel; but another reason was, that there was one point in the charge which he did not fully approve. He should not, therefore, deliver his charge at present, but should reserve it until Monday. In the meantime Col. Burr's counsel could have an opportunity of inspecting it, and an argument might be held on the points which had produced an objection from the attorney for the United States."

It does not appear in the report of the case that this charge was ever delivered. The same case discloses, however, that a

4 See Post 126.

5 U. S. v. Aaron Burr, 25 Fed. Cas. 6͙.

communication on the part of the defendant was actually sent to the grand jury by the Chief Justice:

"Mr. McRae hoped that notice of his communication would be sent to the grand jury.

"Mr. Martin hoped that Col. Burr's communication also would go along with it. The Chief Justice was unwilling to make the court the medium of such communications. The Chief Justice subsequently reduced the communications to writing and sent them to the grand jury."

What would seem to be the true rule in such instances was laid down by Judge Cranch, who said;[6] "The court may in its discretion, give an additional charge to the grand jury, although they should not ask it; and when they do ask it, the court may, perhaps, be bound to give it, if it be such an instruction as can be given without committing the court upon points which might come before them to be decided on the trial in chief. When an instruction to the grand jury is asked either by the accused or the prosecutor, it is a matter of discretion with the court to give the instruction or not, considering the extent of the prayer, and all the circumstances under which it is asked."

The fact that a portion only of the grand jurors were specially advised, at their request, as to the law governing the case then under consideration, will not invalidate an indictment found by such grand jury.[7]

The charge of the court delivered to the grand jury will not, in general, be ground for setting aside the indictment even though highly inflammatory language be used,[8] unless the court should so charge with relation to a specific case to come before them.[9] If the charge be in general terms, no matter how impolitic its delivery may be, a defendant can hardly complain that he was prejudiced thereby. Should the court urge the finding of a particular indictment or in any manner

6 U. S. v. Watkins, 28 Fed. Cas. 419.

7 State v. Edgerton, 69 N. W. 280.

8 Parker v. Territory, 52 Pac. 361; Clair v. State, 28 L. R. A. 367; S. C. 40 Neb. 534.

9 State v. Turlington, 102 Mo. 642.

endeavor to influence the finding of the grand jury, a bill so found will be quashed.[10]

When the court has charged the grand jury as to their duties, the jurors then retire to their room to consider the matters which may come before them. They are there attended by the district attorney[11] or one of his assistants, who aids them in examining the witnesses and advises them upon questions of law.[12] At common law the grand jurors conducted the examination of witnesses themselves, not permitting the attorney for the crown to enter the room, and receiving their instructions as to the law directly from the court. In order that the crown officer might know what evidence was given to the grand jury and perhaps with a view of overawing the grand inquest when they should retire to deliberate, they were in several instances in state prosecutions required to hear the evidence in open court, although after so hearing it they were never denied the right to again hear the witnesses in private.[13] In 1794 upon the indictment of Hardy and others for treason, the grand jury requested the attendance of the solicitor for the crown for the purpose of managing the evidence, for which leave of court was first obtained.[14]

It is the general custom at the present day in all jurisdictions to permit the district attorney to attend the grand jury,[15]

10 Blau v. State, 34 So. 153; State v. Will, 97 Iowa 58. And see Hall v. State, 32 So. 750; People v. Glen, 173 N. Y. 395.

11 Byrd v. State, 1 How. (Miss.) 247. A county attorney is in effect the assistant to the attorney for the commonwealth and may lawfully conduct the examination of witnesses before the grand jury: Franklin v. Com. 48 S. W. 986. The district attorney may be present to assist the grand jury in disposing of township applications for bridge appropriations under Act of April 16, 1870, (P. L. 1199): In re Bridge Appropriations, 9 Kulp (Pa.) 427.

12 U. S. v. Cobban, 127 Fed. Rep. 713; Shattuck v. State, 11 Ind. 473. The powers and duties of the grand jury do not cease because there may happen to be no district attorney: State v. Gonzales, 26 Tex. 197. And see U. S. v. McAvoy, 26 Fed. Cas. 1044.

13 Supra. 28, 29, 117.

14 Growth of the Grand Jury System (J. Kinghorn) 6 Law Mag. & Rev. (4th S.) 380.

15 Charge to Grand Jury, 30 Fed. Cas. 992; Ex Parte Crittenden, 6 Fed.

but he has no right to be present during the deliberations of the grand jurors[16] and should withdraw if requested to do so ;[17] nor is it proper for him to attempt to control or influence the action of the grand jury[18] or to say what effect should be given to the testimony adduced before them.[19]   But the fact that the district attorney was present during the deliberations of the grand jury and the taking of the vote is at most an irregularity and no ground for quashing the indictment[20] in the absence of any averment and proof that the defendant was thereby prejudiced ;[21] likewise where after certain persons had testified in a particular case the district attorney said: "I suppose you do not want to hear any more."[22]   If the district attorney should participate in the deliberations of the grand jury, or make any effort to influence their finding, the indictment will be quashed.[23]   Private counsel for the prosecution

Cas. 822; In re District Attorney U. S., 7 Fed. Cas. 745; U. S. *v.* Edgerton, 80 Fed. Rep. 374; Shattuck *v.* State, 11 Ind. 473; Shoop *v.* People, 45 Ill. App. 110; State *v.* Adam, 40 La. Ann. 745; State *v.* Aleck, 41 La. Ann. 83; People *v.* O'Neill, 107 Mich. 556; Com. *v.* Salter, 2 Pears. (Pa.) 461; State *v.* Mickel, 65 Pac. 484; State *v.* McNinch, 12 S. C. 89; State *v.* Baker, 33 W. Va. 319. See Anonymous 7 Cow. (N. Y.) 563. Where the county attorney is disqualified, an attorney appointed to prosecute a case may lawfully appear before the grand jury: State *v.* Kovolosky, 92 Iowa, 498. And see State *v.* Gonzales, 26 Tex. 197; U. S. *v.* Cobban, 127 Fed. Rep. 713.

16 Charge to Grand Jury, 30 Fed. Cas. 992; Lung's Case, 1 Conn. 428; Rothschild *v.* State, 7 Tex. App. 519.

17 In re District Attorney U. S., 7 Fed. Cas. 745.

18 Com. *v.* Frey, 11 Pa. C. C. Rep. 523.

19 Com. *v.* Frey, 11 Pa. C. C. Rep. 523; Com. *v.* Bradney, 126 Pa. 199.

20 Com. *v.* Twitchell, 1 Brews. (Pa.) 551; U. S. *v.* Terry, 39 Fed. Rep. 355; Com. *v.* Bradney, 126 Pa. 199. And see Regent *v.* People, 96 Ill. App. 189.

21 U. S. *v.* Terry, 39 Fed. Rep. 355.

22 Com. *v.* Salter, 2 Pears. (Pa.) 461.

23 Com. *v.* Bradney, 126 Pa. 199; CONTRA Hall *v.* State, 32 So. 750. And see as to the presence of other officers in the grand jury room, Post 139, Note 90. An indictment was quashed where private counsel entered the grand jury room while they were deliberating and advised them as to their duty: State *v.* Addison, 2 S. C. 356. And see Miller *v.* State, 28 So. 208.

have no right to be present in the grand jury room to examine witnesses and the district attorney cannot authorize such action.[24]

The relation which should be maintained between the district attorney and the grand jury is well stated by Mr. Justice Clark:[25]

"The district attorney is the attendant of the grand jury: it is his duty as well as his privilege to lay before them matters upon which they are to pass, to aid them in their examination of witnesses, and to give them such general instructions as they may require. But it is his duty during the discussion of the particular case, and whilst the jurors are deliberating upon it, to remain silent. It is for the jury alone to consider the evidence and to apply it to the case in hand, any attempt on the part of the district attorney to influence their action or to give effect to the evidence adduced, is in the highest degree improper and impertinent. Indeed, it is the better practice and the jurors have an undoubted right to require, that he should retire from the room during their deliberations upon the evidence and when the vote is taken whether or not an indictment shall be found or a presentment made."

The tendency of the modern cases is to hold that it is the "right" of the district attorney to be present to examine the witnesses and conduct the case for the government.[26] That it was not his right at common law was conceded by the abandonment of hearing the evidence in public when the grand jury refused to indict in Lord Shaftesbury's case.[27] In the absence of any statute which grants this right to him, it would

---

24 Durr v. State, 53 Miss. 425; People v. Scannell, 72 N. Y. Sup. 449; State v. Heaton, 56 Pac. 843. But see Wilson v. State, 51 S. W. 916, where private counsel was present on the invitation of the district attorney and examined the witnesses, but was not present when the grand jury was deliberating. And see People v. Bradner, 44 Hun (N. Y.) 233; Blevins v. State, 68 Ala. 92. This forms no ground for reversing a judgment: State v. Whitney, 7 Ore. 386.

25 Com. v. Bradney, 126 Pa. 199.

26 In re District Attorney U. S., 7 Fed. Cas. 745; Com. v. Salter, 2 Pears. (Pa.) 461.

27 Supra. 117.

9

seem that the common law rule is still in force and that the presence of the district attorney in the grand jury room, even for the purpose of examining witnesses, is not by reason of his right, but as a matter of grace on the part of the grand jury.

The Pennsylvania statute under which the office of district attorney was created provides:[28] "The officer so elected shall sign all bills of indictment, and conduct in court all criminal or other prosecutions." This statute does not expressly give him the power to conduct proceedings before the grand jury; can this authority be said to be implied by it? That the grand jury is in court although not in open court will admit of no question. The direction therefore that the district attorney shall conduct *in court* all criminal proceedings, would seem to be ample authority to conduct all parts of the prosecution from the time it first comes into court, usually on the return of the magistrate, until the case is finally disposed of, either by the acquittal, or conviction and sentence of the defendant.[28*]

There are two ways in which a grand jury may act in order to put a defendant upon his trial.

I.   By presentment.[29]

II. By indictment.

A presentment is the notice taken by a grand jury of any offence from their own knowledge or observation upon which the officer of the court must afterwards frame an indictment before the party presented can be put to answer it.[30]

---

28 Act May 3, 1850, P. L. 654.

28* See the discussion in State *v.* Warner, 165 Mo. 413 of the authority of the district attorney in the conduct of criminal prosecutions.

29 In California the constitution of 1879 omits all reference to "presentments," and consequently a "presentment" by a grand jury is unauthorized: In re Grosbois, 109 Calif. 445. In Georgia, Code Sec. 4632, obliterates the distinction between presentments and indictments: Groves *v.* State, 73 Ga. 205.

30 4 Bl. Com. 301; Mr. Justice Field's Charge to Grand Jury, 30 Fed. Cas. 992. And see Collins *v.* State, 13 Fla. 651. In Com. *v.* Towles, 5 Leigh (Va.) 743, the defendant was obliged to answer to the presentment of the grand jury and was tried thereon. For a similar case see Smith *v.* State, 1 Humph. (Tenn.) 396.

The Constitution of the United States provides :[31] "No person shall be held to answer for a capital or otherwise infamous crime, unless on a presentment or indictment of a grand jury." The provision is in the disjunctive and Chief Justice Marshall makes the pertinent inquiry,[32] "Is it the indictment or presentment he is to answer?" Judge Addison expresses the opinion[33] that a defendant under this provision may be required to plead to the presentment without a formal indictment based upon the presentment being submitted to the grand jury and returned a true bill by them. His view undoubtedly receives strong support from the use of the conjunction *or* in this clause; but opposed to it is the practice at common law, which has been universally adopted in this country, of framing an indictment upon the presentment and submitting it to the grand jury for their action.   Chief Justice Marshall observes[34] that the indictment "is precisely the first presentment, corrected in point of form . . . . to be considered as one and the same act, and that the second is only to be considered as an amendment of the first."

Irrespective of the question of the right of the government to require a defendant to plead to and be tried upon a presentment without an indictment being founded upon it, the lack of "technical form" in the presentment makes it necessary that it should serve only as the basis of an indictment, otherwise in many instances a defendant would escape by the failure of the presentment to properly charge an offence against the statutes.

An indictment is a written accusation of one or more persons of a crime or misdemeanor, preferred to and presented upon oath by a grand jury.[35]

In Pennsylvania as a legal presentment can only be made where the offence charged is within the personal knowledge

31 Amendment V.

32 U. S. *v.* Hill, 26 Fed. Cas. 315.

33 Addison, App. 38.

34 U. S. *v.* Hill, 26 Fed. Cas. 315.

35 4 Bl. Com., 301. The court may order an indictment to be sent to the grand jury without a previous presentment: U. S. *v.* Madden, 26 Fed. Cas. 1138; U. S. *v.* Thompkins, 28 Fed. Cas. 89.

of at least one of the grand jurors, and the presentment is the result of his disclosure of knowledge to his associates, it follows that there are no witnesses to testify before the grand jury in support of it,[36] although it sometimes happens when an indictment has been framed upon the presentment and is sent to the grand jury that witnesses are sent before them in support of its averments.[37]

Where the indictment is not based upon the former presentment of a grand jury, it is necessary that witnesses should testify in support thereof; if the indictment be found without hearing evidence it will be quashed.[38]

In Georgia it has been held that an indictment founded on a presentment of the grand jury need not again be sent before them for their action upon it.[39]

If an indictment has been quashed or nolle prossed, a new indictment for the same offence may be found by the same grand jury which returned the former one without hearing evidence in support of the second bill.[40]

In order to procure the attendance of witnesses to testify in support of any bill which may be sent before the grand jury, a subpoena is issued by the district attorney and served upon such persons as are not bound by recognizance to appear.[41] Those who are so bound to appear and testify are re-

---

36 See State v. Love, 4 Humph. (Tenn.) 255; State v. Cain, 1 Hawks (N. C.) 352; State v. Richard, 50 La. Ann. 210.

37 In Com. v. Hayden, 163 Mass. 453, it was held that an indictment is not void because it was found by the grand jury after hearing testimony by one of the grand jurors, since the grand jury may properly act upon the personal knowledge of any of its members. In North Carolina, where a bill is found upon the evidence of a grand juror, he must be regularly sworn as a witness and be noted as such: State v. Cain, 1 Hawks 352. And see In re Gardiner, 64 N. Y. Sup. 760.

38 State v. Grady, 84 Mo. 220. And see State v. Cain, 1 Hawks. (N. C.) 352.

39 Nunn v. State, 1 Kelly 243.

40 Com. v. Woods, 10 Gray (Mass.) 477; State v. Peterson, 61 Minn. 73; Whiting v. State, 48 Ohio St. 220. Contra State v. Ivey, 100 N. C. 539. See McIntire v. Com., 4 S. W. 1.

41 At common law the committing magistrate before whom the case

quired to be produced by their bondsmen upon whom notice is duly served. If the witness cannot be produced the bond will be forfeited and a bail piece issued to bring the witness into court. If the witness is not bound by recognizance and fails to appear after being subpoenaed, an attachment may issue to compel his attendance upon motion of the district attorney. If it is necessary that books or papers be produced in evidence before the grand jury, a subpoena duces tecum may issue but it should particularly describe the books and papers wanted,[42] and if there is any question as to whether or not the books or papers so produced are relevant or material, they may be submitted to the inspection of the court.[43]

A witness before the grand jury who refuses to testify upon the ground that his evidence may tend to convict him of a crime, is not guilty of contempt[44] but if the question propounded to the witness does not disclose upon its face that it will have such tendency and the witness fails to clearly show to the court how it will have such effect, he may be punished for a contempt if he refuses to answer after being directed to do so by the court.[45]

While a witness cannot be compelled to testify as to matters which would tend to incriminate him, there is no duty imposed upon the grand jury to inform a witness, who is prepared to so testify, of his constitutional privilege.[46] This ruling is based upon the theory that every person is bound to know the law and any failure through ignorance or otherwise to claim the constitutional privilege will be deemed a waiver of it.

A witness duly summoned before the grand jury cannot refuse to be sworn or refuse to testify without sufficient excuse. The grand jury may ask the advice and assistance of the court

was heard, in default of bail, can commit the witnesses to await the next term of court: 2 Hale, Pl. C. 52, 282; Bennet v. Watson, 3 M. & S. 1.

42 U. S. v. Hunter, 15 Fed. Rep. 712.

43 Id. In re Archer, 96 N. W. 442.

44 In re Morse, 87 N. Y. Sup. 721; See People v. Kelly, 12 Abb. Pr. Rep. (N. Y.) 150.

45 In re Rogers, 129 Calif. 468. And see Wheatley v. State, 114 Ga. 175.

46 State v. Comer, 157 Ind. 611.

in such case and if the witness still prove recalcitrant he may be punished for contempt.[47]

The bills are sent or brought into the grand jury room by the district attorney and delivered to the foreman. The indictment ought to be signed by the district attorney[48] before being submitted to the grand jury,[49] but should he fail to do so the court will not quash upon that ground after the grand jury find a true bill, but will permit him to affix his signature to the bill in court, and the motion to quash will then be overruled.[50] The district attorney's signature constitutes no part of the indictment. It is only necessary as evidence to the court that he is officially prosecuting the accused in accordance with the duty imposed upon him by statute.[51] In the Federal courts the signature of the district attorney may be affixed by one of his assistants acting under a general authority conferred upon him by the district attorney.[52]

An indictment signed by a person designating himself as "solicitor general" when there was no such state officer was held to be invalid.[53]

47 Heard v. Pierce, 8 Cush. (Mass.) 338; In re Harris, 4 Utah 5.

48 Penna. Statute, May 3, 1850, P. L. 654.

49 Fout v. State, 3 Hayw. (Tenn.) 98; Hite v. State, 9 Yerg. (Tenn.) 198; Teas v. State, 7 Humph. (Tenn.) 174; Jackson v. State, 4 Kan. 150. Contra Ward v. State, 22 Ala. 16; Harrall v. State, 26 Ala. 53; McGregg v. State, 4 Blackf. (Ind.) 101; Thomas v. State, 6 Mo. 457; Keithler v. State, 10 Smedes & M. (Miss.) 192; Anderson v. State, 5 Ark. 444; State v. Vincent, 1 Car. Law R. 493.

50 Com. v. Lenox, 3 Brews. (Pa.) 249; And see Com. v. Brown, 23 Pa. Superior Ct. 470. That the prosecuting officer's signature is not essential to the validity of an indictment. See Joyner v. State, 78 Ala. 448; Watkins v. State, 37 Ark. 370; People v. Butler, 1 Idaho 231; State v. Wilmoth, 63 Iowa 380; State v. Williams, 107 La. 789; Com. v. Stone, 105 Mass. 469; State v. Reed, 67 Me. 127; State v. Murphy, 47 Mo. 274; State v. Vincent, 1 Car. Law R. 493; Brown v. Com. 86 Va. 466. Contra Heacock v. State, 42 Ind. 393; State v. Bruce, 77 Mo. 193; Fout v. State, 3 Hayw. (Tenn.) 98; State v. Lockett, 3 Heisk (Tenn.) 274.

51 U. S. v. McAvoy, 26 Fed. Cas. 1044.

52 U. S. v. Nagle, 27 Fed. Cas. 68; State v. Coleman, 8 S. C. 237. And see Com. v. Brown, 23 Pa. Superior Ct. 470; Reynolds v. State, 11 Tex. 120; State v. Gonzales, 26 Tex. 197.

53 Teas v. State, 7 Humph. (Tenn.) 174. And see State v. Salge, 2 Nev. 321.

Upon the back of the bill, the names of the witnesses should be endorsed by the district attorney,[54] and in Pennsylvania[55] it is provided by statute that "no person shall be required to answer to any indictment for any offence whatever, unless the prosecutor's name, if any there be, is endorsed thereon."[56] Where no prosecutor is proved to exist, then the defendant must plead without the name of a prosecutor being endorsed on the indictment.[57]

In Mississippi,[58] Ohio,[59] Tennessee[60] and Virginia[61] it is also necessary that the name of the presecutor be endorsed on the bill.   In Arkansas,[62] Florida,[63] Kentucky[64] and Mis-

54 Harriman v. State, 2 Greene (Iowa) 270; Andrews v. People, 117 Ill. 195; Bartley v. People, 156 Ill. 234.   It has been held that if this be omitted it will not be fatal to the indictment: U. S. v. Shepard, 27 Fed. Cas. 1056; State v. Scott, 25 Ark. 107; People v. Naughton, 38 How. Pr. (N. Y.) 430.

55 Act March 31, 1860, Sec. 27, P. L. 427.   Memorial of Citizens Association, 8 Phila. (Pa.) 478.

56 U. S. v. Mundell, 27 Fed. Cas. 23; U. S. v. Helriggle, 26 Fed. Cas. 258; U. S. v. Shackelford, 27 Fed. Cas. 1037; U. S. v. Hollinsberry, 26 Fed. Cas. 345.   The omission of the name of the prosecutor is not good ground for a motion in arrest of judgment: U. S. v. Jamesson, 26 Fed. Cas. 585; U. S. v. Lloyd, 26 Fed. Cas. 986; nor for general demurrer to the indictment; U. S. v. Sandford, 27 Fed. Cas. 952.

57 U. S. v. Dulany, 25 Fed. Cas. 922; U. S. v. Lloyd, 26 Fed. Cas. 986; Tenorio v. Territory, 1 N. M. 279; King v. Lukens, 1 Dall. (Pa.) 5.   And see Wortham v. Com., 5 Randolph (Va.) 669.

58 Peter v. State, 3 How. 433; Cody v. State, Id. 27; Moore v. State, 13 Smedes & M. 259; Kirk v. State, Id. 406.

59 Statutes, Sec. 7207.

60 Code (1898), Sec. 7058.   If omitted the objection may be raised at any stage of the proceedings: Medaris v. State, 10 Yerg. 239.   See, however, Rodes v. State, 10 Lea. 414, where the court holds that the policy of the law has changed and rules to the contrary.   If the bill is founded on a presentment, the prosecutor's name may be omitted: State v. McCann, 1 Meigs 91. A married woman is incompetent as a prosecutrix: Moyers v. State, 11 Humph. 40; Wattingham v. State, 5 Sneed, 64; and a husband is incompetent as a prosecutor against his wife: State v. Tankersley, 6 Lea. 582.

61 Code, Sec. 3991.   Haught v. Com. 2 Va. Cas. 3; Com. v. Dove, Id. 29.   But see Thompson v. Com., 88 Va. 45.

62 State v. Brown, 10 Ark. 104; State v. Stanford, 20 Ark. 145.   And see State v. Harrison, 19 Ark. 565; State v. Scott, 25 Ark. 107; State v. Den-

souri[65] the prosecutor's name must be endorsed in cases of trespass not amounting to felony.

In Alabama,[66] the statute requiring the name of the prosecutor to be endorsed on the indictment has been held to be merely directory and the omission of such endorsement will not invalidate the indictment.

In North Carolina[67] the prosecuting officer may, in his discretion, endorse the governor of the state as prosecutor on indictments whenever public interest may require it; and in Mississippi[68] it has been held that the foreman of the grand jury may be endorsed as the prosecutor.

In Massachusetts[69] the practice is in vogue of omitting the names of witnesses from the indictment, the grand jury making a general return of the names of the witnesses examined by them but without in any manner indicating the bills upon which they testified.   In the case of Commonwealth vs. Knapp,[70] counsel for the defendant applied to the court for a list of the witnesses appearing before the grand jury.   The court granted the application, Judge Wilde, before whom the application was made saying that such a request had never been refused.

ton, 14 Ark. 343.   The name of a prosecutor need not be endorsed on an indictment for passing counterfeit coin: Gabe v. State, 1 Eng. 540.

63 Towle v. State, 3 Fla. 202.

64 Bartlett v. Humphreys, Hardin, 513; Com. v. Gore, 3 Dana 474. And see Allen v. Com., 2 Bibb 210.

65 Rev. Code 1899, Sec. 2515.   For cases within the statute see State v. McCourtney, 6 Mo. 649; State v. Hurt, 7 Mo. 321; McWaters v. State, 10 Mo. 167; State v. Joiner, 19 Mo. 224.   Cases not within the statute see State v. Rogers, 37 Mo. 367; State v. Goss, 74 Mo. 592; Lucy v. State, 8 Mo. 134; State v. Moles, 9 Mo. 694; State v. Roberts, 11 Mo. 510; State v. Allen, 22 Mo. 318; State v. Sears, 86 Mo. 169.   The endorsement may be written on the face of the bill: Williams v. State, 9 Mo. 270.

66 State v. Hughes, 1 Ala. 655; Molett v. State, 33 Ala. 408; Hubbard v. State, 72 Ala. 164.

67 State v. English, 1 Murphy, 435.

68 King v. State, 5 How. 730.

69 1 Whart. Cr. Law, Sec. 479. (7th ed.)

70 9 Pick. (Mass.) 498.

In Mississippi,[71] the names of the witnesses need not be returned with the indictment.

Before the witnesses summoned to attend the grand jury are permitted to testify, they must be sworn. At common law the witnesses were all sworn in open court at the one time,[72] and this practice is followed in the Federal courts at the present time, the witnesses there being sworn by the clerk.[73] But this method of procedure is open to the objection that the grand jury have no accurate knowledge as to whether or not a particular witness has been sworn.[74] In some jurisdictions it is customary to summon a justice of the peace as a grand juror, and the witnesses are sworn in the grand jury room by him.[75] But in Pennsylvania[76] it is provided by the act of March 31, 1860:—

"The foreman of any grand jury, or any member thereof, is hereby authorized and empowered to administer the requisite oaths or affirmations to any witnesses whose names may be marked by the district attorney on the bill of indictment."

The inconvenience resulting from swearing witnesses in open court who, subsequently, were to appear before the grand jury, and the ease with which an unsworn witness might present himself and testify have caused similar statutes to be adopted in almost every state.

The power of a grand juror to administer the oath[77] is lim-

---

71 King v. State, 5 How. 730.

72 In North Carolina this method of swearing witnesses has not been abrogated by Act 1879, c. 12: State v. Allen, 83 N. C. 680. If the witness is not sworn in open court the indictment will be quashed: State v. Kilcrease, 6 S. C. 444; Gilman v. State, 20 Tenn. 59.

73 And see State v. White, 88 N. C. 698. It is not necessary that the judge should be upon the bench if his absence be but temporary: Jetton v. State, 19 Tenn. 192.

74 See Duke v. State, 20 Ohio St. 225, where the statute provided against this contingency.

75 State v. Fassett, 16 Conn. 457. And see 1 Whart. Cr. Law, Sec. 488. (7th ed.)

76 Sec. 10, P. L. 433.

77 The witnesses may be sworn by the foreman of the grand jury: Bird v. State, 50 Ga. 585; State v. White, 88 N. C. 698. In Tennessee he cannot swear them in case of a felony: Ayrs v. State, 5 Cold. 26.

ited to those cases where the name may be marked on the bill of indictment.[78]   The presence of the district attorney in the grand jury room during the examination of witnesses should, however, make this clause free from controversy, for if the name of the witness be not endorsed on the bill when he comes to be sworn, it can then and there be done by that officer. The question, however, did arise in the case of Jillard *v.* Commonwealth[79] where the defendant sought to take advantage of the swearing and examining of certain witnesses whose names were not marked upon the indictment, by a plea in bar, but it was held that at most it was only ground for a motion to quash.[80]   It need not appear by the indictment or otherwise that the witnesses who testified before the grand jury were sworn or affirmed.[81]   The presumption is that the grand jury complied with all the requirements of the law before finding a true bill.

Where the grand jury find a true bill and one or more of the witnesses upon whose testimony the bill was found were not sworn, if objection be taken before the defendant pleads, the indictment will be quashed.[82]   If a motion to quash be not made and the defendant pleads, the objection has been held to have been waived and cannot be raised by a motion in arrest

78 Com. *v.* Price, 3 Pa. C. C. Rep. 175; Jillard *v.* Com., 26 Pa. 169; Com. *v.* Wilson, 9 Pa. C. C. Rep. 24.

79 26 Pa. 169; s. c. 13 L. I. (Pa.) 132.   This case arose under the Act of April 5, 1826, which is similar in its provisions to the Act of March 31, 1860, Sec. 10, P. L. 433.

80 Com. *v.* Wilson, 9 Pa. C. C. Rep. 24; Com. *v.* Schall, 9 Lanc. Law Rev. (Pa.) 332; Com. *v.* Frescoln, 11 Id. 161; State *v.* Roberts, 2 Dev. & Bat. (N. C.) 540; King *v.* State, 5 How. (Miss.) 730; Gilman *v.* State, 1 Humph. (Tenn.) 59.

81 Com. *v.* Salter, 2 Pears. (Pa.) 461; King *v.* State, 5 How. (Miss.) 730; Gilman *v.* State, 1 Humph. (Tenn.) 59.   They will be presumed to have been sworn: Com. *v.* Rovnianek, 12 Pa. Superior Ct. 86.

82 U. S. *v.* Coolidge, 25 Fed. Cas. 622; Joyner *v.* State, 78 Ala. 448; Ashburn *v.* State, 15 Ga. 246; In re Lester, 77 Ga. 143.   CONTRA State *v.* Easton, 113 Iowa 516, upon the ground that the failure to administer the oath was not one of the grounds of objection designed by the statute.

of judgment.[83] This may now be considered as the English rule although the decisions have not been uniform.[84] In Rex v. Dickinson,[85] where none of the witnesses before the grand jury had been sworn at all, while a motion in arrest of judgment was overruled, the twelve judges unanimously made application for a pardon.

While it is usual for the district attorney to conduct the examination, any of the grand jurors may fully interrogate a witness.[86] But it is not lawful for one witness to be interrogated by another witness who may happen to be in the room, nor will more than one witness at a time be permitted to be in the grand jury room and an indictment will be quashed if it be shown that this was permitted.[87]

An indictment will likewise be quashed where a person, other than a grand juror is present in the grand jury room during their deliberations[88] and participates in the voting.[89] But where a stenographer in the employ of the district attorney was present and took notes of the testimony of a witness, it was held that such stenographer was an assistant to the district attorney and the court refused to quash the indictment.[90]

83 Rex v. Dickinson, Russ. & Ry. Crown Cases 401; Reg. v. Russell, 1 C. & M. 247; 1 Whart. Cr. Law, Sec. 489 (7th ed.)

84 Id.

85 Russ. & Ry. Crown Cas. 401.

86 An indictment will not be set aside because the clerk of the grand jury was a practicing attorney and asked the witness some questions at the request of the foreman: State v. Miller, 95 Iowa 368.

87 U. S. v. Edgerton, 80 Fed. Rep. 374; Com. v. Dorwart, 7 Lanc. Bar (Pa.) 121; And see State v. Fertig, 98 Iowa, 139. Contra Bennett v. State, 62 Ark. 516; Mason v. State, 81 S. W. 718; State v. Wood, 84 N. W. 503.

88 State v. Watson, 34 La. Ann. 669; State v. Clough, 49 Me. 573; Wilson v. State, 70 Miss. 595; People v. Metropolitan Traction Co., 50 N. Y. Sup. 1117; Rothschild v. State, 7 Tex. App. 519; Doss v. State, 28 Id. 506. And see Sims v. State, 45 S. W. 705. A judgment will not be reversed upon the ground that a stranger was in the room during the deliberations of the grand jury where no objection was made to such irregularity before trial: State v. Justus, 11 Ore. 178.

89 State v. Fertig, 98 Iowa 139; Territory v. Staples, 26 Pac. 166; State v. Tilly, 8 Baxt. (Tenn.) 381.

90 U. S. v. Simmons, 46 Fed. Rep. 65; State v. Brewster, 42 L. R. A.

Neither the defendant nor any of his witnesses will be permitted to appear before the grand jury.[91] Upon this point Chief Justice McKean thus expresses himself :[92]

"Were the proposed examination of witnesses on the part of the defendant to be allowed, the long established rules of law and justice would be at an end. It is a matter well known and well understood, that by the laws of our country, every question which affects a man's life, reputation or property, must be tried by twelve of his peers; and that their unanimous verdict is alone, competent to determine the fact in issue. If then you undertake to inquire, not only upon what foundation the charge is made, but, likewise, upon what foundation it is denied, you will in effect usurp the jurisdiction of the petty jury, you will supersede the legal authority of the court, in judging of the competency and admissibility of witnesses, and having thus undertaken to try the question, that question may be determined by a bare majority, or by a much greater number of your body, than the twelve peers prescribed by the laws of the land. This point has, I believe, excited some doubts upon former occasions; but those doubts have never arisen in the mind of any lawyer, and they may easily be removed by a proper consideration of the subject. For the bills, or presentments, found by a grand jury, amount to nothing more than an official accusation, in order to put the party accused upon his trial: till the bill is returned, there is therefore, no charge from which he can be required to exculpate himself; and we know that many persons against whom bills were returned, have been afterwards acquitted by a verdict of their country."

444; State v. Bates, 148 Ind. 610; Thayer v. State, 138 Ala. 39; And see Courtney v. State, 5 Ind. App. 356. CONTRA State v. Bowman, 90 Me. 363. And see as to the presence of other officers in the grand jury room: State v. Kimball, 29 Iowa 267; Richardson v. Com., 76 Va. 1007; State v. District Court, 55 Pac. 916; Cross v. State, 78 Ala. 430; Bennett v. State, 62 Ark. 516; Raymond v. People, 30 Pac. 504; State v. Bacon, 77 Miss. 366. See as to presence of interpreter: People v. Ramirez, 56 Calif. 533; People v. Lem Deo, 132 Calif. 199.

91 Supra. 103. CONTRA In re Morse, 87 N. Y. Sup. 721.

92 Res. v. Shaffer, 1 Dall. (Pa.) 236.

The same question was considered by Judge Addison[93] whose opinion is well expressed in the following language: "But if witnesses, brought forward by the accused person, were to be heard in his defence before the grand jury, and they should find the charge true, this would approach so near to a conviction, that the traversing of the indictment afterwards, and the trial by the traverse jury, would appear nugatory, and might be abolished. The finding of the bill would raise such an opinion and presumption of the guilt of the accused person, as must be a bias in the minds of all men; and the prisoner could not come before the traverse jury with a hope of that impartiality in his judges, which the constitution of a jury trial supposes him to expect."

The duty of the grand jury is to determine whether or not the evidence presented by the state raises a prima facie presumption of the guilt of the defendant, or, in other words, is the evidence for the prosecution sufficient to sustain a conviction. If it is, then a true bill should be returned; if not, the bill should be ignored. With this intermediate stage of the prosecution a defendant has no concern except that it shall be according to law. He has secured to him the constitutional right of trial by jury and not trial by grand jury, and until he shall have been indicted he is not called upon to make defence. Until he is thus called upon to face a petit jury he is neither entitled nor will he be permitted to present any evidence in his own behalf.

In the Federal courts it was formerly held that the defendant's witnesses might go before the grand jury with the consent of the district attorney;[94] but it is now held that the district attorney cannot give permission to the defendant to send witnesses in his own behalf before the grand jury.[95] Only in the event that the testimony of any of defendant's witnesses is essential to make out a case for the government will this rule be departed from.

In the hearing of the testimony of the witnesses appearing

93 Addison, App. 41.
94 U. S. v. White, 28 Fed. Cas. 588.
95 Supra, 103.

before them, the grand jury should be governed by the ordinary rules of evidence and no indictment should be found upon evidence, which, before the petit jury and uncontradicted, would not support a conviction.[96]   It is the duty of the district attorney to permit the grand jury to receive no incompetent evidence,[97] but the restriction which prohibits him from taking any part in their proceedings after adducing all the evidence for the government, would likewise prevent him from expressing his opinion as to the insufficiency of the evidence to warrant a conviction.   While it is the duty of the district attorney not to proceed further when he knows the evidence insufficient to convict, it is at the same time the exclusive province of the grand jury to determine the sufficiency of the evidence to justify the indictment.   Should an indictment be found upon insufficient evidence, it is within the province of the district attorney to enter a nolle pros which he may do with leave of court.   In this manner he would leave the grand jurors to arrive at their own conclusions without interference from him, while at the same time he could observe the duty imposed upon him by his oath, and relieve the defendant from an unsupported accusation.   But while he expresses no opinion as to the sufficiency or insufficiency of the evidence to justify the finding of a true bill, he should advise them as to the legal requirement.

The grand jury should, therefore, receive only the best evidence which can be procured, being admissable evidence before the petit jury.[98]   They should not receive hearsay or irrelevant

96 Supra, 105, 141; People v. Stern, 68 N. Y. Sup. 732; People v. Harmon, 69 N. Y. Sup. 511.

97 2 Hawk. Pl. C. c. 25, s. 138-139. Davis' Precedents of Indictments, 25; 1 Whart. Cr. Law, Sec. 493 (7th ed.); Denby's Case, 1 Leach C. C. 514.

98 1 Chitty Cr. Law, 319; 1 Whart. Cr. Law, Sec. 493 (7th ed.); U. S. v. Reed, 27 Fed. Cas. 727; U. S. v. Kilpatrick, 16 Fed. Rep. 765; Sparrenberger v. State, 53 Ala. 481; Washington v. State, 63 Ala. 189; Bryant v. State, 79 Ala. 282; People v. Sellick, 4 N. Y. Cr. Rep. 329; People v. Strong, 1 Abb. Prac. Rep. (N. S.) 244. The court will not pass upon the sufficiency of the evidence heard by the grand jury: Stewart v. State, 24 Ind. 142; Com. v. Minor, 89 Ky. 555; State v. Lewis, 38 La. Ann. 680. And see U. S. v. Cobban, 127 Fed. Rep. 713; State v. Fowler, 52 Iowa 103; People v.

evidence, but if they do receive it, this will not of course be sufficient ground for quashing the indictment,[99] and cannot be availed of on motion in arrest of judgment.[100]

In North Carolina[101] it was held that an indictment would be quashed where it was found upon the testimony of interested or incompetent witnesses.

Where a paper is sent before the grand jury it should be relevant to the matter then under consideration, although its materiality may not appear.[102] When a subpoena duces tecum has issued, the court will decide whether the books, papers and documents ordered to be produced are relevant and material, and whether or not they are privileged communications.[103]

Where the grand jury suspect that a witness has been tampered with by the prisoner, they will not be permitted to receive in evidence his written examination before the committing magistrate in lieu of his parol testimony.[104]

An indictment found upon the evidence of a person who is an incompetent witness by reason of his conviction of an in-

---

Lauder, 82 Mich. 109; State v. Logan, 1 Nev. 509; Hope v. People, 83 N. Y. 418; Morrison v. State, 41 Tex. 516; Cotton v. State, 43 Tex. 169; Terry v. State, 15 Tex. App. 66; Carl v. State, 28 So. 505; Hall v. State, 32 So. 750; McIntire v. Com., 4 S. W. 1. But see People v. Metropolitan Traction Co., 50 N. Y. Sup. 1117.

99 U. S. v. Jones, 69 Fed. Rep. 973; State v. Fasset, 16 Conn. 457; People v. Lauder, 82 Mich. 109; State v. Dayton, 23 N. J. Law 49; People v. Molineux, 58 N. Y. Sup. 155; Wadley v. Com. 35 S. E. 452; Buchanan v. State, 52 S. W. 769; Territory v. Pendry, 22 Pac. 760. But see CONTRA State v. Robinson, 2 Lea (Tenn.) 114; People v. Metropolitan Traction Co., 50 N. Y. Sup. 1117.

100 Com. v. Spattenhover, 8 Luz. Leg. Reg. 101. In this case the defendant's wife was called as a witness against her husband before the grand jury which found the indictment.

101 State v. Fellows, 2 Hayw. 340.

102 U. S. v. Aaron Burr, 25 Fed. Cas. 68.

103 U. S. v. Hunter, 15 Fed. Rep. 712; Hartranft's Appeal, 85 Pa. 433.

104 Denby's Case, 1 Leach C. C. 514. In California the depositions of witnessses taken before a magistrate upon a criminal charge may be used before a grand jury: People v. Stuart, 4 Calif. 218. And see State v. Marshall, 74 N. W. 763; Hope v. People, 83 N. Y. 418.

famous crime will be quashed[105] as will one founded upon the testimony of a witness who has been convicted of perjury.[106] But where an indictment was found upon the uncorroborated evidence of an accomplice the court refused to quash.[107] The court has also refused to quash where an indictment has been found after the defendant voluntarily testifies before the grand jury.[108]

In England an indictment for treason will be quashed unless it is founded on the evidence of two witnesses to the same overt act [109] but the rule is otherwise in the Federal courts.[110]

It would seem, however, where the grand jury find an indictment either upon the evidence of a single witness who is incompetent, or after hearing the evidence of more than one witness, one of whom is incompetent, that it should be quashed if these facts be made to appear.[111] While an opposite view

---

105 2 Hawk. Pl. C. Ch. 25, Sec. 145; 1 Whart. Cr. Law, Sec. 493. (7th ed.)

106 The Penna. Act of May 23, 1887, Sec. 2, P. L. 158, provides that a person convicted of perjury shall not be a competent witness for any purpose except in cases of violence done or attempted to be done to his person or property.

107 King v. Dodd., 1 Leach C. C. 155.

108 People v. King, 28 Calif. 265; State v. Trauger, 77 N. W. 336; People v. Willis, 52 N. Y. Sup. 808; Lindsay v. State, 24 Ohio Cir. Ct. Rep. 1; State v. Comer, 157 Ind. 611; People v. Lauder, 82 Mich. 109; State v. Hawks, 56 Minn. 129. And see People v. Hayes, 59 N. Y. Sup. 761. CONTRA People v. Singer, 18 Abb. N. C. 96; State v. Froiseth, 16 Minn. 296.

109 1 East's Pl. C. 128. In 1 Chitty Cr. Law 320, it is said that it will be sufficient if there is one witness to one overt act and another witness to another overt act.

110 The Constitution of the United States, Art. III, Sec. 3, provides, "No person shall be *convicted* of treason unless on the testimony of two witnesses to the same overt act." . . At common law one witness was sufficient to support a conviction in cases of treason: 1 East Pl. C. 128.

111 People v. Price, 2 N. Y. Sup. 414; People v. Briggs, 60 How. Pr. (N. Y.) 17; State v. Lanier, 90 N. C. 714. This common law principle is recognized in New York by the provisions of Cr. Code, Sec. 256, providing "the grand jury can receive none but legal evidence," and in People v. Metropolitan Traction Co., 50 N. Y. Sup. 1117, the indictment was dismissed upon the ground that the grand jury had been allowed to receive illegal evidence.

has been taken in some of the states,[112] it can hardly be said that their position is well founded in reason. If the grand jury should not be permitted to receive evidence inadmissable before a petit jury, if they do receive it the indictment should be quashed upon the same theory which prompts the award of a new trial when the trial judge against the objection of counsel permits an incompetent witness to testify. If, as the courts have said, it is impossible to say what effect the testimony of the incompetent witness may have had toward influencing the verdict of the petit jury,[113] which hears the evidence in the presence of the judge, how much more strongly the same reason applies where an incompetent witness testifies before the grand jury and his evidence is heard in secret.

The same reason which has moved the court to quash an indictment when it was based upon the testimony of a single person and he incompetent,[114] should also apply in cases where there is more than one witness some of whom are and one or more of whom are not competent. It may well be that the testimony of the incompetent witness formed the principal evidence against the defendant, or it may have been the necessary connecting link in the chain of circumstances, without which the grand jury would have ignored the bill, and it would be manifestly unjust to compel a defendant to answer to an indictment found in such a manner. That the tendency of the cases in general may be said to accord with this view will be seen in the fact that although other witnesses were examined at the same time, an indictment was quashed where the defendant was compelled to testify against himself,[115] and

---

112 Bloomer v. State, 3 Sneed (Tenn.) 66; State v. Tucker, 20 Iowa 508; Com. v. Minor, 89 Ky. 555. And see 1 Whart. Cr. Law, Sec. 493 (7th ed.) ; U. S. v. Brown, 24 Fed. Cas. 1273; U. S. v. Smith, 27 Fed. Cas. 1186.

113 Grier v. Homestead Borough, 6 Pa. Superior Ct. 542; Rahlfing v. Heidrick, 4 Phila. (Pa.) 3; Railway Co. v. Johnson, 55 Kan. 344; Mussey v. Mussey, 68 Me. 346; Hamblett v. Hamblett, 6 N. H. 333; Sherman v. Railroad Co., 106 N. Y. 542; Penfield v. Carpenter, 13 Johns. (N. Y.) 350.

114 State v. Fellows, 2 Hayw. (N. C.) 340; and see Lennard v. State, 30 S. E. 780.

115 U. S. v. Edgerton, 80 Fed. Rep. 374; State v. Froiseth, 16 Minn. 296; State v. Gardner, 88 Minn. 130. And see Counselman v. Hitchcock,

where an unsworn witness testified before the grand jury.[116]

The ground upon which the contrary view is based is that the court will not inquire whether or not the evidence was sufficient to justify the finding.[117] But this can hardly be said to be either an accurate or an adequate reason. If the witness be incompetent, then to sustain the indictment the court must assume that it was found upon the evidence of the competent witnesses only and that the evidence of the incompetent witness was disregarded; if this be not assumed, then we have the condition of an indictment being sustained although founded wholly or in part on incompetent evidence. While in sustaining the indictment all intention to weigh the evidence is disclaimed, in assuming the sufficiency of the evidence the court necessarily weighs it in favor of the commonwealth. If the sufficiency of the evidence be not assumed, then the court should not permit the indictment to stand.[118]

After the grand jury have had all the evidence in the particular case under investigation presented to them, they are then prepared to consider the bill and endorse thereon their finding. They may find a true bill as soon as they have heard enough evidence to convince them that a prima facie case has been made out but they must not ignore a bill until they have

---

142 U. S. 547; State *v.* Frizell, 111 N. C. 722. CONTRA U. S. *v.* Brown, 24 Fed. Cas. 1273. In State *v.* Krider, 78 N. C. 481, the indictment was quashed where the grand jury examined each of two persons against the other in order to obtain a true bill against both.

116 U. S. *v.* Coolidge, 25 Fed. Cas. 622. In Com. *v.* Price, 3 Pa. C. C. Rep. 175, where a witness testified before the grand jury without being legally sworn, Judge Sittser quashed the indictment, saying: "We cannot tell whether the grand jury found the indictment upon the testimony of this witness alone or upon that of others, nor can we inquire into that."

117 Turk *v.* State, 7 Hammond (Ohio) part 2, p. 240; People *v.* Hulbut, 4 Denio (N. Y.) 133; State *v.* Logan, 1 Nev. 509; State *v.* Boyd, 2 Hill (S. C.) 288. In New York even though illegal evidence was introduced before the grand jury, if legal evidence was also presented, which if unexplained, would warrant a conviction, the indictment must be sustained: People *v.* Winant, 53 N. Y. Sup. 695. See people *v.* Metropolitan Traction Co., 50 N. Y. Sup. 1117; People *v.* Molineux, 58 N. Y. Sup. 155.

118 See remarks of Judge Sittser in Com. *v.* Price, 3 Pa. C. C. Rep. 175.

examined all the witnesses, for the last examined may supply the evidence necessary to make out the case.[119]   If twelve or more, but not exceeding twenty-three, agree to find the bill, the return was anciently at common law "billa vera," but now the return is expressed in English, "a true bill."[120]   If less than twelve agree to find the bill, it is then said to be ignored, and while anciently the return was "ignoramus," it is now "ignored," or what is a better return "not found."[121]   But if an indictment be found with less than twelve grand jurors concurring, the finding is bad[122] and a motion in arrest of judgment will be sustained.[123]

A grand jury may find a true bill as to one or more counts of an indictment,[124] but the finding is bad if they return a true bill as to part of a count and ignore the balance of the same

119 Com. v. Ditzler, 1 Lanc. Bar. (Pa.) Aug. 28, 1869. After an indictment has been dismissed and the case again referred to the grand jury, they need not hear all the witnesses: McIntire v. Com., 4 S. W. 1.

120 Where a bill is erroneously returned endorsed, "a true bill," it may be shown on motion to quash that the grand jury voted to ignore the bill and their clerk was directed to endorse it "not a true bill;" State v. Horton, 63 N. C. 595.

121 4 Bl. Com. 305; 1 Chitty Cr. Law 324.

122 People v. Roberts, 6 Calif. 214; People v. Butler, 8 Id. 435; People v. Gatewood, 20 Id. 146; People v. Hunter, 54 Id. 65; Lung's Case, 1 Conn. 428; State v. Ostrander, 18 Iowa, 435; State v. Shelton, 64 Iowa, 333; Donald v. State, 31 Fla. 255; State v. Copp, 34 Kan. 522; Wells v. Com. 15 Ky. Law Rep. 179; Low's Case, 4 Greenl. (Me.) 439; Barney v. State, 12 Smedes & M. (Miss.) 68; State v. McNeill, 93 N. C. 552; State v. Barker, 107 Id. 913; Turk v. State, 7 Ham. (Ohio) part 2, p. 240; In re Citizens Assn., 8 Phila. (Pa.) 478; State v. Williams, 35 S. C. 344; State v. Brainerd, 56 Vt. 532; Fitzgerald v. State, 4 Wis. 395. In English v. State, 31 Fla. 340, the court held that Stat. 4015, Sec. 5 (1891) was unconstitutional upon the ground that it authorized the finding of an indictment upon the concurrence of eight grand jurors. And see State v. Hartley, 40 Pac. 372. A grand jury of seven persons does not conflict with amendments V and XIV of the U. S. Constitution: Hausenfluck v. Com. 85 Va. 702.

123 2 Hawk. Pl. C. Ch. 25, Sec. 16; 2 Hale Pl. C. 161; R. S. U. S., Sec. 1021; Clyncard's Case, Cro. Eliz. 654; Sayer's Case, 8 Leigh (Va.) 722.

124 1 Chitty Cr. Law 323; 1 Whart. Cr. Law., Sec. 504 (7th ed.); Rex. v. Fieldhouse, 1 Cowper 325.

count:[125] and if the bill charges more than one person, they may find the bill true as to some of the defendants and ignore it as to the balance.[126]   And where the grand jury upon a bill for murder find "billa vera se defendo" the finding is bad;[127] and so where the bill charges murder and the jury find for manslaughter only;[128] or where the finding avers that the offense was committed while the defendant was insane.[129] Where the finding is incomplete or insensible it is bad.[130]

The finding of the grand jury is then endorsed on the bill accordingly as they may have acted, and this return must be signed by the foreman[131] or the foreman pro tem.,[132] as the case may be.   In some states it is not essential to the validity of the indictment that it should be signed by the foreman,[133]

---

125 1 Chitty Cr. Law 322; 1 Whart. Cr. Law, Sec. 504 (7th ed.) ; 2 Hale Pl. C. 162; King v. Ford, Yelv. 99; Shouse v. Com. 5 Pa. 83; Com. v. Keenan, 67 Pa. 203; Com. v. Gressly, 12 Lanc. Bar (Pa.) 52; State v. Wilhite, 11 Humph. (Tenn.) 602; State v. Creighton, 1 N. & McC. (S. C.) 256; State v. Wilburne, 2 Brevard (S. C.) 296. And see Hall's Case, 3 Gratt (Va.) 593.

126 1 Chitty Cr. Law 323; 2 Hale Pl. C. 158; 1 Whart. Cr. Law Sec. 504 (7th ed.)

127 Powle's Case, 2 Rolle Rep. 52. In U. S. v. Elliott, 25 Fed. Cas. 1003, the grand jury made a presentment that the defendant acted in self-defence and the court thereupon ordered his discharge from custody.

128 2 Hale Pl. C. 158; State v. Cowan, 1 Head (Tenn.) 280; Compare People v. Nichol, 34 Calif. 211, where on an indictment for murder, the grand jury found a true bill for murder in the second degree.

129 Reg. v. Hodges, 8 Car. & P. 195.

130 2 Hawk. Pl. C. Ch. 25, Sec. 2; 1 Chitty Cr. Law 323; 1 Whart. Cr. Law, Sec. 505 (7th ed.) ; R. v. Cooke, 8 C. & P. 582; U. S. v. Levally, 36 Fed. Rep. 687; Frisbie v. U. S., 157 U. S. 160.

131 U. S. v. Plumer, 27 Fed. Cas. 561; Com. v. Sargent, Thach. Cr. Cas. 116; Com. v. Ditzler, 1 Lanc. Bar. (Pa.) Aug. 28, 1869; Com. v. Diffenbaugh, 3 Pa. C. C. Rep. 299. That the foreman's name was signed by the clerk will not invalidate the indictment, it appearing that it was done at the foreman's request and in his presence: Benson v. State, 68 Ala. 544.

132 White v. State, 93 Ga. 47; State v. Collins, 6 Baxt. (Tenn.) 151.

133 McGuffie v. State, 17 Ga. 497; Com. v. Ripperdon, Litt. Sel. Cas. (Ky.) 194; Com. v. Walters, 6 Dana (Ky.) 290; State v. Cox, 6 Ired. (N. C.) 440; State v. Calhoon, 1 Dev. & Bat. (N. C.) 374; State v. Creighton, 1 N. & McC. (S. C.) 256; Pinson v. State, 23 Tex. 579; State v. Flores, 33 Tex. 444; Robinson v. State, 24 Tex. App. 4; State v. Hill, 35 S. E. 831.

but the ruling in these cases is not to be commended. It is at variance with the common law rule, and if the signature be omitted, there is nothing upon the bill to attest the fact that the finding was duly authorized or placed thereon by a competent person.

A variance between the name of the foreman as shown by the record of his appointment and by the attestation of the finding on the bill is, in general, immaterial.[134] It is not material where the signature of the foreman may be placed,[135] and if he omit to add his official title and merely affix his signature to the finding it has been held that such endorsement can only relate to his official act as foreman and the indictment will be sustained.[136] And likewise if he sign his surname and use the initials of his Christian name only[137] or abbreviate his Christian name.[138]

The omission of the words "a true bill" has been held in some states not fatal to the indictment[139] although the weight of authority is to the contrary, if advantage be taken, before verdict, of the omission of such finding.[140]

134 State v. Stedman, 7 Port. (Ala.) 495; State v. Taggart, 38 Me. 298; Com. v. Hamilton, 15 Gray (Mass.) 480; Geiger v. State, 25 Ohio Cir. Ct. Rep. 742; State v. Calhoon, 1 Dev. & Bat. (N. C.) 374; State v. Collins, 3 Dev. (N. C.) 117. And see People v. Roberts, 6 Calif. 214; Deitz v. State, 123 Ind. 85; Green v. State, 4 Pickle (Tenn.) 614.

135 Goodman v. People, 90 Ill. App. 533; State v. Bowman, 103 Ind. 69; Overshiner v. Com. 2 B. Mon. (Ky.) 344; Blume v. State, 56 N. E. 771; State v. Shippey, 10 Minn. 223.

136 McGuffie v. State, 17 Ga. 497; State v. Chandler, 2 Hawks (N. C.) 439; State v. Brown, 31 Vt. 602. And see State v. Sopher, 35 La. Ann. 975; Whiting v. State, 48 Ohio St. 220.

137 Wassels v. State, 26 Ind. 30; Zimmerman v. State, 4 Ind. App. 583; State v. Groome, 10 Iowa 308; State v. Granville, 34 La. Ann. 1088; Com. v. Gleason, 110 Mass. 66.

138 Studstill v. State, 7 Ga. 2; State v. Folke, 2 La. Ann 744.

139 Com. v. Smyth, 11 Cush. (Mass.) 473; State v. Freeman, 13 N. H. 488; Price v. Com. 21 Grat. (Va.) 846; White v. Com. 29 Id. 824; State v. Hill, 35 S. E. 831. And see State v. Magrath, 44 N. J. Law 227, where the indictments were drawn after the investigation by the grand jury.

140 Alden v. State, 18 Fla. 187; Gardiner v. People, 3 Scam. (Ill.) 83; Nomaque v. People, Breese (Ill.) 109; Johnson v. State, 23 Ind. 32; Cooper v. State, 79 Ind. 206; State v. Buntin, 123 Ind. 124; Denton v.

It has been said "the endorsement is parcel of the ·indict-ment, and the perfection of it,[141] but the name of the offence thus endorsed thereon forms no part of the finding of the grand jury.[142]

The foreman must thus attest the return even though he voted in a manner opposite to the majority of the jurors. And it was held to be proper for him to· so attest the return, not-withstanding he had been directed by the court to take no part in the consideration of that particular bill.[143]

It is no ground of objection to the finding of the grand jury that they had at first voted to ignore the bill and afterwards reconsidered their decision and without hearing any additional evidence voted to return a true bill.[144]   After the grand jury have found a true bill and presented it, they cannot thereafter vote to ignore the bill and recall it.[145]

While it is the usual course, if the bill be found, for the foreman to endorse thereon "a true bill" with his name and "foreman" annexed, it has been held a sufficient return where the endorsement was simply "a bill" without the word "true,"[146] and signed by the foreman.   The endorsement of the words "true bill" omitting the letter "a" is likewise a suf-

State, 155 Ind. 307; Com. v. Walters, 6 Dana (Ky.) 290; Oliver v. Com., 95 Ky. 372; State v. Logan, 104 La. 254; Webster's Case, 5 Greenl. (Me.) 432; Spratt v. State, 8 Mo. 247; State v. McBroom, 127 N. C. 528; Gunkle v. State, 6 Baxt. (Tenn.) 625; Bird v. State, 103 Tenn. 343.

141 King v. Ford, Yelv. 99.   See State v. Thacker, 38 S. E. 539.

142 State v. Rohfrischt, 12 La. Ann. 382; State v. Valere, 39 Id. 1060; State v. DeHart, 109 La. 570; Collins v. People, 39 Ill. 233.   And see Cherry v. State, 6 Fla. 679; Humpeler v. People, 92 Ill. 400; Com. v. English, 6 Bush (Ky.) 431; Thompson v. Com., 20 Gratt. (Va.) 724.

143 State v. Lightfoot, 78 N. W. 41.

144 U. S. v. Simmons, 46 Fed. Rep. 65.   And see State v. Clapper, 59 Iowa 279; State v. Parrish, 8 Humph. (Tenn.) 80; State v. Brown, 81 N. C. 568.   In People v. Sheriff of Chautauqua County, 11 Civ. Proc. Rep. (N. Y.) 172, it was held that the grand jury had full control of every charge presented for its investigation until its final discharge, and before that time may reconsider and change any of its former acts.

145 Fields v. State, 25 So. 726.   And see In re Morse, 87 N. Y. Sup. 721.

146 Sparks v. Com., 9 Pa. 354.

ficient return.[147]   And it has been held that judgment would
not be arrested because the words "a true bill" were printed
on the back of the bill when it was sent to the grand jury
room.[148]

Where there is no endorsement of their finding and the name
of the foreman only is written thereon, or where the return is
not signed at all, a motion to quash the indictment or a plea in
abatement will be sustained.[149]   The court, however, has refused to arrest the judgment where the endorsement, instead of
being upon the bill, was upon the envelope in which the bill was
enclosed.[150]

Where a statute sets forth the manner in which the foreman
of the grand jury shall endorse the indictment, if the act be
not substantially complied with, the indictment must be
quashed.[151]

The indictment never alleges the organization and action of
the grand jury.   The signature of the foreman vouches for the
regularity of the proceedings after the jury is empaneled, and
the records of the court show the venire[152] and the appointment of the foreman.[153]   It has been held that the indictment
need not show when it was found,[154] although it is now the
usual practice for the foreman to endorse upon the bill the
date of its finding.

Where a bill contained ten counts and the grand jury found

147 Martin v. State, 30 Neb. 507; State v. Elkins, Meigs, (Tenn.) 109;
State v. Davidson, 12 Vt. 300.

148 Com. v. Usner, 7 Lanc. (Pa.) 57.   And see Tilly v. State, 21 Fla.
242; State v. Hogan, 31 Mo. 342; State v. Elliott, 98 Mo. 150; State v.
Williamson, 4 Weekly Law Bulletin, (Ohio) 279.

149 U. S. v. Levally, 36 Fed. Rep. 687; Frisbie v. U. S., 157 U. S. 160.

150 Burgess v. Com. 2 Va. Cas. 483.

151 Cooper v. State, 79 Ind. 206; State v. Bowman, 103 Ind. 69; Strange
v. State, 110 Ind. 354.

152 U. S. v. Laws, 26 Fed. Cas. 892.   And see Conner v. State, 4 Yerg.
(Tenn.) 137; State v. Davidson, 2 Cold (Tenn.) 184.

153 If the indictment be returned endorsed by one of the grand jurors
as foreman, the record need not show his appointment as such: Yates v.
People, 38 Ill. 527.

154 Burgess v. Com., 2 Va. Cas. 483; CONTRA Com. v. Schall, 9 Lanc.
Law Rev. (Pa.) 332.

a true bill and returned it with the endorsement "a true bill on both counts," the finding was held to be bad.[155]

If the grand jury return an indictment against a defendant by the initials of his Christian name only, a plea in abatement will be sustained unless the indictment shows that his name is not known to them otherwise than as set out.[156] And where the grand jury set forth in the indictment that the names of the persons from whom the defendant had received certain contributions were unknown to them, but on the trial it appeared that the names were known to the grand jurors, the court directed a verdict for the defendant.[157]

Should they happen to ignore a bill, a new bill charging the same offence may be submitted to the same or a subsequent grand jury; but in England a new bill cannot be sent before the same grand jury although it may be found by a subsequent one.[158]

The practice of submitting a new bill to the same or a subsequent grand jury has nothing in it to commend it, while it has been very severely criticised. That such, however, is the law is undoubted[159] and Mr. Justice Woodward says,[160] "If

155 R. v. Cooke, 8 Car. & P. 582. See People v. Hulbut, 4 Denio. (N. Y.) 133.

156 U. S. v. Upham, 43 Fed. Rep. 68; Gerrish v. State, 53 Ala. 476; O'Brien v. State, 91 Ala. 25; Gardner v. State, 4 Ind. 632; Jones v. State, 11 Ind. 357. And see Skinner v. State, 30 Ala. 524; Levy v. State, 6 Ind. 281; Wilcox v. State, 34 S. W. 958. Contra State v. Webster, 30 Ark. 166; Com. v. Kelcher, 3 Met. (Ky.) 485; State v. Johnson, 93 Mo. 73.

157 U. S. v. Riley, 74 Fed. Rep. 210. And see Cheek v. State, 38 Ala. 227; Winten v. State, 90 Ala. 637; Blodget v. State, 3 Ind. 403; Yost v. Com., 5 Ky. Law Rep. 935; State v. Stowe, 132 Mo. 199; Sault v. People, 34 Pac. 263.

158 4 Bl. Com. 305; Reg. v. Austin, 4 Cox C. C. 385; Reg. v. Humphreys, Car. & M. 601. Contra 1 Chitty Cr. Law 325; R. v. Newton, 2 M. & Rob. 503; Queen v. Simmonite, 1 Cox C. C. 30.

159 U. S. v. Martin, 50 Fed. Rep. 918; Christmas v. State, 53 Ga. 81; State v. Green, 111 Mo. 585; State v. Brown, 81 N. C. 568; State v. Harris, 91 N. C. 656; Ex Parte Job, 30 Pac. 699; State v. Reinhart, 38 Pac. 822; 1 Chitty Cr. Law 325. Mr. Chitty, however, states, p. 324, when the bill is ignored "the party is discharged without further answer," which is inconsistent with his subsequent statement.

160 Rowand v. Com., 82 Pa. 405.

the question were an open one, there would be little doubt as to the rule it would be the duty of this court to lay down. On principle, the return of "ignoramus" made on an indictment by a grand jury ought to be the end of the prosecution originating in the information returned by the committing magistrate. The defendant has complied with the conditions of his recognizance. The prosecution has failed with the failure of the bill. The sureties of the defendant are released, and he is entitled to be discharged.[161] In analogy to the rules by which other judicial proceedings are governed, this ought to be the end of the case founded on the complaint he was called on in the first instance to answer."

It has therefore been held to be error, where, after a grand jury had ignored a bill, a defendant was held in bail to answer the same charge without a new prosecution being instituted.[162]

Where the grand jury ignored the bill and an application was made to the court by private counsel for the prosecutor for leave to send a new bill before the next grand jury, the court held that in the absence of any allegations of irregularity or fraud it had no jurisdiction to review the proceedings of the grand jury or direct the sending of a new bill to the next grand jury.[163]

In some states, it has been provided by statute that a bill once ignored shall not again be submitted to the grand jury except by leave of court;[164] but this has been construed not to apply to a bill charging a different offence arising out of the same assault[165] nor to a case where the grand jury on their own motion find an indictment which has once been dismissed.[166]

---

161 In U. S. v. Bates, 24 Fed. Cas. 1042, it was held that a prisoner was not entitled to be discharged because the grand jury ignored the bill.

162 In re Moragne, 53 Pac. 3.

163 Com. v. Priestley, 10 Dist. Rep. (Pa.) 217. And see Com. v. Allen, 14 Pa. C. C. Rep. 546; Com. v. Charters, 20 Pa. Superior Ct. 599; In re Moragne, 53 Pac. 3.

164 State v. Collis, 73 Iowa 542; People v. Clements, 5 N. Y. Cr. Rep. 288; People v. Warren, 109 N. Y. 615.

165 People v. Warren, 109 N. Y. 615.

166 State v. Collis, 73 Iowa 542.

When the grand jurors have completed their findings, they are prepared to return into court and make their present-ment. They therefore proceed from their room to the court room where they were empaneled, and the names of the grand jurors being called, those present answer thereto. They are then asked by the crier if they have agreed upon any bills and bade to present them to the court.[167] The indictments having been brought in by the foreman,[168] they are handed by him to the crier, who asks if they agree that the court shall amend matter of form altering no matter of substance. To this the grand jury signify their assent. This assent it has been said was necessary to be had at common law in order that clerical errors in the indictment might be corrected; without the consent of the grand jury, the court was powerless to make any alter-ation in the bill as found, and with it, cannot alter the indict-ment in matter of substance.[169]

In Pennsylvania,[170] in view of the act of March 31, 1860, which allows the court for any formal defect appearing on the face of the indictment to forthwith cause such defect to be amended, it would seem no longer necessary to obtain the as-sent of the grand jury to the making of a change which the law directs shall be made. And this would also seem to be the law in the Federal courts.[171]

Where it becomes necessary to alter an indictment in matter of substance, the bill may be re-submitted to the same grand jury which originally found it, if they are then in session, and they may find a true bill in its altered form without hearing

---

167 1 Whart. Cr. Law, Sec. 500. (7th ed.)

168 Laurent v. State, 1 Kan. 313; Com. v. Cawood, 2 Va. Cas. 527. They should not be brought in by the foreman alone, but by the grand jury as a body: State v. Bordeaux, 93 N. C. 560. People v. Lee, 2 Utah 441.

169 1 Chitty Cr. Law 324; Ex Parte Bain, 121 U. S. 1; Sparks v. Com., 9 Pa. 354. In Harrison v. Com., 123 Pa. 508, where the district attorney amended the indictment by inserting "copper" before "lightning rod," without submitting the amended bill to the grand jury, this point was raised, but the court below awarded a new trial upon other grounds.

170 Sec. 11, P. L. 427.

171 R. S. U. S. Sec. 1025; Caha v. U. S., 152 U. S. 211.

any further evidence.[172]   If the grand jury which found the
bill has been discharged, then the altered bill, or what is better,
a new bill may be submitted to a subsequent grand jury,[173]
but, in either event they cannot find a true bill unless evidence
is heard in support thereof.   In Ex Parte Bain[174] the district
attorney amended the indictment in matter of substance by
leave of court and without re-submitting the bill to the grand
jury.   The defendant was tried, convicted and sentenced to
the penitentiary.   Upon habeas corpus proceedings, the defendant was discharged, the United States Supreme Court
holding, "Upon an indictment so changed the court can proceed no farther.   There is nothing (in the language of the
Constitution) which the prisoner can be held to answer.   A
trial on such an indictment is void.   There is nothing to try."

If the grand jury after hearing the evidence find a true bill
without it being read to them, it has been held not to afford
ground for setting aside the indictment so found.[175]   It is
difficult, however, to reconcile this decision with the ruling in
Ex Parte Bain.   It can hardly be said that the finding of a
bill, the contents of which are unknown to the grand jurors, is
any more their finding than the bill altered in substance after
presentment.   The grand jury have no knowledge of the nature of the charge to which they give their sanction.   They
may vote to find a true bill upon the evidence they have heard,
while the allegations of the bill to which their sanction has
apparently been given may present a totally different offence,
and which, if known to the grand jurors upon hearing the evidence, they would have ignored.   But the reading of the en-

172 Com. v. Woods, 10 Gray (Mass.) 477. In Com. v. Clune, 162 Mass.
206, the same ruling was made, although some of the grand jurors who
found the former indictments were absent and their places were filled by
jurors who had heard no evidence. See State v. Peterson, 61 Minn. 73.

173 1 Chitty Cr. Law 325; State v. Allen, R. M. Charltons Rep. (Ga.)
518; Com. v. Woods, 10 Gray (Mass.) 477; see State v. Davidson, 2 Cold.
(Tenn.) 184; Lawless v. State, 4 Lea (Tenn.) 173.

174 121 U. S. 1; and see Watts v. State, 57 Atl. 542.

175 U. S. v. Terry, 39 Fed. Rep. 355. And see U. S. v. Farrington, 5
Fed. Rep. 343, where the court directs attention to this fact, but quashed
the indictment upon other grounds.

tire bill may be dispensed with providing the material por-
tions of the bill charging the offence be read to the grand jury.

They are not required to read in open court their finding
upon the various bills of indictment presented by them.[176] The
handing of the bill to the crier or clerk and the entry made by
him on the records is a sufficient publication of the finding of
the grand jury.[177]   And where indictments, when found,
were sent into court by the district attorney or a messenger
and they were neither presented by the grand jury or a member thereof, the court refused to quash, the indictments having been recorded by the clerk.[178]

The finding of the grand jury should be recorded by the
clerk of the court and a failure to do this cannot be excused
by the defendant pleading not guilty, and a motion in arrest
of judgment will be sustained upon this ground.[179]   And

---

176 U. S. v. Butler, 25 Fed. Cas. 213; Hopkins v. Com. 50 Pa. 9.

177 Id.. And see Hogan v. State, 30 Wis. 428.

178 Com. v. Salter, 2 Pears. (Pa.) 461; Danforth v. State, 75 Ga. 614;
Laurent v. State, 1 Kan. 313.

179 Holcombe v. State, 31 Ark. 427; Thornell v. People, 11 Colo. 305;
Gardner v. People, 20 Ill. 430; Kelly v. People, 39 Ill. 157; Aylesworth
v. State, 65 Ill. 301; Adams v. State, 11 Ind. 304; Heacock v. State,
42 Ind. 393; State v. Glover, 3 G. Greene (Iowa) 249; State v. Sandoz,
37 La. Ann. 376; Jenkins v. State, 30 Miss. 408; Pond v. State, 47 Miss.
39; State v. Brown, 81 N. C. 568; State v. Davidson, 2 Cold. (Tenn.) 184;
Rainey v. People, 3 Gil. (Ill.) 71; Chappel v. State, 8 Yerg. (Tenn.)
166; Brown v. State, 7 Humph. (Tenn.) 155; Hardy v. State, 1 Tex. App.
556; Simmons v. Com., 89 Va. 156; Com. v. Cawood, 2 Va. Cas. 527; State
v. Gilmore, 9 W. Va. 641; State v. Heaton, 23 W. Va. 773. CONTRA Moore
v. State, 81 S. W. 48; State v. Crilly, 77 Pac. 701; People v. Lee, 2 Utah
441; Mose v. State, 35 Ala. 421. And see as to a sufficient record of the
finding: McCuller v. State, 49 Ala. 39; Robinson v. State, 33 Ark. 180;
Johnson v. State, 24 Fla. 162; Fitzpatrick v. People, 98 Ill. 269; Kelly v.
People 132 Ill. 363; Wall v. State, 23 Ind. 150; Beavers v. State, 58 Ind. 530;
Clare v. State, 68 Ind. 17; Reeves v. State, 84 Ind. 116; Heath v. State, 101
Ind. 512; Millar v. State, 2 Kan. 174; Patterson v. Com., 86 Ky. 313; Nich-
ols v. State, 46 Miss. 284; State v. Vincent, 91 Mo. 662; State v. Gainus, 86
N. C. 632; Hopkins v. Com., 50 Pa. 9; Bennett v. State, 8 Humph. (Tenn.)
118; Maples v. State, 3 Heisk (Tenn.) 408; Peeples v. State, 35 So. 223;
Pearce v. Com., 8 S. W. 893; State v. Jones, 42 Pac. 392. In State v. Muz-
ingo, 19 Tenn. (Meigs) 112, it was held that a presentment of the grand
jury need not be entered on the minutes of the court.

where several persons are indicted in the one bill and the finding is recorded as to one only, the court will sustain the indictment against the defendant as to whom the finding was properly recorded, and quash as to the other defendants.[180]

When the finding of the grand jury has been recorded, the bills of indictment should be filed. In some states the statutes make provision for the filing of indictments. Such provisions, however, may in general be regarded as directory[181] and courts are disinclined to invalidate an indictment where the statute has not been complied with.[182] If the date of the filing has not been endorsed on the indictment, the court may thereafter direct that the actual date of filing be endorsed thereon.[183]

When the grand jurors have completed all the duties which will devolve upon them, it is now customary for them to prepare a written report of their work, which is signed by their foreman and handed to the court crier with the indictments. In this report they frequently take occasion to discuss various matters affecting the public welfare, criticise public officials, act as censors of the morals of the community, and make recommendations which it is impracticable and impossible to carry into effect.

That they are acting outside of their duties as grand jurors in making such presentments will hardly be doubted. As the official accuser for the government, their duty is to present persons not things. That this practice should be continued upon the ground that it calls to the public eye abuses in the administration of government or the existence of vice in the community, is a proposition which rests upon no logical basis. If they have any evidence of the things which they thus set forth,

---

180 Drake and Cochren's Case, 6 Gratt (Va.) 665; State v. Compton, 13 W. Va. 852. CONTRA State v. Banks, 40 La. Ann. 736.

181 Stanley v. State, 88 Ala. 154; Dawson v. People, 25 N. Y. 399.

182 Pittman v. State, 25 Fla. 648; Engelman v. State, 2 Cart. (Ind.) 91; State v. Jolly, 7 Iowa 15; Com. v. Stegala, 8 Ky. Law Rep. 142; Reynolds v. State, 11 Tex. 120.

183 Franklin v. State, 28 Ala. 9; State v. Gowen, 7 Eng. (Ark.) 62; James v. State, 41 Ark. 451; Pence v. Com. 95 Ky. 618; State v. Clark, 18 Mo. 432; Caldwell v. State, 5 Tex. 18; Rippey v. State, 29 Tex. App. 37.

it is their duty to the public and to themselves under their oath, to present the individuals guilty of such offences.[184] If they have no personal knowledge of the facts, they are then proceeding in a manner contrary to law.[185] If they know the things which they present, they should present individuals; if they do not know, they are committing a wrong in making broad accusations, which, while they cannot be sustained, grievously injure those to whom they indirectly apply.

This practice received severe condemnation over seventy years ago at the hands of Honorable Daniel Davis[186] then Attorney General for the State of Massachusetts, who says: "The practice, not uncommon in some parts of the United States, of bringing forward, in the form of presentments, what are denominated public grievances, relative to the political or moral state of the country, is altogether extra-official, and may be and has been adopted and pursued for purposes foreign to, and inconsistent with, the nature of the institution; and perhaps it is not too much to assert, that the opportunity has been used and perverted to party purposes, and with an intention to produce an effect upon public measures and the public mind. Whenever this shall be the case it is to be considered in the same light as any other usurpation or abuse of the judicial authority. It may, with the same propriety, be exercised by any other branch of the judicial power, by the court, or the traverse jury, as well as the grand jury."

In the case of Rector v. Smith,[186*] the grand jury made a written report to the court wherein libellous statements were made relating to the conduct of a person then in public office. An action for libel was begun against the clerk of the grand jury who had brought the report into court and there read it.

---

184 See Judge Stowe's Charge to Grand Jury, 3 Pitts. Rep. (Pa.) page 179. It may be doubted whether this charge, so far as it relates to the power of the grand jury to originate prosecutions, is entirely correct; it is at least an inadequate statement of the authority of the grand jury.

185 Case of Lloyd and Carpenter, 3 Clark (Pa.) 188.

186 Precedents of Indictments, p. 11.

186* 11 Iowa 302.

An answer was filed by the defendant who claimed the report was a privileged communication, to which answer the plaintiff demurred but the demurrer was overruled by the lower court. On appeal, the Supreme Court affirmed the judgment and expressly ruled that the report was not a privileged communication. In delivering the opinion of the court, Balwin, J., says:

"The grand jury have no power, nor is it their privilege or duty to present any person for a criminal offence except by indictment. If the misconduct of an officer does not amount to a crime, and is not of such magnitude as will justify the jury in finding an indictment, their powers over the offence complained of, are at an end. . . . . A report by a grand jury, presents nothing upon which the court can act, unless it is in reference to the condition of the prison. The court can take no jurisdiction over the complaint charged by such report. Nor can a person thus presented have an opportunity to show himself innocent of the matters complained of. With this view of the question we conclude that the report presented by the defendant as a juror, was not a privileged communication, and that he cannot plead this in bar of plaintiff's right to recover."

When the grand jury in their presentment thus go beyond their lawful authority, whether they refer to persons by name, title, or by innuendo, or to any particular matter or thing, it becomes a serious question whether or not their presentment should be permitted to stand. Clearly in such instance they have exceeded their authority, and in such event their presentment rests upon no legal foundation. There would consequently seem to be no valid reason why a motion to quash or dismiss the presentment, or strike it, or the objectionable part thereof, from the files should not be made. If the grand jurors have exceeded their authority in making such presentment, it is clearly invalid and illegal and may be subjected to attack either by the attorney for the state or by the person or persons to whom the presentment may relate, in the same manner as any presentment or indictment may be attacked. This course has been pursued in Georgia[186]** where the grand jury made a pre-

186** Presentment of Grand Jury, 1 R. M., Charlt. 149.

sentment reflecting upon the judges of the Superior Court. The attorney general moved to expunge the presentment from the minutes which was accordingly done.

After submitting their report they are then discharged from further service by the court, and go out and mingle with their fellow citizens and their identity as grand jurors is forever lost.[187] But a grand jury cannot legally dissolve itself[188] or dismiss or excuse any of its members.[189] This is the prerogative of the court alone and until the court takes such action, the existence of the grand jury continues during the balance of the statutory period for which it was summoned.[190] It may be dismissed from time to time during the period for which it was convened and again summoned back to duty when any matters are to be laid before it;[191] or it may adjourn upon its own motion and again reconvene and act whether court is in session or not.[192] But when the record shows that the grand jury has been discharged, it will be presumed to have been legally and properly discharged.[193]

Whether or not the members of the grand jury may be again re-assembled after once being discharged is a matter as to which there is considerable difference of opinion. Two

187 Chief Justice Shaw's Charge to Grand Jury, 8 Am. Jurist 216; Addison, App. 75.

188 In re Gannon, 69 Calif. 541.

189 See Gladden v. State, 12 Fla. 562; Smith v. State, 19 Tex. App. 95; Watts v. State, 22 Id. 572; Drake v. State, 25 Id. 293; Jackson v. State, 25 Id. 314.

190 In re Gannon, 69 Calif. 541; People v. Leonard, 106 Calif. 302; State v. Bennett, 45 La. Ann. 54; Com. v. Rich, 14 Gray (Mass.) 335. And see Barger v. State, 6 Blackf. (Ind.) 188; Harper v. State, 42 Ind. 405. R. S. U. S. 811 provides: "The circuit and district courts, the district courts of the Territories, and the supreme court of the District of Columbia, may discharge their grand juries whenever they deem a continuance of the sessions of such juries unnecessary."

191 Ulmer v. State, 14 Ind. 52; Long v. State, 46 Ind, 582; State v. Pate, 67 Mo. 488. That the grand jurors did not return until after the day designated will not dissolve the grand jury: Clem v. State, 33 Ind. 418.

192 Nealon v. People, 39 Ill. App. 481; People v. Sheriff of Chautauqua County, 11 Civ. Proc. Rep. 172. And see Com. v. Bannon, 97 Mass. 214.

193 White v. People, 81 Ill. 333. And see State v. Wingate, 4 Ind. 193.

learned writers hold[194] that "When an emergency arises, requiring the presence of a grand jury after the regular body has
been discharged, in the absence of statutory authority to summon a new panel, the court should set aside the order of discharge and re-assemble the previous grand jury."[195]   But a
contrary and what would seem the better opinion, is held by
Hon. Daniel Davis,[196] who says: "When the grand jury have
finished their business and been unconditionally discharged,
they cannot be re-summoned and reorganized.   No grand jury
can be created or brought into existence but in the manner directed by the statutes of the state."

It would seem that grand jurors in such cases are analogous to petit jurors, who, upon being discharged from further
service and having separated, cannot again be reassembled.
The statutes provide a method for selecting and summoning
grand jurors and the requirements of these statutes must be
strictly followed.   When, therefore, the grand jurors have
been discharged, their official capacity at once comes to an end
and they are but ordinary citizens.   To set aside the order of
discharge would not restore them to their former official position.   Their official capacity having once terminated, it can
only be again created by the method provided by statute.[197]
If there is no statute which provides for setting aside the order
of discharge and the reassembling of the grand jury with the

194 Thompson & Merriam on Juries, Sec. 497.

195 See Newman v. State, 43 Tex. 525.

196 Precedents of Indictments, p. 30.   And see Reg. v. Holloway, 9 Car.
& P. 43.

197 Findley v. People, 1 Manning (Mich.) 234: In Mackey v. People, 2
Colo. 13, the indictment was found by a special grand jury summoned during
the term and after the regular grand jury had been discharged for the term.
The defendant challenged the array upon the ground that the statute provided that the regular grand jurors had been summoned for the term and
that after they were discharged no grand jury could be summoned until the
next term.   The challenge was overruled upon the ground that there was
a common law power in the court to so cause a grand jury to be summoned and that it did not conflict with the statute.   And see Stone v.
People, 2 Scam. (Ill.) 326; Empson v. People, 78 Ill. 248; Freel v. State,
21 Ark. 212; State v. Grimes, 50 Minn. 123.

11

same power as before its discharge, a grand jury thus called back to duty would not be lawfully organized.[198]

The order of discharge cannot be collaterally attacked.[199]

When the grand jurors are in session or during the time they retain their official position their oath restrains them from disclosing to any one out of the grand jury room that which transpires therein, and it is likewise unlawful for any one to approach a grand juror and attempt in any manner to influence his action. When actually engaged in his duties as a grand juror he is prohibited from holding communication with any one except the court, the district attorney, such witnesses as are sent before the grand jury by the district attorney, and his fellow jurors. It is improper for any one else to send communications to the grand jurors, or for them to receive them, whether with a view to influence the action of the grand jury or not.[200] If any person outside the grand jury room has knowledge of any matter proper for their consideration, he should lay such information before the district attorney who will act accordingly, but he must not attempt to have any direct communication with them.

This question arose in Pennsylvania in the case of Commonwealth v. Crans,[201] where the defendant sent a communication to the grand jury, giving his views upon certain subjects which were liable to come before them, and Judge Parsons, there said, "if they (the grand jurors) are to be instructed previous to their retiring by the judge who pre-

---

198 Gay v. State, 49 S. W. 612; Matthews v. State, 58 S. W. 86; Trevinio v. State, 27 Tex. App. 372. See State v. Reid, 20 Iowa 413.

199 State v. Hart, 67 Iowa 142. It is impossible to reconcile the ruling in this case with those cases which hold a new grand jury to be illegally empanelled because the former grand jury was not legally discharged.

200 People v. Sellick, 4 N. Y. Cr. Rep. 329; Charge to Grand Jury, 30 Fed. Cas. 992; Com. v. Crans, 2 Clark (Pa.) 441; Doan's Case, 5 Pa. Dist. Rep. 211. And see Henry Bergh's Case, 16 Abb. Pr. N. S. (N. Y.) 266; People v. Shea, 147 N. Y. 78. The authority of the grand jury to investigate a criminal charge is not affected by an order from the President of the United States to the district attorney directing him not to prosecute the defendant: In re Miller 17 Fed. Cas. 295.

201 2 Clark (Pa.) 441.

sides, it necessarily follows they are not to be instructed after they retire to their rooms by any one else.   Individuals have no more right to appear before them to discuss matters, or send them letters relative to subjects which are before them, or which may come before them, than they would have to communicate with a petit jury after a charge had been delivered from the bench, in relation to a case which had just been tried."

From the time the grand jurors are summoned until finally discharged, they bear an official relation to the court, and while all jurists agree that they are under the control of the court, none have expressed a well defined opinion as to how far the authority of the court over the grand jurors extends, or to what extent they are independent of the court.[202]

In the days of Bracton and Britton and for a long period thereafter, such a question as this would have been easy to determine.   Then, the grand jury was but an instrument wholly under the control of the justices and acting in such manner as they should direct.   If the justices so desired, the grand jurors would hear the evidence (when it became customary for them to hear evidence) in open court.   If they heard any evidence in private or acted as they then most usually did, upon their own knowledge, or upon hearsay, it was optional with the justices to compel them to disclose how they obtained knowledge of the facts which the jurors set forth in their presentment, and the court was at liberty to set this presentment aside.   And it would seem that where a false presentment was made the jurors were liable either to be fined or be imprisoned at the pleasure of the king's justices, and likewise, if the grand jurors refused to present when directed to do so by the justices.

The causes which tended to make the grand jury to a certain extent independent of the court have been heretofore fully considered,[203] and while the court at various times thereafter

---

202 In People v. Sheriff of Chautauqua County, 11 Civ. Proc. Rep. (N. Y.) 172, it was held that the grand jury is not a part of the court in which it is drawn, and that the court has no control over its sittings or adjournments.

203 Supra. 28.

endeavored to compel juries to do their will as we have seen occurred in Pennsylvania,[204] the practice of punishing them by fine or imprisonment for refusal to act in accordance with the wishes of the justices was brought to an end long prior thereto by the resolute action of Sir Hugh Windham.[205] In this case the grand jurors refused to find a bill for murder although they were satisfied that the deceased came to his death at the hands of the defendant. The chief justice thereupon fined eleven of them, among whom was Sir Hugh Windham, and bound them over until the King's Bench should determine the matter. The court relieved them of the fine although holding that the grand jury should have found a bill for murder. The chief justice was afterward accused in Parliament by Sir Hugh, and was obliged to acknowledge, that the fining was unlawful.

That the grand jury from that time has been absolutely free from the control of the court in their findings, there can be no question, and Judge King said,[206] when discharging a prisoner upon habeas corpus proceedings: "I rejoice that our judgment is not conclusive of the subject; the sole effect of this decision, is that in the present state of the evidence we see no sufficient cause to hold the defendant to bail. It is still competent for the proper public officer to submit the case to the grand jury; that respectable body are entirely independent of us; they may form their own view of the prosecutor's case, and may if their judgment so indicates, place the defendant on his trial."

But aside from the independence which they possess in regard to their finding, in what respect, if any, are they independent of the control of the court. Dr. Wharton states:[207] "When the grand jury are in session, they are completely under the control of the court," and in the case of State v.

204 Francis Hopkinson's Works, Vol. I, p. 194. Supra. 31.

205 King v. Windham, 2 Keble 180. And see Bushel's Case, Vaughn 153; 2 Hale, Pl. C. 158 et seq.

206 Com. v. Ridgway, 2 Ash. (Pa.) 247.

207 1 Whart. Cr. Law, Sec. 506 (7th ed.): And see State v. Cowan, 1 Head (Tenn.) 280.

Cowan[207]* the court said: "The grand jury are under the control of the court. And it is the province and duty of the court to see that the finding is proper in point of law; and if not, the court may recommit an improper or imperfect finding, and may, if necessary, exercise the power of compelling a proper discharge of duty on the part of the grand jury."

It was said by Judge Parsons[208] that the grand jury "have no power to compel the appearance of a witness, none to attach him for contempt should he refuse to testify, and even on bills pending before them, it became necessary to pass a special law to authorize them to swear witnesses endorsed on the bills." While they are thus unable to take any legal action on matters not within their own knowledge except with the assistance of the court, the court cannot compel them to receive the witnesses subpoenaed, and while it may recommit to them an imperfect finding,[209] it cannot compel them to alter it if they refuse.

Within their own room they are supreme in their action;[210] within the court room, they are subject to the control of the judge in the same manner as any other officer of the court,[211] but even in the court room, the judge has no authority over the grand jurors in any matter which is in their discretion.

In Pennsylvania[212] a person can only be committed for contempt where the offence is actually committed in the presence of the court, although fines may be imposed for contempts not committed in open court, but in the event of the grand jurors in their own room acting contrary to the instructions of the court all that the judge could do would be to discharge the jurors from further service.

A different rule prevails in the Federal courts, for the judges may commit for contempt where the offence was not committed in their presence. Thus in Summerhayes case[213] the court sen-

---

207* 1 Head (Tenn.) 280.

208 Com. v. Crans., 2 Clark (Pa.) 441.

209 1 Whart. Cr. Law, Sec. 506 (7th ed.); State v. Squire, 10 N. H. 558; State v. Cowan, 1 Head (Tenn.) 280.

210 Allen v. State, 61 Miss. 627.

211 U. S. v. Kilpatrick, 16 Fed. Rep. 765.

212 Act June 16, 1836, P. L. 23.

213 In re Summerhayes, 70 Fed. Rep. 769.

tenced a grand juror to six months imprisonment for contempt in disregarding his oath and the instructions of the court by revealing to persons outside the grand jury room matters which had transpired therein, relating to such persons. And in Ellis' case[214] on motion of the prosecuting attorney, the court fined Ellis, who was foreman of the grand jury, thirty dollars, discharged him from the grand jury and ordered that execution issue to collect the fine.

A different and rather better view was taken by the court of King's Bench[215] which refused to attach a grand juror for certain acts done by him while acting in his official capacity, although they will attach one who had been a grand juror for acting as such after he has been dismissed.

The grand jury has jurisdiction over its own members for any presentable offence which may be committed by a grand juror while acting as such. Thus in Pennsylvania the grand jurors presented one of their number for drunkenness, he being present in the grand jury room in a drunken condition and sleeping by the fire while the inquest performed its duties, and the court held the presentment proper if the jury believed the drunkenness to have been voluntary.[216]

Unlike the private prosecutor a grand juror comes ordinarily unwillingly in obedience to the command of the law to act as an official accuser. If, while so acting, he should disregard his oath and maliciously procure the indictment of any person or persons for some alleged offence, the law affords no redress to the person whom he has wronged. No inquiry can be made as to what he said or how he voted; the veil of secrecy surrounding the acts of grand jurors presents a most complete barrier to any investigation into the motive which inspired his action. Even though it were possible to make such investigation, considerations of public policy would require that no action should be maintained against a grand juror for any act done in his official capacity. The fact that he was liable to answer to a de-

214 In re Ellis, 8 Fed. Cas. 548.
215 King v. Baker, Rowe's Rep. of Interesting Cases, 603.
216 Penna v. Keffer, Add. 290.

fendant for his official acts, would operate as a powerful deterrent to finding a true bill in many cases. The law, therefore, affords a grand juror the most unqualified indemnity for his official acts. "During the whole of their proceedings the grand jury are protected in the discharge of their duty and no action or prosecution can be supported against them in consequence of their finding, however it may be dictated by malice, or destitute of probable foundation."[217]

217 1 Chitty Cr. Law 323. And see Floyd *v.* Barker, 12 Co. 23; Johnstone *v.* Sutton, 1 Term Rep. 513-14; Turpen *v.* Booth, 56 Calif. 65; Thornton *v.* Marshall, 92 Ga. 548; Hunter *v.* Mathis, 40 Ind. 356; Rector *v.* Smith, 11 Iowa 302; Ullman *v.* Abrams, 72 Ky. 738; Griffith *v.* Slinkard, 44 N. E. 1001. In Scarlett's Case, 12 Co. 98, a grand juror was indicted, convicted and sentenced for maliciously causing seventeen innocent persons to be indicted. And see Poulterer's Case, 9 Co. 55b. But this could not be done at the present day by reason of the policy of the law not to permit any grand juror to testify what any member of the jury had said or how he voted. In Allen *v.* Gray, 11 Conn. 95, it was held that where process issues on complaint of a grand juror for an offence of which he is not cognizant, he is liable in trespass.

INDEX

ACTION
>against grand juror, when maintainable, 166.

ACTS
>presumption of regularity of official, 59.
>accused may take advantage of irregular, 64.
>wrongful, of grand jurors, 166.

ADDISON, JUDGE,
>charges to grand juries, 101, 124, 131, 141.

ADJOURNMENT
>of grand jury from time to time, 160.

AFFIDAVIT
>when necessary to sheriff's return, 54.
>in support of challenge to array, 68.

AFFINITY
>grand jurors related to accused by, 81.

AFFIRMATION. AND SEE OATH.
>of grand jurors, 91, 137.

AFFORCIAMENT
>when employed, 24.

AGE OF GRAND JURORS
>exemption by reason of, 72.

ALABAMA
>oath of grand juror in, 95n.
>investigation of sufficiency of official bonds, 122.
>endorsement of prosecutor's name, 136.

ALIEN
>not a competent grand juror, 60, 63, 77.
>cannot demand grand jury de medietate linguae, 64.

AMENDMENT
>of writ of venire, 48.
>of sheriff's return, 50.
>of record nunc pro tunc, 93.
>of indictment, 154, 155.
>Fifth, to Constitution of United States, 32, 131.
>>applies solely to offences against United States, 33.
>>does not apply to Cherokee Nation, 33n.
>Sixth, to Constitution of United States, 57.
>Fourteenth, to Constitution of United States, 33, 66.
>>does not prevent states from prosecuting by information, 33.
>>gives white man no additional rights, 67.

AMERCEMENT
>of hundred for escape of offender, 4.

AMERCERS
>pledges taken by, 20.

ARRAY

    objections to, 65.

    motion to quash, when not sustained, 67.

    if quashed, tales not to issue, 52.

    challenge to, must be substantiated by oath, 68.

        causes of, 66.

        when made, 68, 85.

        how made, 70.

        in Federal Courts, 69, 85.

ARREST

    indictment found without previous, 114.

ARREST OF JUDGMENT. SEE JUDGMENT.

ARSENALS

    workmen in, exempt from jury service, 73.

ARTICLES OF INQUIRY, 11.

    reading of to accusing body, 20.

ASHFORD *vs.* THORNTON, wager of battle, 13.

ASSENT

    of grand jury to amendment of indictment, 154.

ASSIZE

    writs awarding, 17.

    of Clarendon, 7, 8, 11, 14, 17, 18.

      its provisions, 7.

      offenders to be tried by ordeal, 7.

      itinerant courts created by, 7.

      four townspeople referred to in, 7, 23.

      marks important change in law, 7.

      implied prohibition of, 8.

      Prof. Thayer on, 18.

    of Northampton, 7, 11, 17.

      provisions of, 9.

      divided kingdom into six circuits, 8, 9.

ASYLUMS

    investigation into, 121.

ATHENIANS,

    existence of juries among, 1.

ATTACHMENT,

    to compel attendance of witnesses, 133.

    of grand juror for misconduct, 166.

ATTENDANCE.

    of grand jurors, differences in statutes requiring, 47.

        at time fixed by statute, 48.

        before and after regular term, 54.

        immaterial how procured, 54.

        after jury empaneled and sworn, 51.

        of improper person, 49, 139.

CAUSE
> challenge for, 69, 77, 82n.
> individual jurors may be challenged for, 70.
> to be shown on challenge for favor, 74.

CAUSEWAYS
> presentment of inquest in relation to, 25.

CHALLENGE
> error to refuse right of, 65.
> legislature cannot take away right of, 70.
> defendant must demand right to, 71.
> to array, 66, 68.
> when made, 68, 85.
> must be substantiated by affidavit, 68.
> state's attorney cannot challenge panel, 70.
> peremptory, not allowed, 75, 82.
>> unknown in time of Bracton and Britton, 75.
> for favor, 70, 73, 74, 76, 77, 82.
>> how determined, 82.
>> to be made before grand juror sworn, 74.
>> where opinion formed and expressed, 76.
>> upon ground of relationship, 80.
>> examination on voir dire not permitted on, 81.
> of grand juror for cause, 69, 77, 82.
>> how made, 70.
>> by whom made, 71.
>> absence from domicile, 81.
> made and withdrawn cannot be assigned for error, 70.
> exclusion of grand juror on, 72.
> when not allowed in Iowa, 70.
> in Federal Courts, 69.
> Federal grand jury depleted by, 55.
> of petit jurors for cause, 23, 25.

CHARGE OF THE COURT
> when made, 124.
> as means of communication with public, 124.
> effect of omission of, 124n.
> supplemental, when given, 125.
> at whose request made, 125.
> in Aaron Burr's case, 125.
> Judge Cranch's view, 126.
> when inflammatory, 126.
> delivered by Chief Justice Shaw, 43.

CHARGES TO GRAND JURIES, Judge Addison's, 101, 124.

CHARLES II, attack on grand jury, 28, 31.

CHASE, CHIEF JUSTICE, powers of grand jury, 102.

12

COURT—*Continued.*
> illegally impaneling grand jury, 89.
> foreman appointed by, 90.
> matters given in charge of grand jury by, 101, 106.
> to order additional testimony produced, 104.
> district attorney to obtain leave of, 111, 115.
> hearing of evidence in open, 117, 127, 163.
> contempt of, 121, 165.
> charges grand jury when, 124.
> when grand jury in, 130.
> swearing witnesses in open, 137.
> will not inquire as to sufficiency of evidence, 146.
> findings not read in open, 156.
> how indictments brought into, 156.
> relation of grand jury to, 163.

COURT LEET, 5, 8.

COURT ROLLS of the eyres, 11, 24.

COURTS, ITINERANT. SEE ITINERANT COURTS.

CRABB
> on question whether grand jury also tried offenders, 22.

CRANCH, JUDGE, supplemental charge, 126.

CRIMINAL CASES
> disappearance of compurgation in, 8.
> petit jury in, 10.

CRIMINAL PLEAS
> not considered by nambda, 3.

CRIMINATE
> where testimony of witness will tend to, 133.

CROMWELL, OLIVER, oath in time of, 99.

CROWLEY *vs.* UNITED STATES. R. S. U. S. Sec. 1025, 74.

CROWN
> growth of influence of, 8.
> pleas of, administered by itinerant justices, 8.
> authority of attorney general for, 113.

CRY, HUE AND, 4, 12.

CURIA REGIS, sheriff selected from justices of, 8.

CUSTOM
> as to number of grand jurors, 6.
> grand jury a growth of, 26.
> of weregild, 4.
> > disuse of, 9.

DATE
> of finding bill, endorsement of, 151.
> of filing bill, endorsement of, 157.

DISTRICT ATTORNEY—*Continued*.
    presence during deliberations, 128.
    indictments sent into court by, 156.
    may enter nolle pros, 142.
    may not testify, when, 120.
    stenographer as assistant to, 139.

DISUSE OF WEREGILD, 9.

DIVERSE VIEWS,
    as to origin of grand jury, 1.
    as to utility and abolition of grand jury, 35.

DOCUMENTS. SEE BOOKS AND PAPERS.

DOMICILE
    when absence from will disqualify, 81.

DRAWING. SEE SELECTION.

DRUNKENNESS OF GRAND JUROR, 166.

DUE PROCESS OF LAW, 33.
    defined in Hurtado *v.* California, 110 U. S. 516, 39n.

DUTY
    of twelve thanes to accuse, 3.
    of accusing body to present offenders, 11.
    of king's sergeants to enroll appellor's complaint, 12.
    of coroner to enroll appellor's complaint, 12.

EARL OF SHAFTESBURY'S CASE, 29.

EASTERN STATES
    conservatism of, on grand jury, 44.

EDWARD III
    and rise of grand jury, 2.
    development of grand jury in time of, 26.

ELECTION
    by appellor between battle and ordeal, 10.

ELECTOR. SEE VOTER.

ELLIS' CASE, disregarding oath, 166.

EMPANELED
    when grand jurors are, 88, 89.
    grand jury may be, at any time during term, 88.
    when grand jury illegally, discharge of, 89.
    may investigate offence committed after being, 103.

EMPANELING
    irregularity in, 68, 85n, 89.
            witness must testify although, 88.
    objections to grand jurors before, 64n, 69n, 85n.
    talesmen may be added after, 51.
    record must show, 89.
    after new statue prescribes different method, 89.

EVIDENCE—*Continued*.
    sufficiency of, 146.
    to be heard or indictment void, 132, 155.
    when not to be revealed, 118.
    attorney general cannot stipulate as to, 120n.
    hearing of, in open court, 117, 127, 163.
    record offered in, 119.

EXAMINATION
    of witnesses by district attorney, 139.

EXCEPTIONS TO APPEAL, 17, 21.

EXCLUSION
    of negroes from panel, 66.
            white man cannot complain, 67.
    of grand juror on challenge, effect of, 72.
            by district attorney, 84.
    of foreman for disqualification, 90.

EXCUSING GRAND JURORS, 84, 160.
    presumption of in Arkansas, 85.

EXEMPTION
    from service as grand jurors, 72.
    distinction between disqualification and, 72.

EXISTENCE
    of grand jury among Athenians, 1.

EX PARTE BAIN, altering indictments, 155.

EXPUNGING presentment from minutes, 160.

EYRE
    held every seven years, 9, 12.
    held by itinerant justices, 8, 19.
    how held, 19.
    hearing appellor before justices in, 12.
    court rolls of, 11.
    of 1218-19, order of King in Council, 18.

FAME, PUBLIC. See Public Fame.

FAVOR
    grand jurors must stand indifferent, 62, 81.
    individual jurors may be challenged for, 70, 73.
    challenge for, a common law right, 74.
            when prosecutor on grand jury, 78.
            upon ground of relationship, 80, 81.
            examination on voir dire, 81.
            cannot be made after indictment, 85.
            in Aaron Burr's Case, 74, 82.
    conscientious scruples against capital punishment, 76.

FEALTY
    pledge of, by amercers, 20.

FOREMAN

> how selected, 90.
> appointment of, noted on minutes of court, 90, 151.
> to be sworn, 93.
> should not be illiterate, 90.
> pro tem. may be chosen, 90.
> need not be reappointed when vacancy filled, 85.
> receives indictments from district attorney, 134.
> authority of, to swear witnesses, 137.
> hands indictment to crier, 154.
> when to sign return, 150.
> signature of, as evidence of empaneling, 89.
>> vouches for regularity of proceedings, 151.
>> to final report, 157.
> name of, signed by clerk, 148n.
>> variance in, 149.
> when endorsed as prosecutor, 136.
> discharge of, when presumed, 91.

FORM

> amendment of matter of, 154.

FORSYTH

> reference to the four townships, 16.
> participation of grand jury in trial of offenders, 21.

FOURTEENTH AMENDMENT. SEE AMENDMENT.

FOURTH LATERAN COUNCIL

> abolishes ordeal, 18.
> Professor Thayer on, 18.

FOUR TOWNSHIPS. SEE TOWNSHIPS.

FRANK PLEDGE

> system of, 3, 4, 5.
> view of, 5, 8.
> continuance under Normans, 6.
> falls into disuse, 8.

FREE AND LEGAL MEN. SEE QUALIFICATIONS OF GRAND JURORS.

FREEHOLDERS. SEE QUALIFICATIONS OF GRAND JURORS.

FREEMEN

> four of every vill, 14, 15.
> mentioned by Bracton, 15.
> no part of the inquest, 15.
> use of, not obligatory, 16.
> limited to concurrence in finding of inquest, 16.

FRITH-BOT, 6.

FUGITIVE FROM JUSTICE

> district attorney may act when defendant is, 110.

GAOLS
 inquest to inquire as to, 25.
 illegal detention of persons therein, by sheriff, 25.
 escapes from, inquiry into, 25.

GEMOT, meeting of, 5.

GLANVILLE
 institution of prosecutions in time of, 10.
 four townships not mentioned by, 14.
 presentment on suspicion, 15.
 great interest of treatise of, 9.

GEORGIA
 oath of grand juror, 95n.
 grand jurors to revise taxes, 122.
 when indictment founded on presentment, 132.
 expunging improper presentment, 159.

GRAND JURORS
 instructions to, 20.
 number of indeterminate, 6.
 superstition in number of, 6.
 manner of procuring attendance of, regulated by statute, 47.
 names to be set forth in venire, 49.
 impersonation of, 49.
 may act after jury empaneled and sworn, 51.
 selection of, in Pennsylvania, 52.
   in Federal Courts, 55.
   in England, 57.
   from improper class, 52.
 by whom summoned, 59.
 manner of summoning immaterial, 54.
 where incompetent persons summoned as, 52.
 talesmen summoned as, 51.
 qualifications of, 60, 62, 63.
   statute 2 Henry IV, C. 9, 61.
     6 George IV, C. 50, 61.
   in Pennsylvania, 61.
     Federal Courts, 61, 73, 74.
 Blackstone on qualifications of, 61.
 objections to personal qualifications of, 73.
 incompetent, may become competent, 76.
 objections to, when made, 64, 73n, 85.
 challenge for favor, 70, 73, 80, 81.
     by whom made, 71.
 exclusion of, on challenge, 72.
 exemption from service as, 72.
 forming of opinion by, 76.
 absence from domicile, 81.

INDEPENDENCE
    of grand jury established, 28.
                    asserted in College's and Shaftesbury's Cases, 30.
                    from control of court, 163.

INDEPENDENT GAZETTE, Oswald's Case, 31.

INDIANA, oath of grand jurors in, 96n.

INDIAN TERRITORY, oath of grand juror in, 98n.

INDICTMENT
    by accusing inquest, 22, 24.
    upon knowledge of one grand juror, 24.
    no guaranty of, in Constitution of United States, 32.
    where 24 grand jurors sworn and act, 45.
    twelve must concur to find, 26, 56, 108.
    effect of less than minimum number of grand jurors on, 46, 47.
    when no precept issued, 48n.
    error in grand juror's name, 49.
    invalid when selection made from improper class, 52.
    effect of irregularity in drawing and selecting, 57.
    found by grand jury unlawfully constituted, 56.
    by de facto grand jury sustained, 58.
    effect of Statute 11 Henry IV, C. 9, upon, 61.
    disqualification of grand juror, 62, 63.
    failure of defendant to challenge, 71.
    service of exempt person, effect on, 72.
    objections to grand jury before indictment, 73n, 85.
                    after indictment, 64, 73, 85.
            raised by motion to quash or plea in abatement, 86.
            when made by demurrer, 86.
    plea to, a waiver of defects, 87.
    one disqualified person will vitiate, 87, 139.
    void if grand jury organized contrary to statute, 88, 89.
    endorsement on, as evidence of empanelling, 89.
    inability of foreman to write, effect on, 90.
    sustained though no foreman appointed, 91.
    district attorney may submit bill of, to grand jury, 110.
                    to be earmarked, 114.
                    present when vote taken, 128.
                    hands bill to foreman, 134.
                    signature of, 134.
    submitting new, after ignoramus, 112.
    may embrace additional charges, 114.
    not invalidated by failure to charge, 124n.
    and presentment, 131.
    definition of, 131.
    when based upon presentment, 132.

13

MASSACHUSETTS
oath of grand juror, 94n.
names of witnesses not endorsed on bill, 136.
MATERIAL, books and papers when, 133.
MAYHEM
where appellor has a, 10, 21.
McKEAN, CHIEF JUSTICE
Oswald's Case, 31.
explains meaning of "diligently enquire," 101.
presence of witnesses for defendant, 140.
MESSENGER
indictments brought into court by, 156.
MICHIGAN, oath of grand juror, 96n.
MINNESOTA, oath of grand juror, 96n.
MINUTES OF COURT
show appointment of foreman, 90.
grand jury sworn, 92.
expunging presentment from, 160.
MISCONDUCT
of district attorney, 128.
of grand juror, 165.
MISSISSIPPI
coercion of grand jury, 31n.
oath of grand juror, 96n.
examination of tax collectors' books, 122.
endorsement of prosecutor's name, 135, 136.
witnesses' names not returned with indictment, 137.
MISSOURI
oath of grand juror, 96n.
inquisitorial power of grand jurors, 104.
endorsement of prosecutor's name, 135.
MONTANA, oath of grand juror, 98n.
NAMBDA
used by Scandinavians, 3.
civil cases only considered by, 3.
criminal pleas not considered by, 3.
similarity to sectatores, 4.
NAME
error in grand juror's name, 49.
of talesmen not to be furnished by judge, 51.
irregularity in selection, 67.
identity of, in lists, 68.
foreman unable to write, 90.
of foreman, signed by clerk, 148n.
variance in, 149.
abbreviation of, 149.

NAME—*Continued.*
>of witnesses endorsed on bill, 135.
>of prosecutor endorsed on bill, 135.
>of offence endorsed on bill, 150.
>ignorance of, by grand jury, 152.

NEBRASKA, oath of grand juror, 96n.

NEGROES
>exclusion of from panel, 66.

NEVADA, oath of grand juror, 97n.

NEW BILL
>may be sent to grand jury after ignoramus, 152.
>may be found when first bill defective, 155.

NEW HAMPSHIRE, oath of grand juror, 94n.

NEW MEXICO, oath of grand jurors, 98n.

NEW TRIAL, when awarded, 145.

NEW YORK
>Case of John Peter Zenger, 32.
>de facto grand jury, 58.
>oath of grand juror, 95n.

NOLLE PROS
>district attorney may enter, 42, 142.
>prosecution by information after entry of, 115n.
>new indictment for same offence after, 132.

NORMAN
>origin of grand jury disputed, 2.
>institution, petit jury a, 2.
>>grand jury not a, 4.
>appeal, 3.
>occupation, frank pledge continues under, 6.
>laws, introduction of, 7.

NORMANDY
>no itinerant justices in, 8.

NORTH CAROLINA
>qualifications of grand juror, 62.
>Branch's Case, 117.
>endorsement of prosecutor, 136.
>indictment found upon, testimony of interested witnesses, 143.

NORTH DAKOTA, oath of grand juror, 98n.

NORTHAMPTON
>Assize of, 7, 11, 17.
>divided kingdom into six circuits, 8, 9.
>provisions of, 9.

NORTH, LORD CHIEF JUSTICE, in case of Stephen College, 28.

NOT FOUND
>return of, 147.

OBJECTIONS—*Continued.*
    made before verdict, 149.
    incompetent witness testifying under, 145.

OFFICER
    absence of, when selection made, 58.
    cannot delegate authority to another, 58.
    de facto, 58.
    presumption of regularity of acts of, 59.
    irregularity in acts of, 67.
    accused may take advantage of irregular acts of, 64.
    failing to file oath, array not quashed, 66.
    of government, grand jury to summon as witness, 102.
    exceptional power of prosecuting, 112.
    investigating accounts of public, 121.
    of crown attends grand jury, 127.
    presence of, in grand jury room, 128, 140n.

OHIO
    oath of grand juror, 96n.
    endorsement of prosecutor's name, 135.

OKLAHOMA, oath of grand jury, 98n.

OPINION
    forming and expressing, 76, 77.
    district attorney not to express, 142.
    Judge King's, on powers of grand jurors, 106.
    Mr. Justice Field's, on powers of grand jurors, 108.

ORANGE, WILLIAM OF, 31.

ORDEAL
    of fire or water, trial by, 4.
    when awarded or refused, 10, 14.
    assize of Clarendon prescribes trial by, 7, 8.
           Northampton prescribes trial by, 9.
    abolished by Fourth Lateran Council, 18.
    supplanted on presentments by trial by jury, 18.

ORDER. AND SEE PRECEPT.
    directing issuance of venire, 48, 55.
    to whom issued, 48.
    need not be entered of record, 48n.
    verbal, sufficient, 48n, 51n.
    indictment quashed where no order issued, 48n.
    need not be served on sheriff, 48n.
    to summon talesmen, 50.
    directing selection from improper class, 52.
    of King in Council to Eyre of 1218-19, 18, 19.

OREGON, oath of grand juror, 97n.

POLYGAMY

conscientious scruples against indicting for, 76.

challenge to grand jurors on ground of, 82.

POWERS

of ancient grand jury broader than modern, 99.

of grand jury, limitation upon in time of Cromwell, 99.

difference in extent of, 102, 109.

Chief Justice Chase on, 102.

restraint upon, 102, 165.

view of, in Federal Courts, 100.

extent of, to investigate, 103.

to punish witnesses, 104, 165.

inquisitorial, 104.

grant of, in oath, 105.

devolving upon grand jury by statute, 121.

PRATT, JUDGE. Com. v. English, 111, 113.

PRECEPT. And see ORDER.

directing issuance of venire, 48, 55.

to whom issued, 48.

need not be entered of record, 48n.

verbal, sufficient, 48n.

indictment quashed where no, issued, 48n.

PRESENTMENT

by twelve senior thanes, 3, 8.

by seven jurors, 6.

by twelve knights, 8.

by twelve grand jurors, 56, 119.

by accusing body, 10, 11, 21, 24.

upon public fame or suspicion, 13, 15, 19.

made only when appeal failed, 12.

failure of inquest to make, 13.

inquest in King's mercy for false, 13.

part taken by townships in making, 14.

made in writing and indented, 25.

early, in Pennsylvania, 31n.

when made in Pennsylvania, 132.

no guaranty of in Constitution of United States, 32.

remedied by Amendment V, 32.

when void under 11 Henry IV, c. 9, 61.

limitations on power of, 99.

prosecutions instituted by, 107.

grand jurors to make true, 101.

making of by grand jury, 154.

when made, 105.

definition of, 107, 130.

upon knowledge of grand jurors, 119.

PRESENTMENT—*Continued*.

    and indictment, 131.

    when indictment based upon, 132.

    Daniel Davis on improper, 158.

    whether improper, will be allowed to stand, 159.

    making false, 163.

PRESS

    grand jury the defender of liberty of, 115.

    attacks on, by grand jury, 115.

PRESUMPTION. And see INNOCENCE.

    of innocence, 37.

      must be overcome, 105.

    of regularity of official acts, 59.

    that reason existed for excusing grand juror, 84.

    that grand jurors were excused in Arkansas, 85.

    that grand jury was discharged, 89, 160.

    of discharge of foreman, 91.

    that witnesses were sworn, 138.

    prima facie, of guilt, 141.

PRIMA FACIE

    presumption of guilt, 141.

    case made out by evidence, 146.

PRINTED ENDORSEMENT ON BILL, effect of, 151.

PRIVATE COUNSEL

    presence of, 128.

    make application to send new bill to subsequent grand jury, 153.

PRIVILEGE

    of challenge, waiver of, 71, 72.

PRIVILEGED COMMUNICATION. See COMMUNICATION.

PROCESS to summon witnesses, 104.

PROHIBITION, IMPLIED, of Assize of Clarendon, 8.

PROPTER AFFECTUM, 76.

PROSECUTION

    defendant challenging must show he is under, 70.

    evidence for, only to be heard, 103, 140.

    institution of, Judge King's opinion, 106.

    for libel, grand jury defends press in, 115.

PROSECUTIONS

    institution of in time of Glanville, 10.

            in time of Bracton, 19.

    trial awarded with relation to manner of, 21.

PROSECUTOR

    right of, to initiate proceedings before grand jury, 100.

    private, not to intrude upon grand jury, 109.

    presence of private counsel for, 128.

    grand juror may testify who was, 119.

PROSECUTOR—*Continued.*
  asking instruction to grand jury, 126.
  name of, endorsed on bill, 135.
  as member of grand jury, 77, 78.
PUBLIC FAME
  presentment on, 13, 19, 24.
PUBLIC
  institutions, investigation into, 121.
  officials, investigating accounts of, 121.
  improvements, supervision over, 121.
  buildings approved by two grand juries, 121.
PUBLIC POLICY
  examination on voir dire, against, 81.
  wrongful acts of grand juror upheld upon, 166.
PUBLICATION
  of finding of grand jury, 156.
QUALIFICATIONS OF GRAND JURORS
  in Bracton's time, 60, 62.
  in Sixteenth Century, 60.
  Coke's comments on, 60.
  Blackstone's comments on, 61.
  Chitty's comments on, 60.
  Statute 11 Henry IV, c. 9, defines, 61.
  under 6 George IV, c. 50, 61.
  in Federal Courts, 63.
  in Pennsylvania, 61.
  in Tennessee, West Virginia, Arkansas, South Carolina and
    North Carolina, 62.
  in Louisiana and Washington, 63.
  need not be freeholders, 60, 62.
  should be freeholders, 61, 62, 77.
  aliens not competent, 60, 63, 77.
  age as one of the, 72.
  domicile as affecting, 81.
  objections to personal, 73, 77.
  legislature may regulate making of objections to, 70.
QUASH, MOTION TO. And see INDICTMENT.
  where grand jury not summoned at proper time, 48.
  when drawing and selecting irregular, 57.
  where record irregular, 51.
            does not show empaneling, 89.
  array, when sustained, 66.
        when not sustained, 67.
        how made, 68.
  objections after indictment raised by, 86.
  not sustained where no effort to challenge made, 71.

REEVES, MR.
>as to participation of grand jury in trial of offenders, 22.

REGULARITY OF OFFICIAL ACTS
>presumption of, 59.

REIGNERUS LAW OF, 3.

RELATIONSHIP
>when grand juror disqualified by, 80.

RELIGIOUS BELIEF
>of grand juror, 81.

RELEVANT
>whether books and papers produced are, 133.

REPORT
>of grand jurors upon completion of work, 157.
>containing libellous statements, 158.
>whether improper, will be allowed to stand, 159.

RESUBMISSION
>of bill to grand jury, 154.

RETURN
>to writ of venire, 49.
>may be signed after verdict, 50.
>may be amended, 50.
>necessity of affidavit to, 54.
>challenge to array for irregularity in, 66.
>of grand jury, signature of foreman, 148, 150.

REX vs. DICKINSON, witnesses not sworn, 139.

RHODE ISLAND, oath of grand juror, 94n.

RICE, JUDGE, Com. v. Sheppard, 114.

ROLLO carries jury system into Normandy, 3.

ROLLS OF ITINERANT COURTS, 11, 24.

ROWAND vs. COM. Second bill sent to grand jury, 112.

RULES OF EVIDENCE
>grand jury governed by, 142.

SAWYER, SIR ROBERT, Attorney General, 30.

SCANDINAVIANS
>trial by jury among, 3.
>nambda used by, 3.

SCARLETT'S CASE, unlawfully procuring indictments, 42, 117.

SEAL
>venire should be under seal of court, 48.

SECRECY
>in conveying names of evil doers to sheriff, 20.
>observed by amercers, 20.
>purpose of observing, 21, 116.
>did not apply to inquiries made by justices, 21, 27.
>condemned as an evil, 42.
>a bar to inquiry into grand jury's action, 46, 118.

14

SHERIFF—*Continued.*
    cannot delegate authority to another, 58.
    absence of, when selection made, 67.
SHERIFF'S ROLL, reading of, 13.
SHERIFF'S TOURN held semi-annually, 4, 5.
SHIPPEN, MR. JUSTICE, 34.
SIGNATURE
    of foreman as evidence of empaneling, 89.
              when to be affixed to endorsement, 148.
              vouches for regularity of proceedings, 151.
    of district attorney when necessary, 134.
SOLICITOR GENERAL
    no such officer in Tennessee, 134.
SOUTH CAROLINA
    qualifications of grand jurors, 62.
SOUTH DAKOTA, oath of grand juror, 98n.
SPELLING
    error in, name of grand juror, 49.
STANDING ASIDE
    of grand jurors, 83.
STATE *vs.* COWAN, control of court over grand jurors, 165.
STATES
    may prosecute by information, 33.
    prosecution of offences by information in, 115.
    Western, abolition of grand jury in, 44.
    Eastern, conservatism of, on grand jury, 44.
    qualifications of Federal grand jurors determined by laws of, 63.
STATE'S ATTORNEY
    cannot challenge panel, 70.
STATUTE
    of Ethelred II, 2, 3, 5.
    3 Henry VIII, c. 12, 30, 41.
    11 Henry IV, c. 9, 61.
    6 George IV, c. 50, 57, 61.
    when held to be directory, 49, 81, 136.
    selection of grand jurors under unconstitutional, 58.
    grand jurors irregularly drawn under directory, 57, 81.
    disqualification imposed by, 73.
    exempting persons from grand jury service, 72.
    changing method of drawing and summoning, 89.
    of limitations, 103.
    as to disclosure of evidence, 120.
    imposing additional duties on grand jurors, 121.
    allowing eight grand jurors to concur on indictment unconstitutional, 147n.

SWORN—*Continued.*
  grand jurors, as witnesses, 132n.
  witnesses to be, 137.
  when witness not, 138, 146.
  indictment need not show that witnesses, 138.

TALES
  not to issue when array quashed, 52.

TALES DE CIRCUMSTANTIBUS. See TALESMEN.

TALESMEN
  when summoned, 50.
  venire not to issue, 51.
  number to be summoned, 54, 56.
  necessity for, to be shown by record, 51.
  may be summoned when all jurors disqualified, 52.
  selected from improper persons, 52.
  names not to be furnished by judge, 51.
  designated by court to fill vacancy, 84.
  may be appointed foreman, 90n.
  in Federal Courts, 55.

TAMPERING WITH WITNESSES,143.

TANEY, CHIEF JUSTICE, evidence necessary to convict, 102.

TAXES
  payment of, as grand juror's qualification, 63, 81.
  grand jurors to fix rate of, 121.
              as board of revision of, 122.

TECHNICAL FORM
  in presentment, 131.

TENNESSEE
  qualifications of grand jurors, 62.
  grand juror related to accused, 81.
  oath of grand juror, 95n.
  inquisitorial powers of grand jurors, 104.
  investigation of sufficiency of bonds in, 122.
  endorsement of prosecutor's name, 135.

TERM
  two grand juries at same term, 89.

TERRITORIAL JURISDICTION
  inquiry within, 103.

TERRITORY
  admitted as state, how grand jurors empaneled, 89.

TESTE
  venire to bear, 48.
  may be amended, 48.

TESTIMONY

witnesses in contempt for refusing to give, 88, 133.
additional, may be given when required, 104.
presentment made without hearing, 132.
indictment found upon unsworn, 138, 146.
voluntary, of defendent, 144.
of defendant involuntarily given against himself, 145.
when to be kept secret, 118.
of grand jurors, when received, 118.
of clerk of grand jury, 120.
of district attorney, 120.
district attorney not to comment on, 128.

TEXAS, oath of grand juror, 95n.

THANES

presentment by, 3, 8.
duty of, to accuse, 3.
oath of twelve, 98.

THAYER, PROF.

on effect of Assize of Clarendon, 18.
order of Lateran Council, 18.

TOURN. See Sheriff's Tourn.

TOWN MEETING in Connecticut, 122.

TOWNSHIPS

their part in presentments, 14, 16.
did not act in all cases, 14, 16.
until inquest had presented, 15, 16.
not mentioned by Glanville, 14.
identity with four freemen of every vill, 15.
no part of the inquest, 15.
power of, 16.
use of, not obligatory, 16.
limited to concurrence in finding of inquest, 16.
Mr. Forsyth's reference to, 16.
part of trial jury, 23.

TOWNSPEOPLE. And see Townships.

challenge of juror by, 22.
oath taken by, 22.
form part of trial jury, 23.

TREASON

indictment for when quashed, 144.

TRESPASS

when prosecutor's name must be endorsed, 136.

TRIERS

on challenge for favor, 82.

TRIAL JURY. See Petit Jury.

UNANIMITY
    of grand jurors when requisite, 26, 27.
    of petit jurors, 26.
UNCONSTITUTIONAL STATUTE. See STATUTE.
UNITED STATES
    Constitution omits indictment by grand jury, 32.
                    remedied by Amendment V, 32.
    Fifth Amendment applies only to offences against, 33.
    Sixth Amendment to Constitution, 57.
    courts, grand jury in, 55.
    challenge to array in, when made, 69.
    workmen in arsenals and armories exempt, 73.
    rebellion against, will disqualify, 63, 73.
    knowledge of grand jurors of offence against, 109.
UTAH
    unlawful cohabitation in, 82n.
    oath of grand juror, 97n.
VACANCY
    in grand jury, how filled, 84.
VARIANCE
    in name of foreman, 149.
    between indictment and evidence, 152.
VENIRE
    issues upon precept, 48, 55.
    command of, 48.
    should be under seal of court, 48.
    may be amended, 48.
    requisites of, 49.
    return of sheriff to, 49.
    not to issue to summon talesmen, 51.
    to issue when array quashed, 52.
    array challenged for irregularity in, 66.
    selection of foreman from whole, 90n.
    shown by records of court, 151.
VERDICT
    sheriff's return signed after, 50.
    influenced by incompetent evidence, 145.
    objection made before, 149.
VERMONT
    oath of grand juror, 94n.
    act as excise officers in, 122.
VILL
    four freemen of, 14, 15.
VIRGINIA
    oath of grand juror, 95n.
    endorsement of prosecutor's name, 135.